The Prison
Officer

www.penguin.co.uk

The Prison Officer

The Inside Story of Life Behind Bars

GEN GLAISTER

PENGUIN BOOKS

TRANSWORLD PUBLISHERS
Penguin Random House, One Embassy Gardens,
8 Viaduct Gardens, London SW11 7BW
www.penguin.co.uk

Transworld is part of the Penguin Random House group of companies
whose addresses can be found at global.penguinrandomhouse.com

Penguin
Random House
UK

First published in Great Britain in 2024 by Penguin Books
an imprint of Transworld Publishers

A CIP catalogue record for this book
is available from the British Library.

ISBN
9781804992784

Typeset in 12/14.5pt Bembo Book MT Pro by Jouve (UK), Milton Keynes.
Printed and bound in Great Britain by Clays Ltd, Elcograf S.p.A.

The authorized representative in the EEA is Penguin Random House Ireland,
Morrison Chambers, 32 Nassau Street, Dublin D02 YH68.

Penguin Random House is committed to a sustainable
future for our business, our readers and our planet. This book
is made from Forest Stewardship Council® certified paper.

Dedicated to Cosima Glaister and Rosie Carbutt.

My oldest sister, whose contributions to this book have been nothing short of a labour of unconditional love; and one of my most exceptional friends, a fellow ex-prison officer and my greatest source of respite, both then and now.

Contents

1 Imposter Syndrome   1

2 Prison Bound   9

3 Wing Shy   17

4 Calling the Shots   26

5 A&E   35

6 Just a Girl   45

7 A Secret Garden   61

8 Beef   75

9 Bang Up   86

10 Star Signs   105

11 The Mexican Border   118

12 How to Make a Birthday Cake in Prison   131

13 Role Models   143

14 The Strangest Place   154

15 War Poets   163

16 The G-Wing Cycle   170

17 Spice and Prejudice   182

18 Night Shifts   198

19 Code Red   213

20 Staying Alive   222

21 A Study in Scarlet   230

22 The Man Who Hated Carrots   239

23 Gangbangers   258

24 Comings and Goings   273

25 The Hearing   282

26 Counting Straws   293

27 The Infinite Threshold of Shock   308

28 Recycling   321

Acknowledgements   335

The Prison
Officer

1

Imposter Syndrome

'Please, I'm begging you! Please get this man moved, otherwise I don't know what I might do!'

The croaky voice came over the intercom, almost drowned out by the sound of heavy thumping on a door in the background.

A bank of intercoms labelled Emergency Cell Bells was flashing manically in front of two uniformed women who were sitting in office chairs, squabbling over the last energy drink and pausing every now and then to take one of the calls from the growing list.

'Yeah, will do, mate,' one of them said, unconvincingly, before hanging up and answering the next call with two impatient clicks.

'What's your medical emergency, then?' she asked idly.

'Can't you do anything about him?' came another desperate plea over the intercom. 'I feel like I'm going insane. Please help us! I just want to sleep.'

'That's not a medical emergency – nothing we can do,' the woman snapped back.

The next caller was angrier than the others, but she interrupted him straight away. 'Speak to your wing officer in the morning,' she told him casually, then muttered 'dumb prick' just before she hung up. I knew the prisoner would have heard what she said.

I watched on in silence, boiling at their cruelty but not willing to stick my neck out and risk looking even more out of place than I already felt.

Crammed into the prison's central 'bubble' with eleven other trainees who had made it this far, I was on my final test: shadowing a night shift.

The bubble sits at the core of the prison, where its spurs meet. Like a 360° cockpit, it is encircled by tinted windows with a bank of security cameras linked to an intercom system at one end, and some shabby-looking filing cabinets at the other. The two women sitting in front of the intercoms are what's known as 'OSOs' – operational support officers, dressed in the same stiff white shirts and black trousers as the officers. Only their lack of batons signals that they don't have a prisoner-facing role.

Even through two concrete floors and several metal gates we could all hear the relentless pummelling of a cell door coming from one of the wings above us.

Prisoners had been calling continually through the intercoms in their cells for over an hour now, all of them with the same despairing plea for help. I knew the cell bell was their only hope of signalling for help at night, and my heart ached for them over the torture of their sleep deprivation and the brash dismissal which came back at them over the intercom. Still, I said nothing, but managed to fix an unimpressed scowl on my face in the hope that that would count as some kind of protest.

One of my fellow trainees was braver. 'Erm . . . look . . .' he began, 'that's pretty bad, that noise. Can't we – I mean, it must be awful for the other prisoners.'

I nodded vigorously in agreement, glad that someone had spoken up, and there was a murmur of approval from the other trainees around me. We all felt the same. But the OSOs just responded with complacent shrugs.

'Nothing we can do about it,' one of them said with a grimace. 'Just some tapped Polish guy on G-Uppers making a racket. Trust me, you don't wanna see what this guy does.'

I felt my throat close with repulsion at their lack of compassion. *How is anyone supposed to leave this place rehabilitated if they are treated like this?*

I felt powerless. It was as if I was staring into the abyss of an impossible task. I was gripped by imposter syndrome in its most literal sense. Although, I wasn't sure I could really call it imposter syndrome when, right now, my doubts about my ability to do my job in a place like this were actually grounded in indisputable facts.

'Well,' the brave trainee piped up again, 'can't you at least treat them with a bit more respect over the intercom?'

'Pha!' laughed the OSOs, looking at each other and shaking their heads. 'Respect? You won't be saying nothing about respect after a week in this place, mate.'

She said this so cuttingly that the room fell into a strained silence.

The tension was broken a moment later when Jerry, tonight's duty manager, strode into the bubble. I remembered him from my job interview several months earlier, larger than life with an uncombed afro and a booming voice. He walked around the prison like the world's friendliest WWE fighter entering the ring in front of a large audience, his infectious cackle always winging its way around corners before he did.

'Welcome to nights, ladies and gentlemen!' He said this as if he was opening a Broadway show. 'Hope everybody is making you feel at home. Right – searches. Every week, the whole prison is searched overnight. We've got the kitchens, chapel, classrooms, gym, barber's, Visits Hall, Works, reception – have I missed anything out? Oh, and of course the wings. We've got D to H on this block. You'll know that each spur is divided into two wings, Lowers is the first two floors and Uppers is the top two floors. But don't forget about A, B and C on the other side of the jail – that's the segregation unit, the healthcare unit and the addiction wing. This is an area especially close to my heart, because I am head of the security department, so I'm the best person to ask if you've got any questions. My advice to you? Get creative! *Think like a prisoner!* If you wanted to hide your SIM card, or your little stabby-stabby shank, where would you put it? Eyes peeled for drug paraphernalia, bank details, phone chargers – anything that doesn't look quite right. OK?'

He grinned at us as if he was sending children off on an Easter egg hunt. Then he handed over a pile of clear plastic bags with barcodes and forms printed on them, and a bag of cardboard tubes.

'Grab some of these evidence bags and bag up anything pointy in these sharps tubes here. Now, go forth and multiply! Except no multiplying, not inside the prison walls – you'll lose your job for that!'

His chuckle echoed loudly as we scurried off, glad to be given something useful to do and bustling with excitement over what we might find. If there were dangerous activities on the wings – and let's be honest, there probably were – we might actually be able to stop them.

It had gone midnight and the wings were almost dark, each of them only dimly lit by fire exit signs and the orange glow of a lamp post outside the large window at the far end. The prisoners upstairs had gone quiet at last, and apart from the whirr of the air vents and a few TVs crackling behind cell doors, the place was eerily silent. We swarmed from wing to wing, reaching gloved hands into pool tables, running our fingers over the tops of notice boards, tipping out sour-smelling mop buckets and unclipping washing machine parts to reach nooks and crannies. I kept the question in my mind as we moved along each wing: *where would you hide something here?*

As we climbed the stairs to the upper landings, the prisoner's terrible howling began again, and by the time we arrived at the entrance to G-Uppers I felt the clattering of the metal door rattle my bones.

'Every single one of you that's here,' our trainer had told us on the first day our new class assembled, 'has a little dose of clinical madness. You all know that you can stomach that little bit more *nastiness* than the average person. Don't bother telling me you don't, because if you *weren't* like that, you wouldn't be here.'

I'd thought straight away that he was probably right. Now, without even discussing it, all of us moved instinctively towards the source of the noise. A sinister drive propelled us step by step towards those blood-curdling screams. As though we were suspecting, or maybe even hoping, that what we would see behind that door would be a kind of test. That it would give us the toe-curling, gut-wrenching shock that would culminate in – what? A kind of a satisfaction as we pushed the limits of our personal endurance. *Yes. Maybe that's what we are all after.*

We peered through the hatch in the door of his cell, and there he was. Totally naked, his grey skin pulled taut over his bones and dark hair hanging limply around his chin. He was darting about his cell, a toilet brush held to his lips as if it were a microphone. A second or two later he saw us, paused, then hurled himself into the metal door that stood between us with a thud.

We all flinched backwards very slightly – then leaned in again, curiously.

He flew at the door again, this time driving his bare foot into it and turning 180° in the air almost gracefully, like a ballerina. With his back to us he stood quite still for a moment in the middle of the cell, took a slow, ceremonious bow, then reached round and shoved the toilet brush, bristles first, deep into his arse. Nobody moved. There was complete silence for a moment, then he ripped it out and in one swift movement plunged it into his mouth with a gargling roar. He rushed towards us again, his scream muffled by the brush which still protruded from his jaws. I saw the wild look in his eyes as his body hit the door with a crash, and we all felt it shudder.

We recoiled in unison.

From that night on, I knew that our trainer had been right about the clinical madness. No one becomes a prison officer only out of the kindness of their own heart. You have to be here for the gritty parts too.

But if our starting point was a man inserting a toilet brush into himself, where did it go from there? What happens when that sort of scene just becomes a part of daily life? I thought of the OSOs downstairs, about how they seemed so indifferent to the prisoners trapped in a sleep-deprived, hellish nightmare.

What's going to happen to me here? Will I become indifferent like that? Is it inevitable? Do you start off compassionate, then bit by bit that compassion wears away until one day there's nothing left?

One day, will I just shrug too?

2

Prison Bound

I was just twenty-three years old when I applied to be a prison officer at a London prison holding over a thousand men, who had committed crimes ranging from petty theft to human trafficking, rape and murder.

This wasn't a spur-of-the-moment decision. I'd had my heart set on becoming a prison officer since I was fifteen. It was probably quite an odd choice for a teenager at a public school in the rolling hills of Dorset, especially one who found herself in detention most evenings of the week. Much like lots of other teens in the era of *Skins*, I fancied myself a bit of a rebel, clad in scruffy Doc Martens, eyes heavy with black eyeliner and, more often than not, a badly rolled cigarette between my fingers.

In addition to all this normal teenage angst though, I

carried the weight of the world on my shoulders. I worried incessantly about people, mainly my family, and I veered between feeling angry that I had more things to worry about than my friends and feeling powerless to help. I hated not being old enough to know what to do and I hated not being old enough to know how to help, but most of all I hated not being old enough to know what to say.

This culminated in years of me trying to do 'grown-up' things. I pilfered tobacco and alcohol from my parents and smuggled them into school to share among my friends. My ears were laden with home-made piercings and I spent my time with boys who were far too old for me. I developed a reputation: my teachers expected me to misbehave, my friends expected me to misbehave – so I made a point of living up to it. The only thing getting in my way was that, deep down, what I truly wanted was to be liked – and nothing I was doing was making people like me.

I had this inkling though, even then, that prison might be the place where I could be surrounded by all the chaos which my soul craved, except *I* could also be the person who was there to fix it. I could be the person who brought positivity and empathy to a place which lacked both.

Before any successful applicant is let loose into the chaos of a prison, he or she must undergo eight weeks of training. Just eight short weeks – roughly the gestation period of a dog. So, the same length of time it takes to make small, defenceless puppies – and a not altogether dissimilar process. We started off like sixteen bundles of cells, each filled with the potential ingredients to become an officer. We bathed in the safety of our warm, dark classroom located just outside the prison gates, with PowerPoint presentations as our placenta, drip-feeding us information about the prison next door. Then, one at a time, we were clothed in our new black and white pelts which wrinkled around us, too small in some places, too big in others.

In a soft padded room, we wrestled our twenty-stone instructors who taught us how to bring a prisoner under control. They certainly weren't afraid to show us that if you miss a beat you get a fist in the face, but we still knew that one squeal of the safe-word – OXO! – would bring an end to the pain or the disorder around us. We role-played with our teachers to practise de-escalating an aggressive situation or negotiating with a self-harming prisoner, but we knew that if we said the wrong thing the worst that could happen was the teacher drew another line on his wrist in red pen.

We spent afternoons and night shifts shadowing offi-cers on the wings, observing and learning, but having no actual responsibilities ourselves. We saw all the things we were warned we would see – officers not searching prisoners properly, officers who had given up years ago, officers making dark jokes about prisoners who self-harmed. One thing was clear to me by the end of the course. Any privileged sensitivities I might have had were going to be left at the prison gates. I wasn't going to help anyone in this job by being offended.

The dropout rate in training was fairly high. At the end of the eight weeks only ten of us emerged, slippery, squealing and with floundering enthusiasm – and almost totally and utterly blind.

The early morning sun streamed in through the windows in dramatic swathes of gold. It was my first day as a qualified officer, but instead of revelling in this scenic start, I was creeping around the house swearing under my breath, desperately trying to locate the white shirt I had ironed and carefully hung *somewhere* the night before. Finally I found it, still on the ironing board. I pulled it over my head and tugged on the rest of my uniform.

In front of the mirror, I pulled my hair into a plain, low bun and took a step back to check myself. I looked as if I was heading to a canteen shift on a Channel ferry. I knocked back the final swig of my tea and promptly spilled half of it down my front.

'Pull yourself together, Gen!' I muttered at my reflection, before throwing on a coat and turning to head out.

I walked briskly from the train station, through the deserted underpass, to the prison gates. I was puffing on a cigarette, concentrating hard on controlling the butterflies in my stomach, when a car horn blared. I sprang out of its path and caught a glimpse of three scoffing faces inside – prison officers heading the same way. I already knew the narrative that surrounded new PO recruits – *most of them aren't up to it* – and now I looked as though I couldn't even cross the road properly. It could only add to my new colleagues' arsenal of mockery.

In the locker room there were no free spaces, so I shoved my phone and lighter into the pocket of my coat and threw it on top of a cabinet. I checked my pockets, twice, rummaged through my see-through prison-issue bag to check that I hadn't left anything in there I couldn't bring in, and strode over to the entrance, feigning confidence with each step. I joined the queue of officers collecting radios. I focused intently on what each person requested before me so that I would say the right thing.

'Morning, I'll get a beta radio. Cheers.'

I spoke assertively, like the officer before me had done, despite the fact I had absolutely no idea what type of radio I was meant to get.

'None left.'

Without looking up, the woman behind the desk passed me a battered old radio missing three of its buttons.

By the time I reached the first door, everyone else had gone through ahead of me. I saw a sign by the door: PLEASE RING BELL. I did what the notice said, and felt relieved when someone appeared at the window.

'What you ringing the bell for?' she scowled. 'Wait your turn!'

Once I'd got inside, I pressed the big green SEARCH button. The LED light flashed red back at me. I knew that meant I had to be searched. I tugged off my heavy boots, hopping on the spot because the only seat was taken. My heart was pounding.

Have I accidentally left something in my bag? A stray cigarette? A piece of chewing gum?

I thought back to our trainer sternly talking us through the list of items that are prohibited in prison. 'On the outside, chewing gum is just chewing gum. Once you go through those gates, though, it's a material you could use to take an impression of a key.'

I had just slipped my belt off and put everything into a grey airport-style tray on the conveyor belt when I was startled by a shrill voice.

'Odd socks, is it?'

The woman sitting behind the scanner was laughing.

'Oh yeah, I always have odd socks,' I told her. 'No idea how people keep theirs together.'

She ran her gloved hands up my legs, back and arms. I tugged my stiff boots back on and threaded my utility belt through the loops around my waist, then walked through another electric door to the key room. I clipped a set of keys on to my chain, dropped them into the pouch on my belt, and strapped my baton and then my cut-down knife into their holsters. I felt a thrill wash over me that I was arming myself for my day's work not with a laptop and a pen, but with a defensive weapon and a blade I might have to use to cut through a noose at a moment's notice.

When I arrived on H-Wing it was quiet. I made my way to the wing office to find out which officers I was on shift with for the day. The wing office was a small, damp room which sat in line with the cells near the entrance to the wing. There were two desks, a stained sofa and a thickly barred window. Two officers were yawning and checking their emails. Neither of them seemed particularly pleased to see me there and I wondered for a moment if I was even in the right place.

'Hey, I'm Gen. I think I've been assigned to this wing today?'

One of them looked up and pointed at the other officer with a thumb. 'That's Walter,' was all he said. Then he pointed at himself. 'And I'm Steve.'

Walter was a tall, brawny Nigerian man, and Steve a shortish, gaunt-looking man from Essex with sparse ginger hair.

I perched awkwardly on the sofa. I was desperately trying to think of something else to say to break the silence that had descended, but neither of them seemed bothered by it. I rehearsed a couple of questions in my head, but all of them sounded forced, and stupid. I had just settled on *So, anything I should know about the wing?* when Steve turned away from his computer to face me.

'You part of the group that just graduated, then?' he said.

'Yep, first day today actually.' I tried to sound casual about it.

Steve rolled his eyes. 'Half of you'll be gone within the week,' he told me, chuckling dismissively.

And he was right – the eleven trainees I'd graduated with would become six after just one week on the wings. It's why no one would take the time to properly teach us and bed us in: what was the point, if we'd be gone in just a few days? They preferred a 'sink or swim' technique.

'Right,' Walter suddenly said, stretching, then clapping his hands together. 'Let's get on with the day. Jane, right? You can just chill in the office.'

'Um, it's Gen, like G-E-N, but no worries. I mean, put me to work if you need to. Like, I'm up for being busy.'

Steve grinned and batted his eyes at me. 'You can just stay here an' look pretty, Jane!'

I rolled my eyes.

Walter took one look at me and raised an eyebrow. 'OK. Well, follow me. I'm supervising movement upstairs. But you can stay in here if you like.'

I took my chance, jumped off the sofa and followed him through the door before he could change his mind.

3

Wing Shy

Walter and I were standing by the wing door on the upper landing. He and Steve had unlocked the cell doors and the wing had come alive.

'When they call the activity over the net,' Walter explained, 'like Works or Waste or Education, I tick them off this list and they can leave the wing to join freeflow. So yeah, that's basically what's called movement.'

I wasn't yet au fait with prison jargon and felt pretty sure that 'freeflow' wasn't what I thought it was. It didn't matter much if I didn't understand the terminology, though, because I couldn't make out a single word that came crackling over my beaten-up radio.

Prisoners had started to group around us at the door, ears pricked for their own activity.

'You'll get used to it,' one of them said to me warmly.

At first I wasn't sure what he meant, and tried to look non-committal.

'Understanding what they're saying on the radio,' the prisoner added helpfully. There was another loud crackle, and he grinned at Walter. 'That sounded like Works. That'll be me off, then!'

Walter patted him amicably on the back as he ducked out of the doorway. My stomach clenched with the realization that I seemed to be *the only one* who couldn't interpret the instruction.

I gazed back over the landing at the bustling scene of men weaving in and out of each other. The atmosphere was surprisingly buoyant, upbeat, more so than I'd expected. Then one prisoner cheered loudly and I saw him swing his arm around a smaller man's neck and put him in a stiff headlock. *That didn't take long*, I thought to myself, as though sarky inner dialogue would help to brace me for what was surely about to happen. I looked up at Walter for a reaction, expecting him to move rapidly to intervene, but his face remained calm. The prisoner released the smaller man and I saw that they were both laughing.

Walter asked me to search the prisoners who were going off the wing. This at least I felt confident about. We'd spent hours practising on each other in training. We had been warned that many officers on the wings didn't search prisoners properly, and were constantly reminded of how wrong things could go if we let our standards slip. So I put on my plastic gloves, feeling very official, as Walter bellowed 'Edu-edu-educaaation!' down the wing and a few prisoners slunk over to the door clutching textbooks.

The first prisoner looked a bit taken aback when I opened with: 'Have you got anything unauthorized on you?' He shook his head, but a couple of prisoners behind him laughed. However much we had practised doing this in training, it felt awkwardly intimate doing it to a prisoner. I ran the flats of my palms along each of his arms then over the chest and belly and down each leg from the groin to the ankles, feeling my face turning hotter. He spun round and I did the same to his back. The next prisoner stepped into a star position with a mischievous grin. I had barely placed my hands on his shoulders when he cried out, 'Careful, Miss! I ain't bin touched by a woman in three years!'

The queue behind him sniggered.

Another prisoner shook his head. 'What's wiv all these new govs searching us all proper?'

Walter looked at me impatiently and then handed me the clipboard and snapped on his own pair of gloves. He brushed each prisoner on the shoulders, patted their pockets and waved them through.

One of the prisoners who had been watching me from the queue looked at me with something like pity. 'Thing is, Miss, you can search 'em all like that, but if we've got something we don't want you to find it's going up our arse . . . so unless you're going up there, you're wasting your time.'

As quickly as it had begun, movement was over. Now just thirty or so prisoners were milling about the landings and Walter locked the wing door and started heading down the stairs. I followed him, but I didn't turn right into the office at the base of the staircase, resolving not to take the easy way out by hiding in there. There was a term for that kind of behaviour – 'wing shy' – and we'd been warned in training about not getting a reputation for it. The officers all knew which of their colleagues would rather be safely in the peace and quiet of the wing office, taking their time answering emails, rather than out on the wing dealing with whatever was happening there. Pretty soon the prisoners got to know too. If I wanted to prove myself today, I knew I couldn't afford that kind of reputation.

I strolled down to the end of the wing. One prisoner was looking despondent, holding what looked like a heavily dented ping-pong ball in one hand and a peeling bat in the other.

'Ain't my fault you missed my ace, bro!' his opponent was saying, laughing loudly.

I looked more closely at the ball, then noticed the discarded bottle of deodorant on the floor next to them. It wasn't a ping-pong ball at all – they were using the plastic ball from a roll-on deodorant. For a moment I marvelled at their creativity. The prisoner wiped the ball on his T-shirt, then noticed me watching.

'What, Miss? Wanna place bets on who's gonna win?' he said teasingly.

I smiled, but the other prisoner tutted and gave me a disdainful look.

'Why these new govs always so nosey? You've got your own office, man. Go chill there.'

I thought about the first time I ever set foot on a prison wing. I was on work experience during a summer break from university. To this day I still remember everything about it: the sound of the commotion around me, the friendly curiosity of the prisoners quizzing me on who I was, and feeling certainty dawn on me as I thought to myself, *This is exactly what I want to do.*

This time, though, I was on the wing dressed as an officer, and it was completely different. The prisoners around me were looking at me with a mixture of mistrust and expectancy and I didn't feel like a guest any more.

The wing was much wider than the ones you see on TV. The walls were painted a bright white, and instead of eerie recesses, all the doors were flush with the wall. Standing two floors high, the lower landing had fifteen solid metal doors painted baby blue running up each side and a series of tables and chairs, bolted to the ground, dotted down the middle. A wide staircase in the centre of the wing led to the upper landing, where thirty more cells looked over a shoulder-height railing in the same baby blue, and down on to the landing below, as if it were a courtyard.

The space gave me a profound sense that I was being watched. I was grateful for the rigid canvas trousers and the thick belt that sat around my middle, hiding any curve that would signal my femininity. But the bulky kit was taking some getting used to. I was smaller than most of my fellow officers and the utilities along the belt crowded my waist awkwardly. While other officers' batons hung casually from their belts, loosened in their well-worn leather loops and ready to be used at any moment like an extension of their fists, mine just seemed to dwarf me. With each step I took its tip knocked against the small bone on the inside of my elbow, where I could feel a tingling bruise spreading.

I needed a breather. Just a moment of not being watched or stared at. I made my way towards the wing door which led out on to the core, where I knew there was a staff toilet.

When I got to the door, though, I just stared at the lock. I couldn't for the life of me remember which key was which. The electric door which I was used to unlocking was open and secured back against the wall. In its place stood a barred gate. *There's a rule, I know there is.* I was racking my brains while trying not to give away my confusion. *The barred gates have two keyholes in them, which means I use the key which has two holes in it? That doesn't sound quite right though . . .*

I had seen other officers extract their keys from the pouch at their hip and select the correct one with the ease of a penknife connoisseur before expertly planting it in the keyhole and barely rolling their thumb before the door clinked open. The wing doors didn't have handles, so controlling them was quite an art. You had to open them holding your key in the hole at a very precise angle for it to act like a handle, then use just the right amount of force to avoid it swinging open and out of your reach.

The prisoners on my wing were starting to surround me now, reaching their fists over my shoulder and through the bars of the locked gate to touch knuckles with other prisoners walking through the core on the far side. Even if I'd been able to remember the right key – and I still couldn't – now I was nervous that as soon as I opened the door, the prisoners around me would flood out into the prohibited area beyond if I couldn't get my key at that exact precise angle.

As I stood there fumbling through my key chain, now with both hands, the prisoners stopped moshing around me and looked at me, amused.

'Miss, I can give you a hand with those keys if you like,' one of them said through a toothy grin.

I had to laugh, making a point of taking the joke. I thrust one of the keys into the lock and to my delight it clunked open. I squeezed through the gap, not daring to open it wide enough for someone else to slip through, locked it behind me and hurried on straight to the bathroom to regain my composure for a minute.

Come on, Gen. Come on. It all went fine in the end, didn't it?

Not for the first time that day I stared at my reflection in the scratched mirror, dragging my cheeks down with the heels of my hands. *If I was in a film, right now I'd splash my face with cold water*, I thought – but the bathroom was grimy and smelled stale, so I decided against it. Instead I opted for a big stretch, shook all my limbs out, plastered a look of confidence on my face and headed back out on to the wing.

I wanted to look involved and I wanted to look like I knew what I was doing, but I certainly didn't want to look nosey. I adjusted my walk so that I appeared more purposeful, as though I was busy doing something instead of prying or snooping. The problem was that no one had given me anything to do, so I just had to awkwardly pretend to be busy – which made me look even more tense.

I tried to keep my body language composed, but my mind was darting in the direction of every shout or bang. I felt sure my eyes or my twitching head were giving away my racing thoughts. I wasn't frightened. There was no room for fear, like you'd expect. It was just a surreal feeling that I had left my own body and I was looking down on myself.

I leaned up against a table as casually as I could. A group of prisoners near by immediately dropped their voices, but I could still hear them.

'What's she eavesdropping for, man? Jeez these govs are nosey.'

I pretended not to hear, but tried to adopt a pose that said that I was interested but also relaxed, taking things in but not gawping.

'You all right, Miss? You look like you in some dreamland or summin'. You know them lot over there fink you're spying on them? Is it your first day? How come you wanna do this job then?'

I hesitated.

'Well? Why is it then? You like locking doors or you like telling people what to do?'

'Uh, no – no, it's not that,' I replied, faltering. 'I just . . . I, uh, like talking to people. It's an interesting job. Better than working in an office anyway.'

He looked back at me, unconvinced, as I cringed at my answer.

It was a vicious cycle. I stuck out because I felt uncomfortable, and I was uncomfortable because I could feel myself sticking out. I was touched by some of the prisoners earnestly checking if I was OK, but I hadn't heard the word 'nosey' being used so many times since I was six. How was I meant to look like I was paying attention without being accused of being nosey? I'd landed in a world where I just didn't understand the rules.

And it was only lunchtime.

4

Calling the Shots

'You can relax now, that's the busy part over,' Walter said to me after our lunch break, explaining that H-Wing had their association time in the morning, so most of the prisoners were in their cells for the afternoon.

A few prisoners were trickling up and down the wing toting grubby-looking brooms and the odd J-cloth, and I assumed they must be the cleaners. I knew that the prisoners who worked were the more trusted prisoners on the wing, who had earned the privilege of a job and therefore more time out of their cells. Finally I felt like I could relax.

'Anything I can help with?' I asked Walter, feeling emboldened by my new-found state of relaxation.

He turned to me wearily. 'Yep. You cannot unlock any doors.' My face must have fallen, because he softened his tone. 'Nothing against you – it's just there are guys on the wing who've got conflicts and seeing as you don't know who's who yet, I don't want you unlocking doors and causing any madness on your first day.'

At that moment I noticed a change in the air and a prisoner walked into the office. He didn't hesitate or knock like other prisoners did, but strolled in as though he had the keys to the place. He wasn't tall, but he was well built and carried himself as though he was bigger. I immediately noticed that he kept himself better than other prisoners I'd seen. His clothes looked freshly ironed, and his orange polo shirt had 'VR' written on the back of it, meaning he was a Violence Reduction rep – a prisoner who's trusted to defuse issues on the wing.

The VR made himself comfortable on the stained sofa on one side of the office.

'So, you're the new gov on H-Uppers then?' he enquired.

'I sure am,' I replied, with more confidence than I felt.

'I'm Johnson. But people call me Shots. An' I run this wing.'

Walter laughed. 'Ha! Don't talk shit, Johnson.' But there was a strange feeling in the air as he said it. 'Johnson is the VR rep on the wing,' Walter went on, 'and to be honest, he's not bad at keeping the troublemakers around here in line.'

Johnson grinned smugly and put his hand out for me to shake.

'Gen – nice to meet you,' I responded, shaking his hand.

'So how come you wanna do this job then?' Johnson asked me, immediately.

I thought I could see a glint growing in his eye, and in any case I wasn't ready for this question yet again.

'You guys all wanna know that, don't you?' I replied.

'Ha! Have they already laid it on you then? Let me give you a tip. All these youts are gonna be tryna suss you out, tryna figure out what kind of gov you're gonna be. Make sure you let them know where you're at. Like, don't take no shit from them but also be calm with them, you know? Show them you a real person, innit.'

That made sense, and I felt somewhat emboldened by his advice. It was as though he had known that was the type of officer I wanted to be. All the same, there was something about the way he was telling me all this which was making me feel distinctly nauseous.

'Yeah, I get that. It's all good. I'm not gonna take any shit,' I replied carefully.

'I come from the road, you know,' Johnson went on. 'Like I get where all these youts come from, an' you gotta be careful with them, like they ain't playin' in here. But I got your back – don't worry. Any problems an' I got you.'

'Uh – thanks.' It was all I could think of to say.

Johnson turned to Walter and started talking to him in a hushed and serious tone. I caught something about there being beef because a new prisoner on the wing had been in the car in a drive-by when this other guy's brother got shot up. He was using words and names I didn't know but I tried to look as if I understood what was going on. I tried to search for the names on the board but all ninety of them just swam before my eyes and I gave up. Walter sighed thoughtfully, then stood up with purpose and walked out of the office. I felt a sharp pang of panic that I'd been left alone with Johnson.

The second Walter was gone, Johnson turned to me.

'So what do you think of the job so far?'

I shrugged. 'It's good. Lots of interesting people.'

'Yeah? You'll find that. Hey, you wanna see summin' interestin' about me?'

Before I'd even had a chance to respond, he had lifted up his polo shirt and was pointing to four circular scars on his ribcage and one surgical scar running down the middle of his torso.

'Shot four times in the chest. One bullet actually hit my heart. Still here to tell the story though!'

My stomach twisted at the thought of another officer walking in while Johnson was showing me his naked chest. I didn't know how to get out of this situation. Maybe it would be over more quickly if I just played along.

'Shit. Did it hurt?' I instantly realized that this was a ridiculous question, so I quickly followed up with, 'So why'd someone do that to you anyways?'

I could feel myself dropping my grammar and my 't's.

It felt ridiculous to be having a conversation like this one in my middle-class accent. But there was more to it than that. The way Johnson spoke made me feel so exposed, I felt compelled to hide who I was from him.

'Ah – plenty of people would like to do this.' He gestured again to his scars. 'When I was on the roads I was a big man, yeah? You need knives? I got you. You need drugs? I got guys for you. You need guns? I got them comin' out my *arse*, bruv. I can even sort someone out with the best gels. I can make someone disappear in one phone call, you get me?'

'I guess, but why did someone shoot you though?' I was attempting to match his tone of indifference. 'Like, did you shoot first or what?'

'Gen, you don't understand this life yet. I got one of theirs first, innit, couple of months before in a ride-out. That's when one gang goes in another gang's territory with guns and knives and shit and, well, sees who they can find.' He chuckled.

'Is that what you're here for, then?' I asked. I didn't feel as uncomfortable as I thought I would sitting in front of a self-proclaimed murderer.

'Me? Nah, I'm on some bullshit domestic abuse case. Don't even need to tell you it wasn't me, but them police they just wanna get me on anythin' they can. They want me off my streets, ya get me?'

'Sure. So doesn't it bother you that you're serving time for something you didn't do?' I asked, surprised by this carelessness from someone who gave off such an air of control.

'Gen, I bin in an' out of jail for the last twelve years, since I was fourteen, yeah? Sometimes you gotta serve some time for summin' you didn't do. But four murder charges and got off all of 'em, so you win some, you lose some – you get me?' He said the last part with a wink.

Yikes. How do I respond to that one? I wondered. *'Good for you?' Probably not.*

'Anyways you'll get used to scars in this place – there's plenty of 'em! You think these scars are bad, have you met Fingers?'

'Who?' I said, bemused.

'Fingers,' he repeated. 'Hang on.' He stepped out of the office door and shouted up the landing: 'Fingers! Fingers!'

Johnson was right about the scars. Even from the few days I had spent shadowing on the wings I had seen Joker-style scars curling up from the corners of mouths, bite-sized chunks missing from ears, the odd gouged-out eye, and of course more than anything, the marks of rigorous and repetitive self-harm.

Fingers, though, was presumably about to take the biscuit.

Johnson returned and presented to me a friendly, smiling man with a thick Essex accent.

'Pleasure to meet ya, Miss! The name's Fingers. I would shake your 'and but . . .' And he held up both his hands to reveal two entirely fingerless palms. 'Still the best wing cleaner you'll meet in the 'ole slammer, though!' He grinned, then gave me a wink and what I thought was a thumbs up. I let out a bemused laugh before Fingers scooped up his mop, wielding it with unmatched precision as he weaved back off up the landing.

Johnson turned back to me and said in a hushed tone, 'So, what do you *really* think of the job so far?'

There was something about him – the intensity of him – that made me feel uneasy. I was experiencing the unnerving feeling that he was in charge, not me. As we continued to chat I racked my brains for an excuse to leave the office, eventually muttering 'I think I just heard Walter shout for me' somewhat unconvincingly. We both headed for the door, but I was still so flustered that I ended up holding it open for him. He stepped through it with a look of relish on his face.

One nil to Johnson – good start, I thought.

At that moment I did indeed hear Walter's booming voice come from the landing above: 'Gen – crack cell 2 for me!'

I was so glad to be asked to do something that I immediately took the few steps across to cell 2 and unlocked the door. But when I turned back round, Johnson was still there, standing by the open office door, beckoning me over with his hand. I groaned internally, and in a quiet and knowing voice he said to me: 'Gen, never leave the office door open, even with me there. Just always make sure you lock it behind you.'

Fuck, I thought.

'Shit – thanks,' I said. 'That was dumb of me, I know.'

'Don't worry, Gen. See? I got your back. Just make sure you're on the ball, OK?'

From feeling content just after lunch, I now felt like this day couldn't be going any worse. I locked the office door firmly, feeling grateful to Johnson and ashamed all at the same time, then strode up the landing away from him as fast as I could, balling my hands into tight fists to stop my feelings appearing on my face, not concentrating on anything happening around me.

'Gov, unlock this door for me.'

A younger prisoner took me by surprise.

'I'm not unlocking doors, I'm afraid,' I replied, without thinking. I knew it sounded stupid and I immediately wished I'd phrased it differently.

'What? So what's even the point of you!' he spat.

'I – I don't have keys,' I tried again.

'What? Yes you do, pham! Shit – these govs are so lazy, man!' He skulked off and I could feel the lie I'd just told creeping up my face.

A group of prisoners started to flock around me. I wasn't sure where they'd all come from.

'You new, Miss? Where you from?' one asked.

Then another chipped in: 'Yeah, you look like you're from Surrey or sumfin', Miss. Where you from?'

They were all using friendly tones but something told me they had a hidden agenda.

'Um – I'm from South London.' Which wasn't

exactly a lie: I'd recently moved in to a friend's spare
room in Southwark.

'South London? That don't mean nuffin'! Where in
South London?'

'As if I'm telling you guys where I live!' I tried to say
light-heartedly.

'I'm from Walworth, Miss. Gang shit, you know.'
He made a gang sign with his fingers and grinned.

I looked at his hands and tried to look amused but
unimpressed. 'Is that meant to make me wanna tell you
where I live then?'

A couple of them laughed. 'Ha – this gov's got jokes,
you know! How come you wanna be a gov then? You
like lockin' doors or summin'?'

5

A&E

You quickly find out how dispensable you are when you first start. You are forever being slung across to work on a wing that isn't your own, or sent off to trudge around the place escorting prisoners between buildings because another officer is too busy, or just as likely can't be bothered. It happens, bluntly, because you don't know what you're doing yet, so you're not much use on your own wing and won't be missed. Being a newbie, you're also less likely to make a fuss – which is why new officers are often prime targets for hospital escorts too.

After one morning briefing during my first week, instead of being assigned to a wing I was asked to stay behind for more details about going on a hospital escort. I hadn't done one yet, and despite the looks of commiseration I got when they read out my name, I felt a thrill of excitement run through me.

Back in training, our teacher had told us: *when you leave the jail with a prisoner, you become the prison.* In the absence of towering walls and several electric gates, the only things keeping the prisoner 'imprisoned' are the handcuffs and the officer they are locked to.

An hour later, I was sitting in the back of a taxi on the way to the hospital, tightly handcuffed to a bulky man with deep-set eyes hooded by a single bristly brow, and a permanent look of distaste curling his mouth. He was sandwiched by another officer on his left side, and there was one more in the front holding the briefcase-like bag which held the key to the cuffs, the documents we needed and the prison-issue Nokia brick phone. No one seemed to want to introduce themselves, or say much at all, so I kept quiet.

I knew that three officers were sent out instead of two when the prisoner's escape risk was calculated as high. The calculation is usually based on things like the length of their sentence, affiliations with an established gang, previous history of access to firearms or links to foreign countries, all of which could help them to successfully escape. From the look of this man, I thought in his case it might be all of those things.

The cuff was digging into the bones of my wrist and I was squeezed tightly between his right thigh and the car door. I tried to shift as subtly as I could, to give my wrist a moment of relief, sensing that it wasn't in my interest to disturb him. But he noticed this immediately and turned to me with a gruff growl.

'You must be uncomfortable, Miss.' Then his whole face appeared to melt into a soft smile and he added, 'I'm sorry, I'm not the smallest of guys, am I?' I must have looked a bit taken aback because he went on encouragingly, 'Don't worry, I'm a lot nicer than I look. A lot nicer than what it says on my file too, actually.'

The officer in the front chuckled at this. 'Oh yeah, Avaro's a real teddy bear!'

The waiting room at the hospital was packed and chaotic. Sprawled across almost every seat were crying babies or elderly people bleeding and bruised. A couple were arguing in one corner, and several barefoot men with dirt-clogged feet were lying on the floor in between the rows of chairs.

One officer asked the nurse running busily around reception if there was a separate room we could wait in, gesturing his head towards the handcuffed Avaro. She shook her head dismissively – 'Not possible' – and bustled away.

We settled for a couple of chairs at the far end of the room. I sat down next to Avaro, still cuffed to him. The plastic chair was cracked and it creaked as it took his weight. The other two officers stood opposite us. We'd barely sat down when the woman next to us jumped up with her baby and hurried away to stand on the other side of the room, obviously not wanting to be near us.

Avaro chortled awkwardly, but I also saw a flicker of shame in his eyes. I couldn't help but feel pity.

Then one of the other officers leaned into him. 'C'mon, Avaro, why don't you do your thing? You know – get us in that nice side room?'

Avaro grinned. 'If you say so, boss.'

He turned and winked at me, then hesitated. 'I'm sorry, Miss, I haven't even asked you your name.'

'Oh, right, don't worry, it's Gen,' I replied, grateful to him for being the person to ask.

'Got it. I'm Avaro.' He glanced at his cuffed hands, shrugged his shoulders and said, 'Well, I can't shake your hand.'

I smiled and nodded. 'You're off the hook,' I told him.

'Well, Gen,' he went on, 'this is just a little trick of mine you're gonna see now – so play along!'

He stood up abruptly, but I noticed he was careful to lift his right hand gently so as not to yank my wrist with the cuff. He started to yell at the other officer, switching between English and Portuguese, pointing menacingly at the office and then at the hospital door. The yelling continued, flitting eloquently between more languages – I detected a hint of Russian, then another tongue I didn't recognize at all. A toddler in the row behind us started to cry and his mother clutched him closer to her chest. I watched Avaro pause for a moment and turn to the mother, giving her a wink before he kept going.

The nurses started to look concerned and backed away, whispering to each other.

'This is what I was talking about!' the officer said to them. 'This guy – he just kicks off. Is there no way we can go somewhere a bit more private?'

One of the nurses rolled her eyes and hurried us to a room just off the waiting area. Avaro's trick had clearly worked.

The four of us sat there for a few minutes, enjoying the silence.

'I'm not meaning to be a pain,' Avaro said, 'but it's just after all that I need to go to the toilet now.'

I considered for a moment how impressive, almost endearing, his attempts at English turns of phrase were. I imagined the kind of work you'd be able to get if you had that level of skill. What could lead a man who spoke at least four languages to a prison cell?

One of the officers rummaged for something in the bag. 'Not to worry, mate. Let me get the chain out.'

Avaro had one pair of cuffs around his wrists, and then an additional pair attached to one of his wrists and one of mine. For him to go to the bathroom with any kind of privacy, the cuff around my wrist had to be swapped for one with a long chain on it. The officer started to fasten the long chain cuff to me.

'For goodness' sake, don't make the lady do it!' he exclaimed. 'She will not want to come to the toilet with me!'

The other officer shrugged, passed me the escort bag and instead put the long chain cuff on himself.

I watched them trail off together, feeling rather sick.

It's not just freedom you lose when you're imprisoned: it's every last little bit of privacy.

While Avaro was gone, I had a chance to flick through his file, having felt it was somehow too intrusive to do it while he was there. I scanned the first few pages on which were pasted his menacing mugshot and the words WANTED – DO NOT APPROACH – CALL 999 IMMEDIATELY. These were ready for us to hand to the police just in case Avaro did manage to make a break for it. I couldn't help but feel amused by the incongruity between the gentle and seemingly intelligent man I had spent the last hour or so with and the terrifying thug in the pictures. I skimmed over his medical records and then landed on the page I was looking for: his criminal history.

Warnings: Risk to females. 36 counts of arranging or facilitating the travel of an individual for exploitation under Section 2 of the Modern Slavery Act. False imprisonment. Sexual exploitation. Threats to kill.

Disbelief and disgust hit me at the same time. Had Avaro, who'd been careful not to pull my wrist too hard and hurt me, really done all of this? The list went on, culminating with 'sentenced to life imprisonment'.

I slapped the file shut and posted it back into the bag, busying myself with the spare set of cuffs as Avaro and the officer re-emerged from the toilet, chuckling to each other.

Half an hour later the nurse we'd spoken to earlier came over to us, still looking frosty. I got the feeling she had made us wait a little longer on purpose. She wrapped the blood pressure monitor around Avaro's bulky arm.

'Good performance in the waiting room, sir,' she said to him sarcastically, without looking up from the monitor. 'That's a good set of languages you've got in your back pocket too.'

Avaro grinned guiltily and replied, 'Thank you, Miss. Yes, I speak English, Portuguese, Romanian, Albanian, and I'm learning Russian. I travel a lot for work.' Then with genuine graciousness, he added, 'I'm sorry, Miss, but my officers needed a seat. They work almost as hard as you do. And I was hoping to get back to my cell before three because there's a new episode of *Escape to the Country* I haven't watched yet.'

The nurse laughed disbelievingly. 'Well then, I'd better get you in to see the doctor straight away.'

Even once we'd got back to the prison and I was going about the rest of my day on the wing, I didn't stop thinking about Avaro. During my lunch break I grabbed my phone from my locker, hurried outside and sheltered from the early autumn rain under a tree while I typed Avaro's name into Google with chilly fingers.

Sure enough, several news articles appeared immediately showing pictures of Avaro next to his co-defendants. Each of them gave the same details: he was guilty of sexual exploitation, kidnapping and coercive control. There were victim statements from women as young as eighteen whom he'd forced into prostitution.

I spent the rest of the afternoon barely able to concentrate. The facts that I was reading just didn't fit with what I'd seen and heard. This was the first person I had met in prison I'd actually found myself liking, yet he had committed some of the most destructive and abusive crimes against women I could imagine.

Perhaps, I mused, *he didn't take part in the abusive side of the operation*. It didn't make sense for someone like him to be capable of such cruelty and violation – someone so charming and at the same time modest and considerate. *Maybe he thought he was helping the women. Or perhaps what went on just wasn't as bad as the victims in the news articles had said.*

I physically jolted at this thought. Was I really questioning the victims' statements because Avaro had been kind to me for a few hours? Shocked that it had even crossed my mind, I hurried back into the prison, rubbing my hands together to warm them up.

'So you're saying he's a *nice* human trafficker?'

My flatmate, Louis, was looking at me with a mixture of a smile and a frown after I'd told him about my day.

'Well, this is my point: can you actually be a nice human trafficker?' I asked, doubtfully.

'Maybe he was faking it,' Louis suggested with a shrug. 'Making you like him. Fooling you. He's not a nice human trafficker – he's a smart one.'

'That's the thing, though, I think he's genuine,' I responded slowly. 'I think he's charming and kind, or at least he can be, and he isn't trying to deceive anyone. I don't even think he's trying to redeem himself by being nice. I just think he's two things at once.'

Louis was nodding now, but with a grin. He was far more cynical about the human race than me and I knew he was finding it much easier than I was to come to terms with conflicts around the friendliness of a human trafficker.

'What really freaked me out though,' I continued, 'was that he actually made me think for a second that maybe he wasn't guilty. I mean, I know he is. I've seen statements from his victims. But he's not some archetypal cold-eyed, slimy bully. So the crimes – they just don't seem to fit. I mean, obviously I get that people can be charming on the surface and sociopathic behind closed doors. But it never would have crossed my mind that it was possible for someone who was so *authentically* likeable to be capable of what he did.'

'It's a much more comfortable world, Gen,' Louis said, 'if we can just assume that people like that are pure scum of the earth. That way we can just lock 'em up and throw away the key.' He shrugged again.

'Right,' I said, enthusiastically, 'so this is the problem. We aren't doing ourselves any favours by burying our heads in the sand and convincing ourselves that human traffickers are these stereotypes like we see in TV shows. Because if we hold these *totally* two-dimensional and unrealistic images of them, how are we meant to spot them in real life? Our friendly neighbour who's running a brothel? The lady who manages the nail bar but all the girls who work there have been trafficked? The people who do things like that – they can just be normal people, you know? Even nice ones.'

'Shit, yeah – I mean, you're not wrong, Gen. "Know your enemy" is the phrase, isn't it?'

6

Just a Girl

I had survived a full week. It had been disorienting, I had felt horribly vulnerable and I still had absolutely no idea which way was up. I did feel like I was at least getting to know the names and faces of some of the men on H-Wing though – *and that is something*, I thought as I strode purposefully into the morning briefing.

My heart sank when three names were read out for H-Uppers that day and I wasn't one of them. Every time I felt like I was settling into the wing it seemed I was shafted off to the hospital or, worse, to one of the understaffed wings where the officers had given up and the prisoners baulked at being asked to do even the most reasonable things. My disappointment was nothing, however, compared to the look on Reffie's face when my name was called out to work with him on D-Wing for the day.

Reffie was one of those officers who had given up. I'd already learned that he wasn't the only prison officer like this – the ones who'd loudly moan how they were just waiting for trouble to break out because after a 'wrap-up', prison slang for a restraint, they could take six weeks off claiming injury and then not come back. I'd never spoken to Reffie personally, but I'd heard him discuss this exit plan with other officers. He was waiting for his chance, and walking around with an air of defeat and carelessness that made me nervous.

When the briefing was over, he took one look at me and marched over to the manager to complain, with no regard for the fact that I was in earshot. How could he be expected to work with just one new officer? Especially, he added, since the officer was *just a girl*. The manager shrugged, and Reffie stormed off to D-Wing.

I followed him a few minutes later to give him a bit of time to make the phone calls I knew he would be making. I had barely sat down in the office, though, before he strode off again, muttering something about the security office. He had already unlocked a few prisoners who appeared to be workers; some were milling about with brooms in their hands, others were chatting to other prisoners through the hinges of cell doors.

Twenty minutes later, Reffie still wasn't back. I had been lingering in the office, pretending to browse through non-existent emails, but I kept thinking about that term we'd heard over and over again in training: *wing shy*. I knew that it wasn't right for me to have been left on the wing by myself with prisoners unlocked, but I didn't want anyone, staff *or* prisoners, to get the idea that I was wing shy.

I walked out of the office with purpose. I knew that if I was going to make it through the morning I couldn't let on to anyone that I was feeling uncomfortable. Not to mention the fact that it's always best to get at least a couple of prisoners on side – especially if you suspect your fellow officer won't be anywhere to be seen.

One of them was standing at the end of the wing braiding another prisoner's hair. I was taken aback by this seemingly affectionate, almost maternal scene. I wandered over slowly, peering into some of the cells as I went, trying to come across as casual as I could. As I got closer, the man in the chair started eyeing me suspiciously.

'This one of them *nosey* govs or something then?' he hissed to the guy braiding his hair.

'All right, guys – are you both workers then?' I said in the friendliest tone I could muster.

They looked at me defensively.

'Yeah, we're workers,' said the man in the chair. 'Who's askin'?'

'Cool.' I shrugged. 'Not looking to bang you up or anything, just seeing what jobs people got on the wing.'

Their expressions softened. 'What wing you on normally, Miss? I swear I recognize you,' the hairdresser chirped.

'I'm on H-Wing normally,' I replied, hoping I could get away with being from a different wing instead of brand new to the job.

'Ah . . . you new or something? I'm Craig, by the way.' He passed over a bunch of hair from his right hand to his left and put his hand out to shake mine. 'Where's Reffie got to, then? You tellin' me he's left little old you on the wing with us bad men?' Craig laughed.

'Ha! Something like that,' I replied.

The other prisoner smirked. 'He's done out here, pham, that Reffie. The guy don't even care no more.'

'Yeah, Miss – you'll be lucky if you see him again this afternoon. Let me give you some advice though, innit? You're gonna want to keep us two out cos we the peace-keepers on here. You got any problems with mandem on here and we your guys. Craig and Akram, you remember that.'

Akram put a fist out to bump mine. I heard the phone ringing faintly from the office and took my chance.

'Right, well, thanks guys, I'd better get that.'

As I walked away from them I heard Craig teasing Akram: 'Bro, you've got proper baby hair, you know? Real cute and fine! Feel like I'm doin' my daughter's hair, bro! You even got her chubby cheeks!'

I looked back at them to see Akram slapping Craig's hand away from his cheek, both of them giggling like boys. It made me smile and I felt myself relax – for two seconds. The instant I picked up the phone, life on D-Wing was back with a bang.

'Why you not brought the dinner trolley back to the kitchen yet?' a rough voice yelled down the line.

'What? Sorry ... what, didn't I ...' I was taken aback. Sometimes the staff in here were ruder than the prisoners. 'Er, so I'm the only officer on the wing,' I said, as firmly as I could manage. 'I can't leave.'

'Bring it over now or you get no food,' the voice snapped, and the line went dead.

At that moment, Reffie skulked back into the office.

'Reffie, the kitchens just called. Said something about not having the dinner trolley?'

I hoped he might give me some kind of explanation, but he instantly made an about-turn and headed off the wing yet again, muttering over his shoulder, 'OK, OK, I'll get the trolley. Unlock the servery.'

I sighed. *And you're not going to show me how to do that?* I knew that the room off the side of the wing where the prisoners' food was served to them through a hatch from hotplates was called the servery, so I went and unlocked that, still not quite sure I'd understood what Reffie meant.

Some of the prisoners made their way over.

'Is it time for servery already, Miss?' one of them said, a hint of surprise in his voice.

This didn't fill me with confidence. 'Um, what time do you usually have servery on this wing?' I asked him, hoping his response might reveal a bit more about the routine.

'Pha, Miss! It's the same in the whole jail! You the officer – d'you see a watch on my wrist? I go by your time! But if you say it's time for servery then you gotta unlock the rest of the servery workers.'

Ah, I have to unlock the servery workers! *Riddle solved*, I thought to myself. Except . . . how was I meant to work out who they were?

On the H-Wing office board there was a VR next to Johnson's name and a CL next to Fingers' name, indicating respectively that they were a Violence Reduction rep and a cleaner, so I went back to the D-Wing office and stared at the board there for some sort of sign. Finally I noticed a letter S written in red pen next to a few names. S for servery seemed reasonable. But most of the names were illegible – they'd been scribbled out and written over or half rubbed off too many times. Staring at that board was like gazing into Reffie's mind: instead of prisoners' names, the words might just as well have said I DON'T CARE, I DON'T CARE, I DON'T CARE, over and over again.

While I was frowning at the board, an older man strode into the office with a mop in his hands.

'All right, bootiful! What d'you do to end up in 'ere then?'

I felt a queasy stab in my stomach. I had enough to deal with right now without being leered at too. I glared at him. 'Sorry?'

He scowled and moaned. 'Ahhh – you ain't one of these modern ladies that can't take a compliment, is you?'

I shook my head steadily, knowing it was important to stay in control. This wasn't worth starting a fight over, not when I had servery to figure out.

'It's just . . . no woman wants to be called beautiful at work,' I explained pleasantly. 'It's not what we're here for.' I felt quite pleased with the even tone I'd maintained.

His expression turned in seconds to an ugly grimace. 'That it, then? You one of them gels who finks they're better than the rest of us?'

Clearly my words hadn't had the calming effect I'd been hoping for. The expression in his eyes was starting to worry me, turning wild and defensive.

'Look, it doesn't have to be a big deal,' I said. 'It's just condescending, that's all.'

'So you *do* fink you're better than us? Look at that smug look on yer face!' he growled, then spat out: 'You'll regret that, little girl!' He kicked his dirty mop bucket all over the floor, then backed out of the office.

Great, I thought. I'd barely even left the office and I'd already pissed someone off. I felt completely disheartened. I went over what I'd said, and didn't actually think I could have handled the situation any better – but I still felt like a fool. And now there was a big puddle of murky water between me and the door.

Summoning up every ounce of courage I had, I

splashed through the puddle, locked the office door firmly behind me and strode along the landing towards Akram and Craig.

'All right, guys, you're gonna have to help me out. Who's servery on the wing?'

They smiled, delighted to be asked.

'But don't mug me off,' I added. 'I'm not just unlocking all your mates.'

'All right, Miss, we'll show you.'

Craig pointed towards a cell, and he and I went over to it. I cracked the door, and two men stared out of the darkness at me.

'Who's servery in here, then?' I said.

They both started to bustle out of the cell. I stuck my arm across the door.

'Hold on! Which one of you is it?'

I kept my arm across the door, looking to Craig for an indication, but he fist-bumped both of them saying, 'My bruddah!'

'What's going on, Miss? You gonna let us out or what?' one of the prisoners in the cell complained.

'I know it's only one of you for servery, so which one is it?'

I looked them both in the eye, and one of them broke into a grin. *Gotcha*, I thought.

'Ahhh, not so good at lying then, are you? Come on then!'

I beckoned to the one who hadn't smiled and he quickly stepped outside. I locked the door behind him.

'Miss, that's some psychology shit right there!'
Akram exclaimed, laughing.

Akram and Craig went on taking me around, gesturing at cell doors for servery workers. By the time I'd
unlocked five prisoners I knew they were taking me for
a ride.

'Right, guys, that's it, I'm not unlocking any more,' I
said firmly.

'Nah, Miss, you got to!' Craig insisted. 'You got to
unlock my man in cell 20. He's the muscle round here.
I'm telling you, you gotta unlock him. You're not safe
out here without him.'

I groaned. They were the only people helping me –
where the hell was Reffie all this time? – and I almost felt as
though I didn't want to offend them.

'OK, but after that, that's it. No one else is coming
out.'

I flicked open the door to cell 20 and jumped slightly
when I saw the large man standing just the other side of
it. He was brushing his teeth, the toothbrush comically
dwarfed by his enormous hand and arm, which bulged
and rippled with every stroke. He spat into the sink and
grimaced at me with toothpaste dribbling down his
chin.

'All right, Gen! What's taken you so long? Didn't
they tell you I was the muscle around here?'

It was Avaro. He grinned at me broadly. Despite
everything I had read about him, and how sickened I
had felt at liking him so much on meeting him, I felt

like I could breathe again. I suppose that's what a familiar face does to you in a place like this.

Craig slapped palms with him. 'Yo, you good, bro? You already know Miss then?'

Avaro nodded. 'I hope you boys have been good to her.'

Reffie finally reappeared through the wing door, tugging the heated food cart behind him. Filled with food for a hundred people, the carts weigh about as much as a small car and have the wheels of a supermarket trolley. One of the wheels caught on the door frame and Reffie kicked it angrily until it came free with a jolt, and he stumbled through the doorway.

'Why are there so many prisoners unlocked?' he barked at me.

I didn't bother answering.

The man who'd kicked the bucket over in the office marched up to him and greeted him. 'You all right, Ref? Now who's this li'l girl they put you on with today then? What's all that about?'

He touched knuckles with Reffie in a definitely over-familiar way. Reffie turned to me, obviously embarrassed by such inappropriate behaviour.

'Er, OK, Gen,' he said sheepishly. 'You just go and do medication. I'll sort this lot out here.'

Gladly, I thought to myself.

'Thatcher! Mr Thatcher!' I called.

Needless to say, I had never done medication before.

In training we had learned that the supervising officer was there to make sure everyone swallowed the medication they were given there and then, instead of taking it back to the wing. If they got medication back to the wing it might be sold or, worse, stockpiled and used to attempt suicide. Everything is dispensed by prison nurses. They stand in their small surgeries behind a locked door with a small shoulder-height hatch in it. The door's set back slightly from the hexagonal core landing where all the spurs meet.

Thatcher limped over, picking up his ID card and then the small paper cup the nurse had placed on the ledge. He threw his head back, tipping the contents into his mouth. The nurse refilled the cup with water for him to wash down the pills.

'Ta very much!' he said politely to the nurse, tossing the empty cup in a nearby bin. 'Thanks, Miss!'

Prisoners and staff were bustling around me out by the hatch. It was busy, but I was relieved just to step off D-Wing for a moment. A nurse impatiently tapped a prisoner ID card on the metal ledge in the door between her and the prisoners, and I bent down to read the name out.

'Mr Sheeran!' I shouted.

Another man wandered over. I started to relax into the repetitiveness of the process. Here was something so simple that not even I could mess up, and I was enjoying being appreciated for a short while. Then I bent over to look at the next ID card and caught my breath. It was the man who'd kicked over the mop bucket.

I cleared my throat. 'Mr Lane? Mr Lane!' I called, evenly.

Perhaps he's over it by now and won't still be angry?

Fat chance of that. Lane marched up to the counter, glaring at me, making it clear that his grudge after what had happened earlier was very much still being carried. He looked me up and down, knocked his head back and went to tip his meds into his mouth. Something didn't look right. Lane scrunched the cup in his fist and turned to walk away, but he didn't toss it in the bin like the other prisoners had done. On instinct I followed him – *what do I have to lose? He already has it in for me*.

Just around the corner I saw him bend down, revealing half of his pale and hairy back. Then he started to push something under the door to E-Wing. When he saw me coming up behind him, he immediately stood up straight, clenching his fists behind his back.

'Don't think you can try it with me, little girl,' he growled at me.

'What's in your hand, Mr Lane?'

He responded with a sneer.

'Mr Lane! Show me what's in your hand.'

He held it out towards me, spreading his fingers. A couple of pills were stuck to his sweaty palm, along with some scraps of roughly cut paper. I recognized the squares of paper from training.

Spice paper.

Credit-card-sized squares of paper sprayed with the synthetic drug and then passed seamlessly around the prison before they're ripped smaller again and rolled up into vapes to be smoked.

Mr Lane was smiling at me provocatively, daring me to do something.

I went to grab the contents of his hand, but in one swift movement he snapped his hand out of my reach and threw the handful into his mouth. He swallowed, purposefully.

'Look what you've done now, little girl,' he snarled, sticking his tongue out to show me he had swallowed everything.

My fury took over from common sense: I grabbed him by the wrist and led him forcefully back to the office. Reffie was standing by the door looking bored.

'Lane is passing stuff under the door to E-Wing,' I panted.

Lane broke free from my grasp, aggressively shaking me off. 'Reffie, tell this girl to leave me alone, I ain't doin' nuffin'!'

Reffie looked at Lane, and then at me. 'Nah, this guy's fine. Just leave him. He's a cleaner.'

'No!' I said, now adamant. 'He's been passing stuff under the door to another wing!'

There was a silence.

Oh my God, I thought. *Is Reffie actually going to back the prisoner?*

'And he's been a dick to me all day!' I sniffed. I kicked myself for sounding like a child in front of a teacher, but I'd had enough and I didn't know what else to do.

'OK, OK, I'll sort him, leave him with me,' Reffie said reluctantly, but he made no move to do anything.

Lane strolled off to pick up his mop and proceeded to make a display of wandering about cheerfully, chatting to other prisoners. He knew as well as I did that Reffie wasn't going to do anything at all about what had happened. He bounced between different groups, laughing and joking and occasionally lowering his voice and pointing in my direction.

Great, I thought to myself. *He's building up his army.*

I felt powerless, dejected. For the first time since starting the job I had to fight to swallow back tears. I strode away from Reffie – I couldn't even look at him. But the second I was out of Reffie's sight, Lane clocked his opportunity to get me on my own.

I bit the insides of my cheeks, hard, trying to meet him with a stern face as he covered the last few steps between us. He leaned in with me toe to toe, and I felt the hot stench of his breath on my face as he spoke.

'I told you, little girl,' he said softly. 'You messed with the wrong man. It's me who runs this wing, you silly little bitch. An' guess what? I get out tomorrow, and I'll make sure I'm waiting for you when you leave those gates. You're not gettin' 'ome safe tomorrow night, you 'ear me?'

Again, I didn't feel fear. I was far more concerned about *looking* vulnerable than *being* vulnerable. A mixture of humiliation and defiance swirled inside me and, perhaps against my better judgement, I retorted: 'We'll see if you get out tomorrow after threatening a member of staff.'

'You filthy—'

But before he could finish what he was saying, a large hand reached over my shoulder and came to rest firmly on Lane's. I turned and saw Avaro. In a very calm voice, he said, 'Bullying ladies again, Lane? Do us a favour and fuck off now, OK?'

Lane turned on his heel with a scowl and spat on the floor at my feet. I glared after him.

Avaro turned to me with a grin on his face. 'Told you I was the muscle round here, innit,' he said. Then he looked at me more seriously. 'But Gen, for real – you watch who you rub up the wrong way from now on, right? Don't go starting fights you can't finish.'

Once all the prisoners were locked up, I tried to speak to Reffie. I told him what Lane had said to me, but he barely looked up from his microwave meal.

'So yeah, anyway,' I went on, 'can you just remind me, what's the paperwork I need to do to report this?'

Reffie rolled his eyes. 'Tss, this is prison, you know? Just leave it. You're doing too much. You'll burn yourself out.'

So I dropped it. I didn't feel like there was anything else I could do . . . apart from look over my shoulder on my way home in the dark.

It wasn't so much Lane's threat that bothered me, although I did stop taking the short-cut through the underpass on the way to the station. The problem was the total disregard that my colleague had had for me. If even other officers weren't going to support me through the tribulations that crop up daily in prisons, how was I going to survive here?

7

A Secret Garden

'All right, Gen? Haven't seen you in a while!'

Johnson burst through the office door. My heart sank. I didn't have the strength for it.

'Thought it might have got too much for you already!' he went on cheerily.

'Um, yeah – I've been around and about, hospital escorts, did a shift on D-Wing the other day,' I responded flatly.

He seemed unperturbed. 'Ah yeah, they always do that with new officers – it's cos you don't really know the ropes yet. They sling you off anywhere they need another body in a uniform.'

I didn't think anything could have made me feel any smaller than I already did, but at this I shrank a bit more inside my uniform.

'Don't worry though, you're catching on quicker than most, Gen!'

Johnson said it smugly, but I still felt my heart swell ever so slightly with gratification. I tried to fight the feeling. *Can the approval of this man really mean that much to me?*

Johnson sat down on the desk in front of me, tapped the door with his foot so that it swung shut and leaned towards me.

'You all right, Gen, seriously? You seem a bit down today.'

'Yeah, everything's fine. Just tired, that's all.' I added a yawn to my reply.

But a big part of me wanted to tell him what had happened the other day. I wanted to explain that I had stood my ground and that I was happy I had done it, but that what had happened had also made me feel so alone, so neglected. I wanted to confess to him how angry I was that it was an *officer* who had made me feel like that, and a *prisoner* who had come to help me. I wanted him to be pleased with me.

'Gen, you can tell me,' Johnson said softly. 'I can always tell when someone's got summin' they need to get off their chest.'

Once again I felt as though he was looking *into* me, and my stomach knotted. I could tell my cheeks were flushing because my eyes started to water. I thought I saw a hint of something like delight flash across Johnson's face.

If he sees this, he'll know I'm weak.

I felt a sudden, desperate urge to escape the conversation.

'*Shit!* I forgot, I need to do AFCs!' It was the first excuse that came to my head. Flustered, I ushered him out of the office, desperate to get away from his piercing stare.

'Heya, good morning, just here to do AFCs,' I said, opening the door of one of the cells.

'AF-whats?' replied a sleepy voice from the bottom bunk.

AFCs are 'accommodation fabric checks'. It's something that officers are meant to do, in pairs, every day – an inspection of each cell that's not a formal search. It's basically just making sure the cell is in good shape, the lights are working, the toilet flushes, there's no damage to windows and the inhabitants haven't made any holes anywhere they might be able to escape through or hang themselves from. Everyday prison stuff.

Doing this kind of check in pairs daily isn't all that realistic, though. In real life, officers do the checks by themselves, once a week at most, and as a result the prisoners aren't used to them. But in our morning meeting, Kelly, our wing manager, had reminded everyone that in the long lead-up to Christmas and New Year we needed to be on the lookout for hooch.

'The distillers will be getting to work around this time,' she told us. 'Who doesn't like a drink at

Christmas, eh? So I wanna see you all checking under those beds. I'm on duty on Christmas Day and I won't be in the mood for no drunken mess.'

I got to work, starting with the cell bell, located just inside the door, as I'd been taught. I pressed it on and then held the fob on my key chain against the flashing red light which appeared on the other side of the door to turn the alarm off.

'You guys all right? Everything working in here? Anything I need to call Works about? Your phone and TV working OK?'

I was keen to make it clear to the prisoners that I was there to ensure their comfort, not to spy on them. This 'nosey' tag that I'd unwittingly created for myself was starting to get me down.

I unplugged the phone, then plugged it back in again. I checked the taps and the toilet flush, tapped on the window, and bent down to look under the bed. I was careful to keep my back to the wall for this part, not wanting to attract any unwanted attention.

As I continued down the wing, I started to sense more and more that the prisoners weren't used to AFCs.

'Mr Pierre, AFCs!'

I swung his door open with purpose, preparing for him to make a scene out of me coming into his cell. He had arrived on the wing a couple of days earlier, standing at 6ft 5in, laden in tattoos covering him right up to his eyebrows. He'd flashed a grille of gold teeth through a snarl as I led him to his cell. He was registered as *high risk, single cell*, and his file read *threats to kill* and *history of making weapons*.

But I wasn't going to let him know that he intimidated me.

'Everything working in here?'

Pierre had his back to the door and was carefully fiddling with something on his windowsill. I took a few steps towards him and peered over his shoulder. To my surprise, he was tending to the most incredible garden, each plant growing strangely from an empty yoghurt pot or a plastic bottle. I stopped short.

'Did . . . did you plant all these?'

He looked me straight in the eye. 'So what if I did?'

I hesitated, but I couldn't help myself. 'Can you show me around?' I asked.

His scowl froze for a moment and then cracked into a grin. 'Yeah – if you want, gov!'

He showed me a Pringles tube with a flourishing bush of rosemary protruding from it. 'I walked past a bush when I went to court once, pulled a bit off and grafted it. Bin growin' that for nine months now.' Then he pointed to a large Tupperware box, out of which browning stalks towered, weighed down in places by sparsely laden vines.

'Tomatoes!' I said. 'But how on earth are you growing tomatoes in here?'

'Should've seen them a month or two ago. Coming to the end of their season now but I wanted to give these last ones a chance before I cut 'em down an' make compost.'

He'd taken the seeds from the tomatoes in his lunch sandwiches, he explained, carefully selected the bigger seeds, dried them on some toilet paper and let them germinate in the sun before planting them in soil he'd collected from a corner in the yard. The garlic bulb he'd stolen from the kitchens to plant. The daffodil bulb he'd dug up from the only flower bed in the prison.

Finally, now grinning ear to ear, he showed me his pride and joy. He reached under his desk to pull out what appeared to be another small Tupperware box filled with mud. He dug around gently with his finger and delicately plucked out a worm.

'This! This is where the magic happens. Without these worms, you see, I ain't got no compost. These plants, they need the worms to thrive!'

His eyes were alight as he held the worm up to my face.

'It's amazing,' I said. 'But where did you learn to do all of this?'

He tipped his head back and laughed. 'Miss, I grow all my own stuff on the outside! Tomatoes, beans, potatoes.' And then he added with a wink, 'I even grow my own weed, innit.'

After closing up Pierre's cell, I was joined by Steve. At first I was grateful for the help, until I saw who was in tow. It was Clark, one of the wing cleaners. I didn't like him, and the feeling was clearly mutual.

As I had grappled with settling in on H-Uppers, trying to build decent relationships with the prisoners,

Clark had made it clear that he wasn't interested. He couldn't have been older than nineteen but already he was bitter and manipulative. He'd been in and out of prison for the best part of five years already, starting as a young offender, and he took a strange kind of pride in knowing the system better than any officer did. I couldn't understand why the other officers had given him a job: even a novice like me could see that he was clearly dealing drugs on the wing. He was forever sliding things under other prisoners' doors, only for those prisoners to emerge at dinnertime swaying and red-eyed.

But on top of that, Clark was a total dick and a bully.

I was crouching down looking under what must have been my twelfth bed when I felt the room get a bit darker. I looked up to see Clark standing in the doorway. He had a long pale face and a scrawny physique, so it was more his sinister energy that darkened the cell than his physical shadow. I pretended not to have noticed him and looked instead to one of the prisoners who was lying on his bed reading. 'Everything all right in—'

Clark interrupted me. 'Pha, Miss – are you bending down like that so no one's lookin' at your arse or sumfin'?'

I ignored him, but I allowed a sarcastic scowl to cross my face before turning back to the prisoner reading. 'Anyway, everything all right in here? Anything I can get—'

'Cos, Miss, no one's tryna look at your flat arse like that, yeah, so get over yourself!' Clark jeered.

'Shut up, Clark, not today,' I said, visibly annoyed.

Obviously that was the wrong thing to say to someone like Clark, and he seemed to take it as an invitation to ramp things up. He turned to the prisoners in their beds.

'Seriously, mandem – 'ave you noticed that Miss walks around here like everyone's on her tryna get her number or sumfin'?'

The prisoners in their beds laughed awkwardly. They clearly didn't want to offend either of us.

'Thanks, guys, have a good day,' I said, getting up and walking out, pushing past Clark at the door.

I was glad the next cell I walked into was dark because I knew my face was flushed. Clark had followed me. I tested the bell, and he stood there and watched my slightly shaking hands as I tried again and again to turn the cell bell off with my fob which seemed to have chosen this moment to play up.

'Everything working in here, guys? Anything you need?'

'All good, thanks, Miss,' came a sleepy voice from under the covers on the top bunk.

'Anything you *neeeed*?' Clark mimicked in a sultry voice, batting his eyelashes.

Once again I ignored him, busying myself with a stiff tap to avoid meeting his gaze before I pushed out of the cell past him.

'What's up, Miss, not gonna look under the bed this

time?' he crooned at me. 'Is it cos of what I said about you bending over, Miss? Is that it?'

He was practically giddy by now.

'Honestly – fuck off, Clark, or I swear you'll go back behind your door. I'm not in the mood today.'

I had almost shouted it at him, and for a moment he looked a bit surprised, but then that satisfied grin spread across his face again.

Steve came over. 'You two all right?' he asked.

'Blissful,' said Clark.

'Steve, Clark's going behind his door, he's getting in my way. Let's go, Clark.'

'Pfft.' Clark smirked. 'You can't lock me up cos I'm getting in your way. I'm a worker, I know my rights.'

'Right then, you can stay out, but I'll give you a negative IEP,' I retorted bluntly. 'Your choice.'

'Oooh, a negative incentive earned privilege – like I'm scared of one of those,' he simpered.

'Well, congrats on knowing what it stands for, Clark, but you will care about it if you get two cos that means you'll lose your job.'

He smirked again. 'Pfft – you think one of the other officers on this wing is gonna give me one? You're 'avin' a laugh, Jane.'

As he said this, he looked at Steve. Then Steve looked at me, nervously.

'Nah, Gen, he's all right, Clark is,' Steve mumbled. 'He's a cleaner so he needs to stay out.'

'Yeah, well, he's not doing any cleaning, he's just following me around talking about my arse and I'm over it so he needs to go back behind his door.'

Surely Steve will back me up?

But Steve just stared back at me like a rabbit in the headlights, trying to decide which side to pick.

'Don't worry, Jane, he's with me,' he said eventually. 'He's all right, really. You just gotta treat him with respect. You respect him then he'll respect you.'

Steve tried to laugh it off, but by now Clark was beaming at me. I couldn't believe it: once again an officer was picking the side of a prisoner. I clenched my jaw to stop my mouth dropping open.

Was anyone *ever* going to take my side in here?

I stormed back to the office with purpose, desperate not to look defeated. I made myself a cup of tea and put my feet up on the spare chair to make it clear to anyone who came in that I wasn't in the mood to be messed with. Naturally, as soon as I turned to Clark's file intending to write up his negative IEP, Johnson swept in.

'Whoa, Gen, now I know sumfin's up. Your whole vibe today, honestly, I can always tell, you know?'

I groaned internally, but I was craving a release so I blurted out what had just happened with Clark. I left out the bending over bit: I didn't want to enter yet another conversation about my arse with a prisoner, least of all X-ray-eyes Johnson.

'Yeah, Gen, that Clark – he's a prick. Don't let him make you feel any kind of way, yeah? He's just a prick.'

Support. That's what I'm so desperate to hear.

'Pha – yeah he is, isn't he?' I laughed, relieved.

'These other officers, yeah, they give him a job cos they just want him off their backs,' Johnson went on. 'He's a melt, but he knows how to get what he wants round here.' Johnson leaned into me again, as if he was letting me in on a secret. 'That's why govs like Steve give him a job. They can't handle his whining otherwise. But govs like Walter an' you – you put him in his place an' that's why he don't like you.'

Again my heart swelled at the praise – and yet again I got that sickening feeling that I was almost letting Johnson in.

'There's a lot of men in here who won't take word from a female – but with Clark it's all about respect. An' you gotta remember that Walter's our African brother out here too, an' that means he gets respect different from you.'

'Right, of course, yeah ... but – um – Clark is white,' I faltered, not sure if I should point out the obvious. 'Sorry, not that I'm saying that that's got anything to do with who he respects. I'm just saying, is that why he's got less respect for me? Cos I'm white?' I realized I wasn't making much sense, and stopped to take a breath. 'Oh, I dunno, it doesn't matter anyway. Don't worry about it.'

'Ah, Gen – you got so much to learn, you know! I'll put it like this: prison's one of the only places in dis country where Black is king. You see all these white men round 'ere? They talk like they Black, they walk like they Black, we the ones who got the respect out 'ere. You see me, for example. I'm light-skinned mixed race, right, so when I'm on the outside and I see some feds pull up I am white, just like that – I am the whitest version of myself.'

'OK,' I said, suddenly transfixed by what he was saying.

'Soon as they throw me in 'ere though? Bam! Now I'm Black again, right? Don't get me wrong, I'm always careful to keep my manners – keep my good *British* tone.' He enunciated the word 'British' in an almost royal accent. 'I don't talk like them white people on *EastEnders*, but you don't see me talkin' like no full road-man neither.'

I was gripped by everything he was saying. I had never heard anyone talk about race as candidly as this. Johnson could obviously tell that he had intrigued me. Realizing this, I then tried to look as though I wasn't interested, flicking through Clark's profile, working out where to write his negative IEP. *A bit late in the day now, though. Johnson knows I've been hanging on his every word for the last few minutes.*

Then a note popped up in the file. It had been written by Walter.

Negative IEP for Mr Clark for telling an officer to 'suck her mum'. Written on behalf of another officer.

So it wasn't just me who wanted to enforce some

rules around here. Another negative IEP and Clark would lose his job.

'See, Gen, you got stuff to learn, you know, if you don't come from these ends.' Johnson was looking a bit put out that something in the file had taken my attention away from him. 'That's what I'm 'ere for though!' he went on. 'While we're at it, don't try an' hand out negative IEPs. It makes you look like you don't know what you're doin'. Any proper prisoner ain't gonna care about no IEP.'

'Well actually, Johnson,' I responded, 'I just looked on his file and he loses his job if I give him one, so I think you'll find Clark does care about them.'

Johnson chuckled. 'Touché, Gen. Well, that still don't mean you can give me one though!' His smiling face suddenly went deadpan and he hissed harshly: 'You give me an IEP an' I'll make this wing go mad.' His eyes were blazing and I felt a coldness spreading through my stomach. Then just as suddenly he turned again and laughed good-naturedly as if he hadn't said anything at all.

I jumped to my feet and strode over to the office door, muttering something about needing to do AFC paperwork, which as far as I knew didn't even exist.

'Why you always rushin' me out like this, Gen? What's wrong with just enjoyin' a friendly cup of tea?'

Johnson was speaking to me now in an almost singsong voice, and as he spoke I could hear his voice getting nearer behind me. For one second I was sure I felt his breath on the back of my neck. And his fingers, running along the chain that held my keys at my waist.

I reached for my pouch, heart hammering. As soon as Johnson was out I locked the door and strode away as fast as I could.

8

Beef

I had been warned when I first arrived on H-Uppers that there were gang issues on the wing. It had become so overrun with gang-affiliated young offenders, known as YOs, that at times it came close to descending into chaos. The place was nicknamed, first by prisoners and then by staff, the Gaza Strip.

'We're a Do Not Travel zone,' the YOs would say proudly.

Gang-affiliated prisoners from different areas were kept apart in the prison. Despite best efforts, though, that wasn't always possible. Months ago during training my entire class had been called into the prison to help search for a four-inch blade which had been spotted when a brawl broke out between two opposing gangs. We never found it.

Gangs had been one of the things which drew me to prison the most. Just the word itself conjured up images of lawlessness and anarchy for me and I was gripped by the disparity between the headlines, which suggested savage, senseless violence, and what I understood about human nature. I'd read Psychology for my degree and probably the biggest revelation for me was finding out the extent to which we are the product of our environment. We'd learned about the girl who was raised with dogs and the boy who was raised by pumas, and I'd written a painfully ignorant essay on the psychology behind gang membership. But up until now the closest I had got to gang violence was Johnson's show and tell and I was desperate to actually talk to some of these so-called gang members.

So when one day Walter pulled me into the office to explain that the reception staff had just brought on to the wing a prisoner who had serious gang issues, I couldn't help but feel a flutter of excitement.

'You need to be aware, we have a live conflict on the wing, Gen,' he told me, more formally than usual. 'Johnson has explained the situation to me: the prisoner that was brought in last night was involved in the murder of Carter's brother. You know Carter, in the cell next to Johnson?'

I nodded. I knew who Carter was, and I wouldn't want to be the person who'd murdered his brother.

'You would've seen it on the news, it was a big story,' Walter went on. 'Anyway, we need to move this man because I'm pretty sure these guys are gonna kill him.'

This is what I thought gang conflict was going to be like. I knew it was serious, but I felt that flutter of excitement again.

As Walter had told me to do, I walked calmly over to the cell which housed the new prisoner and asked him to come and confirm something with me in the office. I felt a thrill rush through me as we briskly walked the twenty paces back to the office, the prisoner on my right and the rest of the wing to my left. I heard a murmur rumble through the prisoners further up the wing so I bustled the man into the office.

But it was too late – he'd already been spotted. I had only just managed to slam the office door shut behind us before a jeering crowd started to form. They jostled and sneered through the window of the door, their lips wet and their fists bared. I looked at Walter, expecting to see relief on his face that I had got him inside in time, but instead he just looked amused.

'Tss. These boys, they think they are all big grown men. Soldiers! Look at them all, trying to be these big men they are not.'

Bemused, I turned back to look at the growing throng. Walter was right. When I looked at them again it wasn't the mob of cold-blooded killers I had presumed. They actually looked like a deplorable crowd of overgrown teenagers, puffing out their chests and grunting through the door.

Walter smiled, shook his head, picked up the office phone and pretended to type in a number.

'Security?' he said loudly. 'Yes, I need the dogs on H-Uppers. Immediately.'

All the prisoners knew that the prison had a group of highly energetic spaniels capable of sniffing out anything from crack to SIM cards. But there had recently been a new investment: two riot-trained Malinois. Rumours had spread – and I was certain that this hadn't been discouraged – that these dogs had been purposely injected with rabies and even genetically modified to have two rows of teeth. Either way, they were currently a very effective tool, even before they were let out of their kennels.

I heard one older prisoner suck his teeth and spit. 'I ain't out here to get rabies, pham!' And the crowd dispersed, just like that. It was over.

My initial response was to feel a bit disappointed. Perhaps it was the adrenalin which had been coursing through me a moment ago and now had nowhere to go, or perhaps it was the reality of the situation: that these gang members were just a bunch of razzed-up youngsters who were afraid of a couple of dogs.

Then something dawned on me. How differently might that situation have looked if Walter hadn't been there? Would I have read it differently? Almost certainly. Would I have done something different? One hundred per cent.

I had a lot to learn before I could handle a situation like that so efficiently by myself.

Surprisingly, it was Steve who proved quite useful on this front. I had initially baulked at the news that I was on shift with only him all day, but without Walter present he was showing a bit more interest in me. He even took the time to talk me through NOMIS, the Prison Service database, which stored the backgrounds and charges of all our prisoners. Unfortunately, this also meant I had to sit through his intermittent patronizing advice or bizarrely unrelated anecdotes, all of which tended to culminate in prisoners begging for his mercy. And after four weeks on the job he was still calling me Jane.

'Yeah, I was in a gang once, Jane. Got stabbed fifteen times when I was a teen.' He pointed out a few minuscule marks on his hands and arms which looked more like chickenpox scars. 'We used to do all sorts,' he went on nostalgically. 'Selling guns, drugs, you name it. Still, I turned it all around, didn't I?'

I managed to fix on an expression of admiration. Admittedly I wasn't familiar with this world, but Steve, who was a scrawny 5ft 5in and had a grovelling disposition, didn't seem at all like the type of guy to be running around after college selling drugs and guns. In fact, he seemed more like the kind of guy who used to sit with the teachers while he ate his lunch. Nonetheless, I realized that this was my chance. I could ask Steve any question I wanted without so much as a flicker of self-consciousness.

'Wow, that's pretty cool, Steve. So, how is it then that the prison knows who's in which gang?'

He looked practically elated at my question.

'So, I'll start at the beginning. You know on this wing, for example, we've got SW1 from Southwark and Wolves from Walworth?'

'Yep, I remember. But wait, isn't SW1 the postcode for Chelsea or somewhere?'

'Yeah, it is. It's meant to be a joke. Cos where these guys come from, it's nothing at all like Chelsea.'

I nodded. *Quite a bleak joke but pretty funny, actually*, I thought to myself.

'So if someone comes in an' says they got beef wiv, say, Johnson, then the reception guys are gonna see on NOMIS that Johnson's affiliated wiv Wolves so they're gonna know that they come from a different area that's got conflicts with Wolves, yeah?'

'OK.' I nodded. 'But how come Wolves and SW1 can be together?'

'The gangs unit, they really know their stuff. They asked me to be a part of it actually, but Kelly didn't want to lose me as an officer – so, yeah.'

Kelly, our manager, was sarcastic and tough as nails, but she spoke to prisoners with fairness and dignity. I'd liked her as soon as I met her. What's more, I could tell just by the way she looked at Steve that she thought he was a total buffoon – so I thought Steve's claim about her not wanting to lose him was unlikely. I kept the admiring expression firmly on my face so that he'd carry on talking.

'They're like proper specialists on gangs, right? They know the ins and outs, sometimes cos they've worked for police, sometimes cos they've grown up with gangs, right? Like me. Course, I ain't no fed.' He gave a smug chuckle.

'*Right*, of course not. So Wolves and SW1 are good with each other,' I repeated slowly. 'But would they, I dunno, have the same beef with other people? Say Johnson has beef with someone else – would someone from SW1 beef them too?'

He smiled coyly. 'Remember, Johnson's SW1. So of course they would have beef if he had beef with someone.'

'Um, I'm sure you said Johnson was Wolves, no?'

Steve looked flustered and started to turn red. 'Nah, Gen, you must be getting confused. It *is* confusing, but you'll get it when you get a bit more experienced.'

He spun back to his computer screen and refreshed his inbox a few times with no results. 'I'm waiting for an email from this fit bird. We did it in the back of my BMW, she hasn't left me alone since.'

Suddenly Johnson burst in, grinning and shaking his head. He had clearly been listening outside.

'Steve, bruddah! I thought you was a *big man*. What you got to tell stories like this for, bro? The back of your car! You a dad, ain't you? You got kids in this world and you talkin' about ladies like this? To a lady, no less. Fix up, bro!'

I couldn't help but be grateful to Johnson for ending that line of conversation.

Steve just shuffled his feet and muttered, 'Nah, mate, it ain't like that. I was explaining to her 'bout gangs an' all. Jus' lightenin' the mood, ya know?'

'Gen,' said Johnson, turning to me, 'would you mind unlocking some doors for me? I've got laundry to 'and back to people upstairs.'

'Her name's *Jane*!' said Steve, with an exaggerated laugh.

Johnson furrowed his brow. 'It's Gen, mate. Wiv a G. I'm sure she's told you that, you know?'

Upstairs, Johnson took me to a pile of netted laundry bags, each filled with neatly folded clothes.

'Don't worry 'bout Steve, Gen. I swear Hotel 1 needs to come take a look at him, man, he ain't all right in the head.'

I laughed. Hotel 1 is what the duty nurse is called in prison, named after the radio sign they are reached on.

'Not meant to be me that does this job,' Johnson remarked as he folded up a towel neatly, 'but the last laundry guy kept losin' fings. Or nickin' 'em. Either way, the mandem roughed him up for it cos they were sick of the hassle, so I'm fillin' in for now.'

'Good folding skills!' I said, brightly.

'I take pride in my work!' He grinned at me again. 'And Steve, right – he don't know the first thing about gangs, so let me do some correcting on the bullshit he just spun you.'

Johnson picked up two of the laundry bags and pointed at a cell door for me to unlock. A scrawny boy came to the door, yawned and took them both, fist-bumping Johnson as he did. 'Respect, bro. Love, yeah?'

'Love, bro,' Johnson replied. He glanced inside the cell. 'What's my man doin' up there – are you readin'?' he said to the even younger-looking boy on the top bunk.

The boy nodded. 'Yeah, man, reading Malcolm X. My fifth time.'

Johnson nodded appreciatively. 'My brother, knowledge is power. Love that from you, bro. That's how we should all be spendin' our time in 'ere.'

I closed the cell door.

'See, Gen, we ain't just a bunch of men with matching tattoos on our faces who like lookin' threatenin'. Those are some young Wolves – they're good kids, still. Think we should start preachin' this whole readin' fing to SW1 youngers too. It's good for them to know where they came from.'

'You read too, Johnson?' I asked, genuinely curious.

'Me? I read plenty. Oh yes.' Johnson nodded vigorously. 'I done more jail time than some of these kids have bin alive for. All of them growing up on their PlayStations and iPhones – it ain't good for the brain.'

I couldn't help nodding in agreement.

'How old are you, Gen, if you don't mind me askin'?'

'No, that's fine. I'm twenty-three.'

'Is it? You seem older than that, you know – not that you look it!'

I didn't know how to react to that, but it sounded like a compliment. Before I could say anything, he went on.

'Anyways, people in gangs. There's more to us than what they say in the news. But that don't mean you should underestimate no one, you get me? I know these kids. They can cause some madness, if you let it happen.'

We went on delivering laundry. The next door I unlocked, the guy behind it took the bag then walked out casually past us. Johnson said in a hushed tone: 'Careful now, Gen. You can't just be lettin' people out like that now. You give someone an inch in this place and they take a mile. Trus' me, I used to be like dat.'

'Right,' I said, 'yeah.'

'When you don't take no shit, you'll get attitude right back. But if you ain't firm then these men are gonna take you for a ride. Some of these guys could have a degree in negotiatin'. And in manipulatin', you get me? An' that includes me too – remember that, Gen.'

'Yep, yep,' I said, 'I get it.' I swallowed, feeling horribly vulnerable suddenly.

'You stay in charge, Gen. Stand for less shit, you know? Otherwise you'll end up like Steve, innit. Letting all the badmen do what they want an' then exercisin' your power over the tapped ones. That gives you no respect, trus' me.'

He smiled and patted me on the shoulder blade. I flinched, and he whipped his hand away.

'You're doin' better than 'im already though.'

His tone was reassuring, but suddenly I didn't feel so reassured.

I need some reinforcement, I really do — but it doesn't feel right to get it from him. Why does he make me feel so dirty every time he says something nice to me?

9

Bang Up

It was 5.43 p.m.

Walter looked at his watch and inhaled sharply. All the prisoners were meant to be behind their doors in seventeen minutes. We both knew it was an impossible task.

He glanced around him. 'Right, Gen. No sign of Steve. Probably a good thing. So, you and me, let's do this. Whatever it takes, all right? And it's gonna take some pushing and shoving with this lot. If we can get them all banged up by six fifteen, it'll be dinner on me.' He gave me a wink.

'Bang up' is one of those phrases we were told not to use during training because it sounds unprofessional and violent, when really all it means is to lock a prisoner in their cell. So far, though, I hadn't met an officer or a prisoner who didn't use it.

Banging everyone up at the end of the day is a bit of an art, and a couple of months into the job I was finally starting to get the hang of it, even enjoying it. It's almost like doing a giant, fiendish sudoku. You have to hold all the moving parts in your head, know the name of every prisoner on the wing, as well as what cell they live in, or what cell they have just switched to or left, and update the enormous imaginary grid with swaps and releases as you go. Then, you need to remember which direction each of them should be going in, so you know which direction you should be cajoling them in, and keep track of how many times you've already asked them to go back to their cell, so that you're not accused of picking on anyone. On top of that, you need to know who you need to ask politely and who you need to be tough with – if you want to avoid them doing the exact opposite of what you asked, or being spat at in the face.

Prisoners know what time they are meant to go back behind their doors, and if it runs past that time they sense lenience. I'd already learned that the wing moves like a flock of birds: it's hypersensitive to changes in energy. So if that sense of lenience emerges, it spreads fast. As an officer, you've got to nip it in the bud or they'll start to push their luck.

Walter set the tone by bellowing, 'Baaaang up! Everyone to their doors. NOW!'

It had seemed counter-intuitive to me at first, but to get things moving you start by locking every cell, whether they're empty or not. This is to stop the endless flow of prisoners zipping in and out of each other's cells, which is what slows everyone down. The alternative is walking around groups of prisoners asking them to go behind their doors. Their response to this will almost certainly be to ignore you or say 'Yeah, yeah' but not move anywhere, thus maintaining the leisurely energy, which increases with each minute that passes.

Walter and I took a side of the wing each, moving in symmetry, flicking our keys in the locks and snapping the handles shut with a finger or a knee as we went. The prisoners had started to move faster now that we had picked up the pace. Some of them chased after me crying, 'Miss, that's my cell!'

'Well, you going in there?' I replied to one of them, Butler, still on the move.

'Yeah, yeah. I just need to fill my water bottle, then I'll bang up.'

'Nope, you've had all afternoon to do that, you're not filling it up now.'

'Miss! C'mon! Let me get my bottle!' He took a step towards his door.

I spun round to face him. 'I'll be honest, Butler. If I open your door and you go inside, I'm locking it behind you.'

I knew he'd be one of the last to go behind his door so I decided not to fight this battle yet and let him skulk off down the landing. The next cell I locked had four prisoners inside, playing a game of chess.

'Gen! Bruv – what the fuck?' They started banging on the door.

I shouted back to them, 'Finish your game – I'll come grab you in a minute!'

I knew all four of them were masters at dragging their feet at this time of day so I'd come back for them later when there was no one else out to distract them. One of them continued to bang on the door, but I kept moving. As long as we kept on reducing the number of prisoners out on the landing, we were cutting into that feeling of drift. And the more we did that, the easier it would be to get people back behind their doors.

'Miss, let me just grab my laundry from my cell real quick?'

'No chance. You've been gassing out on the landing for the last half an hour, Miller. Do your laundry tomorrow. Which cell are you again – 24?'

I took a few steps towards it and locked it. I wasn't about to let him get in there and start pretending to do his laundry to avoid banging up.

'Pham – are you high?' Miller protested. 'Just let me do my laundry, bruv!' He carried on protesting while I continued down the landing.

An older prisoner called Creighton trotted up to me. 'Gen, did you send that email to Probation for me?'

Shit, I've completely forgotten about that.

'Creighton, I sent it but I got an out-of-office email straight back. Remind me again on Monday, yeah?' I had an excuse for everything these days, but I was always careful to set up a reminder so that I could actually get it done at some point.

'Yeah, course. Thanks for tryin', Miss.'

'No problem, Creighton. Also, did you get your meds this evening?'

He looked guilty. 'No, Miss. You and Walter both looked so busy, Miss, didn't want to give you another thing to do.'

I sighed. 'I'll tell you what's another thing to do, Creighton. All the paperwork we'll have when you pop your clogs cos you didn't take your blood pressure pills. Come on now, let's go before the nurses shut up shop. Quick though.'

'You're an angel, Miss, I don't know what I'd do without you.'

Creighton hobbled behind me, chatting away about the heart conditions that run in his family, as I locked the final few doors on my way off the wing. I was careful to keep the three closest to the office open. Those cells belonged to Johnson and two other workers. The rest of the workers' cells are scattered about the wing, but if one of the numbers slips your mind and you lock it before you lock the rest of the wing up, it is taken as a personal offence. It's a rule created by prisoners that the workers are locked up last, even if they've finished their day of work. It's rarely worth the battle to contradict them on this point.

'Oi, Gen,' Johnson called meekly from his cell. 'Bang me up, will you? I ain't feelin' too good.'

I shrugged. 'Never been asked to bang up by a prisoner before, but sure. See ya tomorrow, Johnson.'

Compelled by Walter's challenge, rather than by what was hopefully a tongue-in-cheek invitation to join him for dinner, after sorting out Creighton I was determined not to lose momentum. The second half of the prisoners are always harder to bang up – the easy ones have already gone behind their doors. I took a deep breath and shouted up the landing.

'Guys, let's go! Come on, everyone, bang up, bang up!'

'Miss, did you sort out my visit for me? I'm not banging up until you get that sorted.'

I turned my head. It was Tisdale – and I knew he really meant it. I relayed to him the conversation I had had on the phone with the Visits officer, trying to appear as if I was giving him my full attention because otherwise I knew he'd kick off with me.

'Anyway, they said your missus didn't have her ID on her and that's why they didn't let her in,' I informed him. 'It was nothing to do with the skirt she was wearing.'

I was still talking to Tisdale when I opened the next door to let a prisoner who was waiting get inside. I also knew his cellmate, Jaydon, whom I'd locked in there a moment ago, was going to try and push out past me – and he immediately did. Although my head was turned away talking to Tisdale, I instinctively put my arm across to stop Jaydon from escaping. He tried anyway and I gave him a shove with my shoulder. It's a judgement thing: some prisoners would have clocked me over the head for physically pushing them like that, but I'd pushed Jaydon back inside the day before too. It was a little routine we did most days. He mainly resisted for his own entertainment.

'Goodnight, Jaydon!' I called to him before turning back to Tisdale, who was still muttering about discrimination against short skirts.

'Tisdale, tell her to google the dress code for prison visits if you're worried. But if you don't get up for your meds tomorrow without me pulling you out of bed, she'll be visiting you in the hospital anyway!'

By this time it was only the really tricky prisoners left out – so I'd have to change tactics again. Now I had to make sure all of their cell doors were open, because I was going to need both hands free to push them in there. I headed back to a group of YOs who'd ignored me five minutes earlier.

'Right, guys, you've had enough chances. I'm gonna start putting hands on you if you don't get moving.'

They just laughed. I started with one of the ones I knew best, because once you've taken down a few, the others tend to walk on their own – it's that flock thing again. I grabbed Shingles by the wrist with my left hand and on the elbow with my right and tugged. Of course, he was stronger than I was – but he also knew as well as I did that if he started to resist I could just press my alarm and it wouldn't end well for him.

He began to walk, but as we got closer to his cell he

tried to pull away again. The group had followed us, so he was playing up to them. As soon as we reached the doorway to his cell I pushed him in the chest with both hands. He let out a cry – 'Ooooh, Miss, I love it when you touch me like that!' – and all his friends howled with laughter.

'What a depressing insight into your life, Mr Shingles,' I retorted, before turning back to the group to find my next target.

'Miss, you're rushin',' he tried. 'Slow down. We don't got nothin' to rush for.'

Of course, he was quite right – they didn't, and that was the whole problem.

'I'm not rushing,' I said briskly. 'You guys can bang up when you want. I've got to stay late to do paperwork anyway, so I'll have a bit of time to write up some negatives on some of your profiles.'

None of them moved. *Shit. I forgot that YOs don't care about that sort of thing.*

I turned my attention to two prisoners walking towards me, swinging their arms and chatting, obviously with no intention of banging up any time soon. I put out my arms to block their path.

'Guys, your cell's the other way. Back you go.'

I walked forward with my arms spread until I collided with them. They resisted, but only briefly before they started to walk backwards. The group of YOs were watching me moodily and when I told them I wouldn't be asking them again, they turned their backs on me, pointedly.

This is where it gets really hard.

I hadn't paused for breath since I'd started doing bang up, but all along I'd been aware that I was saving my energy for this part.

It's almost 6.15. Let's just do this.

I grabbed one of them by the arm.

He shook me off violently, spitting, 'Get the fuck off me!'

'I've asked you nicely five times,' I told him. 'It's time to go – now keep walking.'

YOs are always unpredictable and they often make a point of being aggressive to make up for their age. He shoved past me hard, but I put my arms out to catch him.

'Ridley – don't take it too far,' I warned him.

'I said fuck off!' he snarled again, and pushed me even more aggressively.

But I gripped on hard.

'Listen, Ridley, that's technically two assaults now, but we can forget about both of them as long as you get back to your cell without any more trouble.'

I could see Walter coming towards us over Ridley's shoulder. Ridley saw where I was looking, spun round sharply, and held up his hands in defeat. The rest of the group started to disintegrate.

Now almost all of the prisoners were behind their doors. The whirlwind of bang up, thinking and moving at a hundred miles an hour, combined with the satisfaction of the landing eventually falling quiet had given me a warm buzz of adrenalin. Now I marched towards the servery where I knew the workers were avoiding being asked to bang up and were cooking on the hot-plates of the warming trolleys.

Some of them were melting cheese sandwiches into toasties. Others were rehashing the food they'd been serving up for dinner. They'd extracted some carrots from one dish and some chicken from another, mixed them with some Pot Noodles, and now they were re-frying the lot and adding jerk seasoning they'd bought on the canteen. I never stopped being impressed by the things they could create.

'OK, guys, don't make me ask you to bang up. You're all grown men – now get moving.'

They all glanced at each other, waiting for someone to move first. Then I noticed Clark leaning against a table on the far wall.

He shouldn't be here. He'd lost his job when I'd put in that report about him, but I knew Steve kept letting him out.

My heart thudded with a sense of dread. But instead of making things between us worse, I decided to try a different tactic.

I smiled at him genuinely and said, 'Clark, thanks for your help tonight, but that means you too, I'm afraid.'

He didn't reply, and pointedly refused to meet my gaze. Instead he idly picked up a magazine from the table and lifted it up in front of his face, pretending to read it with the insolence of a sulky child. The other prisoners looked at me, waiting to see what I'd do next. The tension in the room felt suffocating. They knew as well as Clark did that I'd just offered him an olive branch, and even some of *them* seemed a bit taken aback at his brazen rejection of it.

I took a few steps towards him, calmly took the magazine out of his hands and placed it back on the table. He stared back at me venomously, then without taking his eyes off mine he slowly picked the magazine up again and held it back in front of his face, inches in front of mine.

I could feel myself starting to get angry. I could feel heat flaring up the back of my neck.

'Right, my camera is going on, Clark,' I said, trying to keep my voice steady as I fumbled with the ON button of the body camera clipped to my shirt until the LED light flickered. The camera would record what I was seeing, and the mic would pick up every word that was said. 'It's nearly half past six and I've asked you to go behind your door twice now. You're not a worker, so please will you get going to your cell?'

I said all this clearly, mainly for the benefit of the video. He lowered the magazine and looked straight at the camera.

'Has Miss here told you that she's having inappropriate relations with a prisoner?'

I snorted a laugh in surprise and heard a couple of the other prisoners sniggering and saying, 'Oh shiiiit . . .' Clark was certainly escalating the situation – and they were as surprised by it as I was.

'Clark,' I said, 'you can say that as much as you like but it's not going to get me to turn the camera off. Now, please go back to your cell.'

I was speaking and acting with confidence, but inside I was growing more wary.

Clark smirked. 'With Cane Johnson on H-Wing. You should check his phone records. You'll find her number on there for sure.'

I laughed again in disbelief.

He's trapped himself, I thought, *while he's trying to trap me. He's talked himself into a confrontation in front of witnesses. Now he'll feel that he's lost face if he backs down. So what will he do? Storm off? Spit in my face?*

Clark raised the magazine again, making sure he got me on the chin with it on the way up. Now I'd had enough. This time, without missing a beat, I snatched it and threw it on the floor. Clark's eyes blazed. In a flash, he grabbed me by the shoulders and slammed me into the wall, knocking the breath out of me. I heard one of the other prisoners let out a 'Whoa!' Nobody had been expecting that. I think even Clark himself was a bit surprised by what he'd done.

For a second I felt panicked. Then more adrenalin flooded through me and my panic turned to defiance. I drove myself into him in an effort to get him off me. He let go of me almost instantly, as though he'd just realized what he'd done.

'Everyone out! I'm fucking serious!'

I made sure I sounded angry, not scared. I glared at

Clark as I spoke, and saw a flash of confusion in his eyes before his face twisted into bitter frustration.

He's disappointed that he hasn't frightened me off. That means I've still got the upper hand.

The other prisoners quickly shuffled out. Now it was just me and Clark. He looked me in the eye, shrugged and sat down at the table, crossing his arms in front of him. I felt a kind of calm wash over me – a clear determination that I wasn't backing down, and wouldn't be leaving this room without him.

'You think I'm not gonna come and get you after that?' I asked him, scathingly.

'Shut the fuck up, you bint.' He spat on the floor at my feet.

I lunged forward, grabbed him by the arm and prepared for the other one to swing at me, but just that second Walter appeared in the doorway. He dived for Clark's other arm, but Clark was stronger than he looked and he pulled free of my grasp and drove his head into my chin. I bit my tongue and winced. I was desperately trying to get hold of his arm again, but every time I got a grip on his wrist he twisted it violently and slipped out of my grasp. I saw him sink his teeth into Walter's arm, drawing blood.

Walter grunted, and then I heard a hard thump. Clark howled, 'You fucking prick!' But he stopped thrashing for a second, just long enough for me to clasp on to his hand, twist it against his wrist and yank it round behind his back before he could regain his composure. Walter and I looked at each other for a moment across Clark's back. Then Walter hit the personal alarm on his radio.

Personal alarm on H-Wing! Personal alarm on H-Wing!

I could hear the message being broadcast, and as we walked Clark out of the servery door, still yelling profanities at us, black and white uniforms began to pile in.

'Careful!' Walter shouted to them. 'He's a biter!'

'You fucking piece of shit – get off me!' Clark yelled. He kicked out behind violently, narrowly missing Walter's shin, and then I felt his whole body drop and the muscles in my back snag as I struggled to hold his weight. He had picked his feet off the floor, and his entire weight was now hanging between Walter and me.

'Mr Clark,' Walter said firmly, 'will you put your feet down so we can walk you back to your cell? I won't ask you again, Mr Clark.'

Clark stayed exactly as he was.

'Mr Clark!' Walter repeated, louder this time, panting under the weight.

Clark lashed out again with his foot, this time managing to kick Walter hard in the shin.

'Fuck!' Walter shouted.

I heard our manager Kelly's voice behind me as she arrived: 'All right, guys – he lives upstairs, don't he? You're gonna need to drag him. Everyone else here, I want you anchoring the stairs while they go. All right?'

Clark pulled his knees up to his chest, making it as hard as he could to move him. Like one enormous creature, we all shuffled over to the stairs. The other officers were crowding around now, lining the stairs for reinforcement. The adrenalin that had been coursing through me up until now had suddenly drained away and left me feeling shaky and nauseous. My arms began to tremble. I could feel my cheeks heating up.

Drawing on my last ounce of energy, I heaved him up the first step, and then up the second. Just one jerk from him and I wouldn't be able to hold on any more. I focused hard, trying to recycle my anger at him into strength – but I barely had any more of it. By the time we made it to the top step I knew that I had only seconds left in me.

'Let go of me, you pigs – let go of me!' Clark shrieked.

We practically dived towards his cell but he started to writhe again, screaming. As we reached his doorway we lurched forward and I hit the door frame hard, dropping him completely.

Feeling almost delirious by this point, my arms weak as jelly, I tried in vain to grab hold of him again before he could lash out. Kelly was behind me and she expertly grabbed his arm in a tight lock.

'If you haven't told us summin',' she said to Clark, 'and we find out you've given Walter summin' nasty by bitin' him, I'll personally make sure you go down for GBH. D'you 'ear me, Mr Clark?'

A few minutes later, I was sitting in the wing office.

'Don't worry, Gen,' Kelly said, 'you done good. Just

catch your breath. You all right? I heard he roughed you up a bit.'

'Yeah, he's a prick.'

'Any injuries?' she asked casually. It was part of protocol.

'Nope, none. Been waiting for that wrap-up for a long time though!' I grinned through the exhaustion.

'That's the spirit!' She patted me on the back. 'Now, we need to get Hotel 1 down here ASAP. I want Clark's medical record checked in case he's got anything nasty, and I want Walter straight to the hospital to get that bite looked at.'

Walter came in the office door, rubbing a purple welt on his arm and shaking his head.

'Now, guys,' Kelly said to us, suddenly stern, 'where was our VR? Where was Johnson while all this was going on?'

'I'd locked him up,' I replied. 'He asked me to do it – said he wasn't feeling so good.'

I was cringing inside. I was certain this situation wouldn't have escalated so badly if Johnson had intervened. It's because things can kick off unexpectedly that the VR is meant to be the last prisoner locked up.

Kelly nodded. 'Listen, we can't always predict these things. What we can do is learn lessons, though. And speaking of learning lessons – Walter, you're going straight to the hospital. You wouldn't be the first one of my officers to get Hep B from a biting prisoner.'

'I don't need to go to the hospital,' Walter said

resolutely, 'as long as he has had his checks here and he's clean. We'll leave it there.'

I felt horribly guilty, but still unsure what I should say. 'Shit, Walter – that looks bad, though,' I managed. I took a closer look at his arm, which he was icing with a daggy-looking carton of juice from the fridge. 'The nurses are on their way, so you shouldn't have to use that juice box much longer.'

He smiled. 'I've had worse, Gen, never you worry.'

I hesitated, then forced myself to say what I was thinking: 'I'm sorry though, Walter. I feel like this one's on me.'

'It was you that bit my arm, was it?'

'I should've pressed my alarm for backup way earlier instead of trying to handle it myself. I just didn't want him to think I was scared of him – but if there'd been all three of us, he might have gone behind his door without a fight.'

I was racking my brains, trying to remember the sequence of events – the point at which the situation had escalated. Now the adrenalin had worn off, it was strange how foggy and confused my recollections were.

Walter gave me a thoughtful look. 'So, what would you have done differently?' He didn't say this in an accusing way, as though I'd made a mistake, but as though he wanted me to think about it.

Clark's smug, mocking expression swam into my mind.

I really let him get to me. That was the problem. That was how it went wrong.

I wrinkled my nose. 'Differently? Probably nothing. I wanted to make a point, though. And that's not exactly professional, is it?'

'What would have been more *professional*, then?' Walter asked, gently pushing me to arrive at an answer.

'Well . . . um, I could have, you know, calmly told him that he was being disrespectful and that I would be nicking him for refusing a direct order. And then I could have called you guys for support to get him banged up. But yeah, I got angry. I didn't want him to think I needed help.'

Walter was nodding now. 'You were angry, Gen, and you showed him that. Anger is a human emotion, an emotion these men understand. As long as you save it for when you really need it, and you take people by surprise with it, anger can be a very useful tool in this place.'

That wasn't at all what I'd expected him to say.

'It's your job to get wound up all day,' Walter went on. 'It is, isn't it? These guys know how to press our buttons, right?'

I gave a little smile. 'They certainly do, yeah,' I agreed.

'So it's important to let it out occasionally. This evening you showed those boys that you can't be pushed over, and I think that was the right thing for you to do.'

Walter raised his eyebrows as if to see whether I agreed with him, and I nodded gratefully.

'It was the *safest* thing for you to do, in fact. For yourself. Of course, my arm wasn't so lucky,' he added with a wink. 'Now, how do you feel after that?'

'I'm gonna be stiff tomorrow, but otherwise, good!' I said, brightly.

Walter gave a knowing smile. 'Good to hear. Cos no one lasts very long in here if they don't enjoy getting their hands dirty now and again.'

10

Star Signs

Over the weeks I'd been on H-Wing I'd become used to opening the cell doors each morning to be greeted by pitch darkness, barely able to make out the mound protruding from each bunk which told me everyone was where they should be. You can't really blame the prisoners for lying in as long as possible: unless you have a job or you're in education, there's really no reason to be awake for most of the day.

There are plenty more reasons to stay up late at night. Firstly, it makes the days shorter; secondly, there are better programmes on TV at night; and finally, of course, if you want to get away with smoking a joint or catching up with your girlfriend on your recently-smuggled-in iPhone, then night-time is the best time to do it.

This morning, though, instead of the unstirring

mounds in beds I was used to, I was met by prisoners waiting at their doors, bleary-eyed but eager, as if they'd just woken up for an early morning flight. Most of them rushed out past me without acknowledging me.

I thought of what Johnson had told me. *Stand for less shit, you know?*

I decided to take this advice, and called out to a couple of them in a sing-song tone as they passed: 'Hi Miss, thanks Miss, good morning Miss!' To my surprise, this was mostly reciprocated straight away with a good-natured 'Oops – morning, Miss!' in a 'sorry I forgot my manners' sort of tone. *Interesting*, I thought. *A bit of sarcastic prompting goes a long way.*

Most of the prisoners were making their way to one cell door in particular, talking in excited tones. I was starting to feel a little unnerved by this energy, imagining what could possibly be about to happen and preparing myself for whatever it might be. Then Johnson came out of his cell. His timing really was always impeccable.

'What's gwarnin', Gen?'

'Yeah, good, Johnson. But what's going on?'

He grinned with delight at my request for information. 'You don't listen to drill, then?'

'Drill music? Nope,' I replied, a little impatiently. Nervousness about what was happening was still bubbling within me.

'It's all right, Gen. Nuffin' to worry about. I can always tell when you get a bit worried, you know. You should try and sort that out – you don't want some of the guys in here pickin' up on that, you know.'

I wasn't in the mood for another lesson on how to do my job. My mind was racing and I felt like I was running out of time to get in the know. 'Well, Johnson, it's kind of my job to worry . . . and I do need to pick up on—' I suddenly realized I was explaining myself to a prisoner, so I stopped. 'Can you just tell me what's going on?'

He grinned again and let out a cackle. 'Ha – Gen, you know I got you! You know about the Wolves, yeah, the other gang on this wing? Most of 'em are on 'ere, right?'

'Yeah, I know about them.'

OK. So whatever's going on, it's something to do with the main gang on the wing. That can't be good news. I was really uncomfortable, yet again, with Johnson's knowing tone.

'Well anyways, the Wolves – they rap and shit, you know? And my guy in the cell over dere, he's one of their best rappers. He's mad famous, you know? So yeah, he's a big guy for them an' he got in last night so they all rushin' to see their guy, pay their respects, you get me?'

I glanced over. I couldn't see which guy he was talking about because of the bustling group around him, but I could certainly see Steve standing on his tiptoes, trying to get in on the excitement with the prisoners. He was plainly being ignored.

Then I heard Walter's booming voice: 'Excer-excer-eeeexercise! Exercise is early today, so out on the yard or back behind your doooors! I said out on the yard or baaaack behind your doors!'

He yelled it authoritatively but shook the out-stretched hands of a couple of prisoners who passed him with a friendly smile. Walter had a different way of interacting with prisoners, and I couldn't help but envy it. He had such charm, such a natural air of kind, strict fairness about him. He respected the prisoners, I could tell, and in return they respected him.

Walter's booming voice even brought Steve to his senses: he stopped fan-girling the drill artist and started cajoling prisoners towards the door of the exercise yard.

'Medi-medi-medicaaation!' boomed Walter's voice again. 'You can go out on the yard after your medi-caaaation! You will *not* be allowed medication after exercise! Anyone for medication come now!'

I looked down at him on the landing below as he greeted a few sleepy prisoners cheerfully while they leaned up against the wall to queue as he had requested. Then he beckoned me downstairs.

I hurried down. 'You want me to take meds, yeah, Walter?' I turned on my heel and felt my ponytail swing around with me as I escorted the waiting prisoners out of the landing door and on to the central core.

While I was supervising medication at the hatch, Walter had been efficiently locking up prisoners who'd chosen not to exercise, having wisely sent Steve down to the yard to supervise there. When I returned to the wing, it was quiet and almost empty, save for a slight figure sitting on the table opposite the entrance. He was wearing a sunshine-yellow matching tracksuit, and a pair of Balenciagas dwarfed his twiggy legs. He watched me intently while twirling a neat braid absent-mindedly with two fingers. As I got closer I noticed his lips were pursed in a mischievous pout.

'So . . . you must be Gen.' He said the words slowly, lifting his chin up slightly.

'Yep, that's right,' I said, as casually as I could manage, trying not to reveal my surprise that he already knew my name.

'You don't know who I am, then?' he said with a smile.

'I do not, no.'

He cracked into a boyish giggle. 'Not a fan of drill then, Gen?'

'Well, I just don't really listen to it.'

'You don't listen to it *yet*!' he corrected me, flicking his wrist and snapping his fingers.

I laughed and put my hand out to shake his, but he put his fist out. I bumped my knuckles into his as he said, 'Rimez. R-I-M-E-Z. That's what they call me. Cos that's what I do – you get me?'

'Good to meet you, Rimez. But I'm not calling you by your street name, so what's your actual name?'

He didn't answer straight away, but seemed almost to stare into me. There was a scrutinizing but not unfriendly look on his face.

'So – the boys haven't got you figured out yet, I'm

hearin'. Some of them say you a nosey gov, and some of them say you chill. You've got them arguin' out there 'bout you.' He giggled again. 'So instead of Miss I'ma call you Miss *Mys*terious, 'til I get you figured out.'

I paused for a second. 'I thought you said you're a rapper! Can't you do better than that?'

He tipped his head back and laughed, revealing a row of unruly white and gold teeth. 'I like that, you know, Miss. You got a fire in your belly. You must be some kind of Aries or sumtin', am I right?'

I'd not met many men in my life who talked about star signs, so I didn't have much of a reference point. But I definitely hadn't expected a rap-spitting, gang-affiliated drill artist to be discussing the alignment of my stars on a prison wing, of all places.

'Libra, actually,' I replied, raising my eyebrows slightly.

'OK, so now we startin' to understand each other! That's cool, that's cool.' He nodded his head slowly. 'Anyways, you're all right, Gen, I like your vibe, ya know? So you can call me Domingo, if you like – but hey, make sure you give me a google when you get home, yeah? Rimez, Wolves. You can't miss me on YouTube. Let me know if you like my tunes, yeah?'

He mimed taking a shot at me with his hands, winked and then skipped off down the landing.

Domingo swung his frame around the office door grinning from ear to ear and wearing a frilly floral shower-cap. 'So, Gen, did you look me up over the weekend, then?' He crossed his arms over his chest to wait for my response.

The thing was, I had. I was so intrigued by him after our first meeting that I'd had a look on YouTube just like he said. I'd occasionally heard some drill music before I started in prison, but I couldn't understand a word and thought it was pretty uncreative and repetitive. But this time after listening to Rimez I felt like I could speak a new language and I was suddenly in awe at how he had constructed the lyrics, dancing around metaphors and the beat of the bass. I'd loved it. But I wasn't going to let him know that.

'Yeah, I looked you up. Gabriel Domingo, right? But I couldn't find a thing.'

He let out a laugh. 'Come on, Gen – you kill me. I'm all over the web, you can't miss me!'

'Nope, couldn't find a thing!' I repeated mock-defiantly.

'You know, I can't even tell if you're jokin' wiv me!' He shook his head.

'Anyway, why are you unlocked at this time of day? And, actually, why are you wearing your grandma's shower-cap?' I added with a grin.

He stuck his bottom lip out and imitated my accent: 'I am wearing my grandma's shower-cap because I have managed to misplace my durag. And I am unlocked on this *fine* day because I bang up with Fingers and when Steve unlocks 'im in the morning he lets me out and about too.'

I rolled my eyes. As Fingers was a wing worker he was let out of his cell to do cleaning, but Domingo should have still been in there with the door locked.

Domingo grinned broadly. 'And,' he went on, 'Steve's given me a job as Healthcare Champion.'

I felt a surge of irritation. 'Course he did!' I blurted out, before I could bite my tongue.

Just like Steve to give the most popular kid in school a job in his first week on the wing. It was going to cause problems. There was always a list of prisoners who'd earned the right to a job through good behaviour and were waiting patiently for one to become available. So when officers shunted someone else to the head of the line like this, it caused a potentially disastrous trickle-down effect: those of us who'd promised jobs weren't able to keep our word, and prisoners who'd tried to behave well weren't rewarded.

The job of Healthcare Champion wasn't a must-have anyway. The prisoner with the role was meant to promote healthy habits like giving up smoking and exercise on the wing, or signpost other prisoners towards available health services. In reality, though, it was one of those policies which never really landed, and jobs like these which don't mean a huge amount were mainly useful because they could be given to prisoners as a reward: a job provides a prisoner with more time out of their cell, a little bit of responsibility and, of course, a bit of pay.

Domingo again grinned back at me. It was obvious

he knew what I was thinking about Steve. 'Anyways, what's got into you today? Are you in a bad mood cos o' that big old zit on ya forehead?' he sniggered.

It was true. I did have an enormous spot above my nose, so big that it was making me go cross-eyed because I could see it with both eyes. The grit and grime of prison, combined with a lack of sleep and sunlight, inevitably equalled bad skin.

'Yeah, yeah, I have a big spot, you don't need to remind me.'

I laughed it off. I was getting good at that.

Steve clattered through the wing door with the enormous dinner trolley.

Normally the wing would be unlocked at lunchtime and the prisoners could come and collect food from the servery. They could sit and eat at the shabby tables and chairs which lined the lower floor of the wing, each of them built into the ground so there was no way they could be picked up as weapons, or thrown. A couple of missing plastic seats, which had clearly been ripped off with force, were a good reminder of exactly why they were fixed to the floor. But at the moment, at least several times a week the prisoners weren't allowed to use them because the prison was short-staffed and the managers had to try to reduce the number of prisoners unlocked at once. Today was one of those days.

On these occasions we unlocked rows of five or six

cells at a time for prisoners to come out and get their food, to avoid the queue getting too unmanageable, then we leaned up against the pool table to supervise. They filed out holding their plastic plates and bowls, heading towards the servery window where the servery workers stood behind a bank of hotplates, slopping spoonfuls of food on to people's plates.

'OK, everyone, straight back to your cells with your food today, I'm afraid,' I instructed. 'There's no dinner on the landing.'

I knew that no one was going to be happy about this, and the prisoners did what they often did when they didn't like what they were being told to do: they flat-out ignored me.

I walked over to a group of younger prisoners who had gathered outside the locked office door.

'Hey – are you all right to bang up now?' I said to them. 'I'm sorry, I know it's not great having your food behind your doors, but it is what it is.'

They took no notice.

I tried again, with a little more authority this time. 'Guys? You need to go behind your doors now.'

'Tsss!' a lanky baby-faced boy spat back at me. 'Miss, we heard you the first time. Stop gettin' all in our faces. Jeez.'

Another one, just as baby-faced but slightly rounder, added, 'I need a new fork anyways. Miss, get me a fork from the office, will you?'

'What happened to your last one?'

I was starting to get the hang of challenging prisoners' requests. There was always something more going on.

'I never had one, innit. Bin usin' a spoon. Can't eat my kiev with no spoon, though, can I?' he retorted.

I sighed. I knew he wasn't telling the truth but I couldn't actually dispute that.

'Fine, but all of you are waiting outside the office – I don't want you getting your sticky fingers on the store cupboard.'

A moment later I emerged from the office and the young prisoner put his hand out expectantly.

'No way,' I said. 'We'll walk back to your cell and I'll give it to you there.'

He smiled sheepishly and headed towards his cell, but the lanky boy snapped at me again: 'These govs love this power trip t'ing, man. Jeez – ain't the keys and the baton enough for you lot?'

I shrugged. 'I'm using a plastic fork as a bargaining tool, mate. I'm hardly withholding water from him, am I?'

In they went, and I shut their door behind them, somewhat triumphantly.

Domingo skipped over. 'Gen, let me pop that spot for you! C'mon, let me pop it!'

I heard the boys I'd just locked away cackling behind their door.

'Domingo,' I said, with little choice but to laugh too, 'it's not happening.'

'But Gen, it'll only take a second! I'm Healthcare Champion, remember! I'm qualified!'

He was still grinning and trailing behind me as we passed his cell. He dipped inside, and I took my opportunity. I spun round and locked the door behind him in a flash.

'That's enough from you today. See you tomorrow, Domingo!'

I heard him howl with laughter again and bang on the door. 'Gen! Man, when did you get so sneaky? What's this about?'

I paced away, chuckling to myself.

In that moment I felt a sudden sense of contentment. Like I suddenly knew how to do this job, like I knew how to *enjoy* this job. I realized, with what felt like a breath of fresh air, that this protective exterior I had been forcibly building was now fully constructed, and with that in place I could finally be myself for the first time.

I thought back to the time when one of the governors had said to our training group: 'The best piece of advice I have is to bring your sense of humour to work. It makes you human, and it makes it easier for everyone to cope.' When he'd said it, I'd practically glowed at his words, thinking to myself that this was *exactly* what I was good at. But since the first day I'd set foot on the wing I'd been unable to shake off a stiff, awkward version of myself who was constantly trying not to do or say the wrong thing. Now that the out-of-place, every-single-moment-something-bad-might-happen feeling was lifting, I realized how exhausting all that non-stop effort had really been.

11

The Mexican Border

The cry of 'Jummah!' was coming over the prison radio. Muslim prisoners could attend prayers in the chapel at lunchtime every Friday.

I was waiting by the wing door to send them down there when Johnson suddenly took the opportunity to corner me.

'So if you was doin' roll count and you saw me smokin' a spliff, would you report it?' he asked, as if he were daring me. His question immediately caught the attention of Fingers who was near by, rolling a mop between his stumps to wring out the water.

I'd been thinking about Johnson recently and I'd decided to be more wary of him, and to try to stay more centred in myself when I was dealing with him. That feeling of needing his approval, of becoming dependent upon him, was something I needed to resist. I'd also had some ideas about how I might handle our conversations. *Put a pause in. Take a beat. Don't just immediately react. That's how he gets you off balance.*

'Gen ain't that kind of officer that writes up on a prisoner smoking a li'l spliff!' Fingers protested. 'C'mon, bro!'

I realized what Johnson was doing. *He's trying to get me to slip up in earshot of other prisoners*, I thought to myself. *The more beef I've got going on in this place, the more isolated and stressed he knows I'll feel – and the more reliant on him he thinks I'll be.*

'Hmm,' I said. 'Actually, Gen *is* the kind of officer that writes up on people smoking spliffs.' I didn't say it unkindly, because I did appreciate Fingers' attempt to stick up for me. But I made sure I said it very firmly.

'Tss!' Johnson hissed. 'You know smokin's part of some people's religion, Gen? An' for some people it's their medication for mental health or pain. The mandem's right, you know – you *are* too nosey.'

The more I stood up to him, the more I was noticing how quickly he turned unfriendly. *Manipulating me – keeping me off balance.*

Rather than reacting emotionally, I stayed detached, more observing what was happening than taking part.

'It's nothing to do with that at all, Johnson,' I responded coolly. 'I think prisoners probably should be allowed to smoke if they want to. They're actually talking about trialling it in some prisons to help reduce the issue with spice.'

Johnson looked put out by my knowledge of the subject, which gave me the upper hand in the conversation. It spurred me to go on.

'But right now it's still illegal, so I know that somewhere along the way someone's been bullied into bringing it in. That's the bit I'm not OK with. End of.'

Fingers was nodding profusely now. 'Yeah, I like that, Gen. I ain't thought about it like that before, but I like that.'

Johnson puffed his cheeks out and muttered something about human rights under his breath.

Just then, the cry of '*Jummah! Final call!*' came over the radio and I took my chance to end the chat.

'Right, Fingers and Johnson, you've got work to do, and that doesn't involve bothering me!' I said.

Fingers chuckled and gave me a salute before trotting off down the landing, putting WET FLOOR signs out as he went. Johnson headed after him, presumably disappointed with his latest attempts to get to me.

Now Domingo was approaching, a mischievous grin plastered across his face, tapping knuckles with prisoners in the queue for Jummah and greeting them with 'As-salamu alaikum, brother' as he went. As Johnson reached Domingo, I saw him take a quick look over his shoulder, grab Domingo by the arm and tug him into a nearby cell. It might have been nothing, but straight away my instincts told me that Johnson was up to no good.

I should go and take a look. But I hesitated. I was still trying to shake this nosey reputation.

Think about it. Neither of them is the type to be beaten up or taken advantage of. They can both look out for themselves. So whatever's going on, it can't be too bad.

I turned to open the wing door and the queue of prisoners merrily flooded out on to the core. As I watched them affectionately greeting those from other wings, what I'd just seen between Domingo and Johnson completely evaporated from my mind.

Supervising exercise was a drag.

The exercise yards sit almost phallically like bulbous, semicircular afterthoughts on the tip of each spur. They're enclosed by impenetrable, tight-knit metal fences topped with spiralling razor wire. They're roughly twenty metres wide and they all follow the same simple design: two pull-up bars for exercise, and an eternally freezing metal bench in the middle of the solid concrete floor for the supervising officer.

We were moving into winter now, and from this point on, supervising exercise became an unpopular duty. It usually meant forty-five minutes turning to ice on that miserable bench, counting the seconds until it came to an end on a beat-up old radio which probably showed the wrong time anyway.

But there was more. The exercise yard also had a

major design flaw. I'm not sure who thought it was a good idea to build a window which opens from one wing directly on to an exercise yard used by prisoners from another wing – somebody who'd never worked in a prison, perhaps? They might just as well have installed a hatch there and let everyone pass drugs and phones through it to their hearts' content.

When the prison authorities had noticed the problem, they'd tried to do something about it. They built wire cages around the window on both sides, which gradually filled up with crisp packets and tins of energy drinks. They were – naturally – riddled with fist-sized holes. Just due to wear and tear maybe, I'd thought when I first saw them – but of course wear and tear had nothing to do with it. Those holes had been made deliberately.

When I'd talked this through with Walter, he'd laughed.

'Oh, you mean the Mexican border?' he said with a chuckle.

'What do you mean?' I asked, confused.

'Well, just think of H-Lowers as Mexico and us on H-Uppers as the US of A. An' that fecking window is what everyone calls the border!'

For the last couple of days, though, I hadn't minded supervising the yard at all, despite the chill. There were two reasons for this. The first was that it gave me a break from being incessantly followed around by Johnson, who was becoming increasingly hard to shake off. He had made it clear that he felt exercise on the yard was for the common prisoner, so at least there I knew I could escape from his mind games. The second reason was more positive: those forty-five minutes could fly by with the ceaseless fount of debate and discussion that was Gabriel Domingo.

We chatted out there most days. First of all we covered his early childhood in the Dominican Republic. He discussed opportunity – the desperate lack of it – in the places where 'people like him' grow up, whether that is an estate in London or a Caribbean island. The clearest route out of poverty for him, and others around him, is crime.

'Are you religious, Gen?' he asked me one day.

I shook my head. 'Nope. Not at all.'

He looked slightly taken aback. 'So where do you get your guidance from?'

I thought for a moment. 'My family and my friends. Or sometimes people I don't know but who I respect, like activists or scientists. Which is a bit like religion, I guess.'

'OK, but tell me then, who are your *role models*?'

He asked this with a sincerity which made me feel slightly put on the spot. I felt like I wanted to give him an answer he liked.

'Uh, so . . . my mum, my sisters. I have lots of strong women around me. I guess they're my role models. I see parts of them that impress me. You know – they're driven, they're interested, they're kind, but also they're funny. So yeah, I suppose I want to be that way too.'

Domingo nodded slowly. 'That's cool, Gen. That's really cool you have that. So these strong ladies, I bet they ain't shippin' no guns or crack around, innit?'

I laughed and shook my head. 'Definitely not.'

'So you see then. People like me – I looked up to people too. For the same reasons: cos they're funny, cos they're successful, cos they can look after their mum. Problem is, though, they ain't doin' all that stuff with no legit job. You get me?'

'Would you say God is your role model then?' I asked.

Domingo nodded energetically. 'Hundred per cent I would. Cos if I follow him, I know I can't go wrong.'

I bit back the urge to remind him where he was. We fell into silence for a moment.

'So, what's your favourite hymn?' I asked instead.

He leaned forward laughing, then burst into 'Morning Has Broken' in an immaculate pitch.

'Really?' I asked.

'Nah!' he replied. 'Jus' that was the only white-person hymn I could think of. Still though, I like it, I like that one. I love to sing, you know?'

These were the types of conversations I'd never expected to have in prison. Domingo had an astonishingly engaging manner. Sometimes he had so much to say that he would hardly draw breath, but at the same time he would always be bringing my opinion to the forefront of the conversation, listening and toying with ideas philosophically.

With every week that passed now I was finding more and more ways to be myself in prison without giving too much away. Safely within the realms of debate and beliefs or even humour, I could let down my guard a bit.

So, when Walter asked me to go and supervise exercise after Jummah, I skipped out on to the yard willingly and sat myself down on the bench to wait for the prisoners to start trickling out. I was surprised when Domingo appeared but didn't take up his usual spot on the other side of the bench from me. Instead, he adopted a casual lean-up against the window, twiddling one of his braids, flanked by two younger prisoners wearing surly expressions on their faces, their hands shoved firmly down the fronts of their tracksuits.

I was cross with myself that I felt slightly hurt by this. *Hurt at being rejected by a prisoner?* I cleared my throat briskly and looked around the yard. After a couple of minutes, I glanced back at Domingo.

That was when I saw it: a figure in the window behind them. I clearly saw Domingo's hand pass back inside, and then come out clenched. I got up and went to do a lap around the yard so that I could subtly take a better look, but one of his guards gave him a firm nudge of warning. He looked up at me with a toothy grin, then turned round and laughed with the figure behind the window.

He's hiding in plain sight, I thought, *making it look as if they're just chatting.*

'Domingo, what are you doing? I'm literally sitting right opposite you,' I called across the yard to him.

His grin widened to reveal even more teeth. 'Nothin' at all, Miss,' he said, in a naughty-schoolboy tone, holding his hands firmly behind his back.

'An' it's none of your business anyway, Miss,' said one of the others defensively.

I strode over with my hand out, and Domingo whipped a piece of paper, the size of an envelope, from behind his back, popped it in his mouth, chewed a bit and swallowed, not dropping that beguiling grin for even a second.

'What was it, Domingo?' I tried to remain casual but stern.

'It was my phone number, Gen.'

'Your phone number? Domingo, you're in prison for four years. You don't have a phone number, and if you did you wouldn't be telling me about it. I'm not buying it.'

'OK then – it was *his* phone number.' He jerked his head back towards the window, chuckling.

I felt a pang of annoyance, realizing I hadn't expected this kind of trouble from him. Then I felt a stab of disappointment at myself. *When am I going to learn* always *to expect this?*

'Come on, guys. You're doing it in front of me *and* it's on camera. It's really disrespectful. So move to the other side of the yard, or I'll get you all searched off the wing.'

The younger two skulked off, one spitting on the floor as he did so, but Domingo lingered.

'Come on, Gen, it's not a big deal. We gotta live a little in 'ere too, you know,' he said.

'It's not about it being a big deal. I'm not gonna turn a blind eye to stuff. It's embarrassing that you think I would, Domingo.'

'Gen, you wastin' your time, you know. It's the people dressed like you that are the problem. We just playin' the game.' He shrugged, then he skipped off, and I was left there, wiggling my toes in my boots to try to keep the blood circulating.

It's the people dressed like you that are the problem.

My heart sank. I felt embarrassed, dejected and powerless. Domingo wasn't wrong. How many times had I felt that it was some of my fellow prison officers who were the root of the problem? Why was it that most of the time I felt more supported by certain prisoners than I did by them?

Perhaps it was that sudden negative train of thought that triggered my memory. When Johnson and Domingo had slipped into a cell for a discussion earlier, what exactly had been going on?

What if they are testing me out? What if Johnson told Domingo to do something suspicious in front of me and see if I reported it? Was this yet another of Johnson's mind games? Was Domingo in on it? Or had Johnson asked him to do it without telling him the reason?

Back on the wing I told Walter what I'd seen, and asked him what he thought I should do.

'You should always trust your instincts, Gen,' he told

me. 'If you think you saw something going on, you should report it.'

As I travelled home that night I tried to rationalize what Domingo had done. I kept ending up back at his final comment: *it's the people dressed like you that are the problem.* He saw it as a justification for whatever it was that he was doing, I could see that now. Then I thought about what he had said to me about role models a couple of weeks earlier. *I looked up to people too*, he'd told me. *For the same reasons: cos they're funny, cos they're successful.*

What troubled me the most was his reference to success. What even is that? Obviously the answer is that it means different things to different people, and I certainly saw how different success looked for people in his world compared to the people in mine.

The drill artists I had met so far in prison had had success that my musical friends could only dream of, with Spotify streams in the multi-millions and diehard fanbases. Yet the majority were banned from performing their music by law, or were serving long stretches in prison, or were imprisoned by their postcodes, unable to leave their neighbourhood block without the risk of being murdered by an opposing gang.

And what alternatives had they witnessed? It's not like they had friends from school who were bankers or business owners or family members who were university professors. They had seen people around them make thick wads of cash or become experts in their fields, but they did that by selling illegal things or rapping about guns on YouTube. That was the kind of opportunity they were exposed to, the kind of success they could look up to.

I recalled walking a new prisoner to the Visits Hall about a month or so earlier. He'd only just arrived on H-Uppers, facing ten years on arms charges. But I knew that it was an amazing day for him: his partner was waiting to see him, and she'd brought their newborn baby. It was the first time he would see his son. I'd tried to imagine how he felt, how excited he must have been to meet his child for the first time – but at the same time, in his situation, so deeply sad. How could he be a dad? How would his son even know him?

He was walking in silence, and I wanted to check that he was OK.

'How you doing?' I asked. 'Big day for you, I know.'

He glanced across at me. 'OK, Miss. I'm OK.'

'It will be good to meet your baby,' I said.

'Yeah. Yeah, it will.' Then he gave a half-smile. 'You look so stressed, Miss. Don't worry, I'm not goin' to hang myself after.'

'No – well, OK. Good.'

'It's an occupational hazard for people like me, you see, Miss.'

'You mean – prison?'

'Yeah. For some people it's hittin' their head on a scaffolding pole on a building site. For me, it's doin' jail time.'

I was dumbfounded by how casually he said this.

'But Liam — ten years away from your missus and your kids. What is worth that?'

'Gen, when I was at school all those years ago, the teacher would read the register out in front of the whole school every morning. Most of the kids just had to stand up and reply "Here" when their name was read out. Me? Me and my little sister had to stand up and say "Free school meal" when our names was read out.'

He met my eyes for a moment. Even now, I saw in him the scorching shame he'd felt back then.

'Do you know how *embarrassin'* that was?' he added quietly. 'My dad worked in a garage and my mum was a secretary in the local surgery. But they was poor. I saw where honest work got 'em, Gen.'

I got it. It was the same for so many of the other men on H-Wing. When they looked around their world, what had they seen? Parents and neighbours stuck eternally below the poverty line. Crippled by a lack of hope. Perhaps working two jobs and still barely able to scrape by. I recognized the determination in their eyes. It was the same determination I had seen in lots of my own friends, a dogged drive to make their mark. To succeed in the world the only way they'd ever seen.

But there was something else I remembered seeing in Liam's face. It was fear, and looking back now I suspected it might have been the fear of not having a choice.

12

How to Make a Birthday Cake in Prison

As I climbed the stairs to the laundry room one morning, the stench of weed was heavy in the air. And when I walked past cell 29 I might as well have been holding the spliff between my own lips. Naturally, that cell was home to Domingo and Fingers.

After I'd put in a report about Domingo, his cell had been searched. The security team had found an ounce of weed and a Zanco (a tiny Nokia brick-style phone, not much bigger than a thumb – popular in prison because they can be easily slotted into an arse to be smuggled in). Because of this he had been placed on what was called basic regime, where you are stripped of any privileges and left only with your human rights. This meant he'd been locked in his cell for twenty-three and a half hours a day. His TV had been replaced with a radio. He wasn't allowed to order any extra food on the canteen and he was only allowed out for thirty minutes of solo exercise a day.

I'd only seen him a handful of times over the last week, when I'd opened his door to hand him his lunch. Each time I'd been met by a silence I pretended not to notice.

The thud of hip hop music grew louder as I approached the door. I peeked through the observation panel and saw Domingo and Fingers dancing round their cell, blissfully unaware. I watched for a few moments until Fingers caught my eye, threw himself against the door dramatically and put his eye up to the other side directly opposite mine.

'Gen!' he said in his heavy Essex accent. ''Ello there!'

I was slightly taken aback by the friendly welcome. After all, I was the reason they'd been locked in this cell.

I opened the door and scanned the room. It was quite a sight. There were three TVs balanced awkwardly on the desk. All three were blaring out the same music channel. Domingo and Fingers were holding empty tin cans which they'd been drumming together as they danced. Scarcely a basic regime. In fact, it was so absurd that I couldn't help but let out a laugh.

'So, let's start with the TVs,' I said to them, matter-of-factly. 'You're both on basic, so that should be *no* TVs, not three. I'm not gonna bother asking—'

'Five,' Domingo interrupted with a smile.

'Five what?' I asked.

'We actually have *five* more TVs than we should have,' he said, cracking into an intoxicated giggle as he pointed under his bed.

I took a look, and saw two more TV-shaped lumps wrapped in pillowcases.

'Right. So that's, um, ridiculous. And do you wanna talk about the weed while we're at it?' I said to them.

I used the sarcastic tone I'd learned worked best for these kinds of questions. The tone that says: *I'm not going to tell you off like I'm your teacher but I am going to make it absolutely clear that I am seeing everything that's in front of me.*

I thought back to the time not so long ago when I had declared that I absolutely was *the kind of officer that writes up on people smoking spliffs*, and I wondered when I had realized that there were just bigger fish to fry. Probably somewhere in between being reminded that it was my colleagues bringing it in anyway and the general madness of prison life which saw me being thrown around in brawls on a weekly basis. It all puts things in perspective.

'Firstly,' Domingo drawled, 'it's my birthday, innit. So the mandem give me these tellies as a gift. You ain't gonna take away my gifts, are ya? And thirdly, this *weed*, if that's what you wanna call it, well – that's a gift from the mandem too, actually.'

'You missed out "secondly"!' Fingers said, giggling wildly, while Domingo was still babbling on to me about 'how the mandem be shapin' up this year'.

'Bruddah, this is gettin' to be a good birthday, you know?' he finished, gazing up contemplatively through the smoky haze.

I looked from one to the other.

'OK, Domingo. One – happy birthday. Two – don't be a dick and smoke in the day. Three – hand the weed over and I'll forget about the TVs 'til tomorrow.'

'Ah, Gen – you can't get your hands on ma weed, an' I'll tell you why.' He mimed his actions as he spoke. 'That weed comes outta my arse jus' long enough for me to roll up my joint and then it goes right back up there before I even light up. That's a lesson I learnt recently!'

I screwed up my face and turned to go.

'Hold up, Gen!' said Domingo. 'At least stay for a piece of home-made birthday cake!'

He held out a large Tupperware box.

'What are you talking about, "birthday cake"?' I asked him.

'All right, so it's not *home-made* – but it is *prison*-made! See!'

I looked into the Tupperware and saw what appeared like the top of a pretty nice-looking banana cake. It was the last thing I'd expected.

'What on earth is this, Domingo?'

'Birthday cake! For real! You got the mashed-up digestives on the bottom, an' you mix that in with some peanut butter and squish that down. Then you gotta melt the Cadbury's in the kettle 'til it's all nice an' soft, like, pour that over, chop the banana – an' voila, banof-fee pie! Take a piece!' He thrust it towards me again.

In training you're taught never to take anything from a prisoner, let alone eat anything they give you. But this seemed like a good time to make an exception. While I was hesitating, he chuckled, 'An' don't go worryin', Gen – I washed my hands proper after I spun that spliff!'

I bit into the cake, and it was hands down the best birthday cake I'd ever tried.

'Baker made it, an' he ain't called Baker for nuffin'!' said Domingo proudly. 'Not all of us just bakin' crack, you know? He's got a proper business on the outside an' all – he bakes and delivers to your door, innit.'

'Impressive,' I said. 'Now sober up, both of you. It's exercise in an hour and you're not coming out for it unless you can walk in a straight line.'

It was 9 a.m. on a Sunday morning. I was alone in the wing office, sitting slumped over the desk with my face in my hands, hoping that no one would notice if I just shut my eyes for a moment. I'd woken up at five that morning, waited for my connecting bus with the wind and rain howling down around me, before completing the last leg of my journey on a damp bus seat – accidentally falling asleep on the man next to me.

The night before I'd left my friend's birthday at 1 a.m. – just as they were getting started – to cash in on a few hours of sleep before my blaring alarm signalled the start of another twelve-hour day in prison. It can be hard to fit in a social life around shift work, or rather fit in shift work around your social life.

As I sat in the stale-smelling office, I felt the night's beer swirling threateningly in my stomach.

Maybe some cereal will help. Soak up some of that alcohol. I could only hope.

Cereal packs are given to the prisoners with their evening meal for breakfast the next day, but you can always find plenty of extra ones lying about the wing. The trick is to find one a rat hasn't got to yet.

In a cardboard box on the floor I spotted what I was looking for: a small plastic bag, knotted at the top, containing a handful of Rice Krispies and two teabags, all miraculously rat-free. I couldn't find a bowl in the office cupboard, so I poured the cereal into a plastic mug and rummaged for a spoon in the drawer. No metal cutlery is allowed into the prison and each prisoner is issued with reusable plastic cutlery when they arrive. But you don't want to use theirs, not after you've seen how many different ways they've been used: unblocking toilets, slashing wrists, stabbing cellmates.

My head was in the office cupboard searching for a plastic spoon when Johnson poked his head round the door.

'Morning, Gen! What you lookin' for?'

'Morning, Johnson, tryna find myself a spoon.'

'So – Gen. A li'l dicky bird told me that someone ain't happy with you. Do you wanna know why?'

Of course, I already knew that Domingo hadn't been

happy with me, but that was old news. The last time I saw him things had seemed to be improving on that score. So why was Johnson bringing it up now?

'Do you mean about his cell getting spun? That was a while ago, Johnson. You're losing your touch.' I knew that Johnson wasn't good at being teased, but I couldn't help myself.

He raised his eyebrows. 'It ain't just that, you know. You don't even know that I stopped you from gettin' potted.'

I felt my throat suddenly go dry.

'You ever seen someone get potted, Gen?' he said softly. 'It's *humiliatin'*. Walkin' up the wing and havin' some nitty chuck a pot full of their hot shit and piss at you. Most officers don't come back after that.'

Could it have been Domingo? Surely not. Not after those conversations we had, surely? I thought we were cool now anyway. Clark, though — he might want me potted. That I could easily believe.

I shrugged, trying not to give my racing thoughts away to Johnson. 'Clark's probably been planning that for months,' I said calmly.

'It weren't even Clark, you know?' said Johnson. 'I keep fings quiet on this wing, Gen, you know? So quiet you wouldn't even know this guy's got beef wiv you.'

Now I know he's playing with me. So relax. Take a beat. Don't be rushed into making a response.

I took a nonchalant sip from my mug, giving myself time to consider my reply. But I'd forgotten it wasn't tea in the mug, and instead I inhaled a mouthful of dry Rice Krispies. I felt the bottom of my lungs hurl upwards and was sure that the contents of my stomach would follow. My eyes began to stream and soon I could hardly see the room in front of me. Clutching at the desk to steady myself as I choked uncontrollably, I felt a hand pat my back hard, but instinctively batted it away. When I finally began to compose myself, Johnson thrust a carton of juice into my hands.

'Here, drink this. Wow – you all right, Gen? That was proper! Sorry about tryna pat you on the back there – just tryna help, of course, but I get 'ow some of you female officers gotta be careful about touchin' us. Or us touchin' you!' He laughed.

I tried to croak a reply but felt my lungs surging again, so I just wiped my eyes and took a long draught of the juice.

'Still, I forgot you weren't like that,' Johnson went on. 'That was a little trick of mine though, back in the day. I slept with bare officers – an' you wouldn't believe it, Gen, how many officers are out there like that. Pham – it's easier to get girls in prison sometimes than on the road! It's easier to get *drugs* in prison than on the road!'

I seriously considered inhaling another mouthful of Rice Krispies just to avoid having this conversation with him, but he looked me straight in the eye and went on.

'You start off with the small stuff, Gen, you know?

Give 'em a little touch here an' there. Maybe a stroke of their key chain – just to see if they let you get away with it.'

A jolt fired up my spine. *Just to see if they let you get away with it*.

That was exactly what he'd done to me.

He paused then, and I knew he was examining me for a reaction. I kept perfectly still, focusing on last night's beer, which was sloshing around in my stomach.

Just at that moment Walter strode into the office. He was studying a piece of paperwork in his hand and thankfully he couldn't see the discomfort on my face. But naturally Johnson grabbed his moment.

'Is everything OK, Gen? You seem a bit flustered. A bit off today.'

'Fine! Absolutely fine! I'm just tired. Didn't sleep much last night.' I tried to sound as bright as I could.

'Word of advice. You don't want to do this job on a hangover.' Johnson's voice was cheerful but his eyes were still on me. 'Where were you out last night then?'

He's still testing me, I thought. I kept my voice casual, conscious that Walter was overhearing this conversation now.

'I just went to the pub with some mates.'

'Ahh – I miss the pub, you know,' Johnson said. 'Where d'ya go, then?'

'Some pub in Bermondsey.'

'Bermondsey! What pub were you at? Those are my ends, you know?'

I'm certainly not telling him that — me and my friends go there all the time.

'Just the Spoons, you know.'

'Ah, Gen, I thought you was a classier bird than that. But Bermondsey's my ends, still — you know what I mean? Like, I *ran* that area, you get me? I done some big man shit around there, ya know.'

There was another pause before he went on.

'An' that's why you don't see no officers snitchin' on me, you get me? You got yourself in a bit of trouble with Domingo, you get yourself in trouble with some other nitty who wants you potted, an' I can sort that. But there ain't no one above me on this wing. So you get in trouble with me and then you really do got trouble, you get me?'

I'd stopped listening to what he was saying. How had I even allowed myself to think it might be Domingo that wanted me potted? I felt the relief flow over me after what Johnson had said.

'Look,' I said to him, 'I just wanna say that I'm here to do my job, which I actually really care about. I don't know what you mean by "get in trouble" with you.' Then I looked him straight in the eye, just as he had done to me. 'And I'm also not here to let anyone "get away with" things either.'

Johnson didn't respond immediately. It looked like he was thinking about what to say.

'All I'm sayin', Gen, is you want me on your side. So be careful who you go reportin', all right?' He sounded defensive now.

Walter looked up from his paperwork for the first time. 'Leave this girl alone, Johnson. What you talkin' about? Trouble wiv you? Tsss. Silly man.' He kissed his teeth.

Johnson raised his eyebrows. 'I'm tryna help her out, Walt. I was tellin' her how I saved her from getting potted this week.'

Walter interrupted sharply: 'I said leave the girl alone! She's one of the only ones on this wing doing her job. I won't have you telling her this madness. Now be gone wi'ja.'

Johnson's face turned stony.

'No offence intended, Gen,' he said to me. 'Jus' remember – I know what pub you an' your friends hit up now, innit.'

He gave a slow, satisfied nod and turned to walk off. I knew I shouldn't blow my story, but I couldn't help wanting him to know that I'd been smarter than he thought.

'Johnson?' He looked over his shoulder. 'What makes you think I told you the truth about which pub my friends and I go to?'

He snorted. 'Ha – I knew you was one of the smart ones, Gen.'

'Did you 'ear then?' Steve looked up at me, clearly buzzing to tell me something.

It was Tuesday morning, just a couple of days later, and I was on my knees with exhaustion. I'd had one day off in nine – sometimes that's just how your shift pattern falls, and it's brutal. The last thing I needed was Steve spinning me crude prison gossip.

'Johnson got shipped out yesterday afternoon!' he burst out.

My heart started thudding so loudly I was sure Steve would hear it. *Why? Who made that decision?* And then, to my horror, I realized that I felt disappointed. Despite everything, despite the way he could send a chill down my spine just by walking into the room, I understood in that moment how much I still felt like I relied on Johnson. The thought made me feel queasy.

'Something about Security receiving intelligence on him grooming a female officer,' Steve explained.

My stomach jumped into my throat.

Was this about me? It can't have been. I never actually let him in. Was it to do with what Clark had said on camera? Did someone think that Johnson was grooming me? Or even . . . did they think that he'd succeeded? That he had indeed corrupted me?

The final thought I had was the most sickening one of all: *was it possible he actually had?*

13

Role Models

I'd heard only negative things about Ellen from the prisoners. That's what made me certain, before we had even worked together, that I'd like her.

Our shift patterns didn't match up, so only rarely had we been on together, but when we were, I found her a welcome break from Steve. Unlike him, there wasn't an ounce of her that wanted prisoners to like her: she was there to do her job and she didn't curry favour, or care about which prisoner was the coolest.

A prisoner called Porter, who was a big dog in SW1, was always rubbing her up the wrong way. Every time someone mentioned her name, he'd cross his fingers up in front of him as though he was warding off a bad spirit. Once I actually saw him do it to Ellen's face, and without missing a beat she retorted: 'Yeah, you should do that, mate. Don't fuck with a witch like me unless you got all your protections in order.'

She was enviably sassy. I regularly wished I could swap her for Steve, with whom I seemed to be incessantly on shift. She also made it clear that Steve's ingratiating targeting of weaker prisoners while he let the alpha types get away with much worse was as sickening to her as it was to me.

One day a new prisoner, who couldn't have been older than nineteen, was clearly having a mental health crisis. He was begging Steve to get him a new mattress, because the one in his cell was so threadbare. Steve told him that there weren't any in the warehouse at the moment. But the prisoner knew – and so did Ellen – that Steve was lying. He just couldn't be bothered to walk over to the far side of the building. Steve had never been a good liar.

The prisoner started to get agitated with him, tugging at his own hair in distress, calling Steve a 'lazy prick'. That's mild as far as things go in prison, but there was an audience of some younger SWIs standing near by, and Steve blatantly took offence to being talked to like that in front of them. 'Who you calling lazy, you dumb fuck?' he spat back, defensively. 'Shut up, you dumb crackhead!' Then he slammed the cell door in his face.

Now, it's a golden rule in prison that you never undermine your colleague in front of a prisoner. I knew too well already that not every officer kept to it, but I also knew that Ellen certainly did. I didn't expect her to say anything, and she didn't. But she beckoned Steve to come to the office with her, lips pursed and disgust plastered on her face.

Then she handed him the phone. 'It's the warehouse. Now just get that boy a mattress.'

Steve flushed bright red.

As he headed out of the door to collect it, I heard Domingo, who had only recently come off basic, say almost musingly, 'I don't like *bullies*, you know. It was my job in school to beat up *bullies*.'

He left it there. There was nothing directly threatening about the way he spoke, but there didn't need to be. Steve got the message, and he started steering clear of Domingo.

When I arrived for my shift a few days after Johnson had been shipped out, I found Ellen in the office, deep in consultation with Walter and Steve. They were talking about who should take over the Violence Reduction role now that Johnson was gone. Walter and Ellen were both pushing for Domingo, but Steve seemed staunchly set against it.

It made sense. The last thing Steve would want was for Domingo to be placed in a more important position on the wing. What was strange was to see Steve standing up to someone who wasn't a weak and defenceless prisoner.

Walter's vote for Domingo puzzled me, though. I couldn't work it out. Why was he supporting him for this VR job? I usually trusted his judgement, but he was the one who had advised me to write the report about Domingo passing contraband through the window in the yard. *So how come now he wants the guy to get a job?* I didn't think Walter could be so easily swayed by his charms. I liked Domingo a lot, but he was dodgy as hell. Even my novice eyes could see that.

The office phone rang and Steve picked up, nodded a few times in agreement, and then said, 'No problem, I'll be there.'

'What was that?' Ellen asked suspiciously.

'Planned removal. Nothing for you to worry about – man's job.'

A planned removal is when three officers get all kitted up and enter a cell to restrain a prisoner and move them somewhere else. Something Ellen and I had both done plenty of times.

Ellen choked on a laugh. 'Pha – are you for real? Didn't know they made riot gear in children's sizes!' she said, looking Steve up and down.

Steve's bottom lip wobbled for a moment, then he turned and hurried out.

Ellen smirked, clearly pleased with her work. 'Right, I'ma go meds hatch. I'm gonna need some paracetamol to take the edge off if I have to put up with Steve all day.'

On my own with Walter, I took my opportunity.

'Um, Walter – that thing with Domingo, you know, the thing that happened on the yard. Don't you think he shouldn't be VR, like, so soon after that?'

Walter nodded slowly. 'My friend, I hear you. But there's a thing about these gangstas. You treat 'em like a prisoner, they gonna act like a prisoner. You see Domingo – he's a leader. You got to give him a bit of responsibility. Let him live up to that responsibility.'

I nodded, but I still didn't get it. It just didn't feel right to reward him with the best job on the wing.

'Besides that, Gen, Johnson's gone. He was one slimy bastard, but he kept the peace on this wing. Just watch now he's not here and see what happens. The dodgy ones – they make for the best VRs, I tell you. Now, do me a favour today, sweetie – can you go on the yard this afternoon?'

I sat on the cold metal bench in the exercise yard as prisoners trickled out around me. One group, led by an energetic prisoner known as PT, set up in a circle, putting their towels on the floor and tying rags of ripped clothing around their hands. At PT's command, the whole group dropped to the floor and started doing press-ups. PT moved between them, offering words of encouragement and occasionally stopping to laugh good-naturedly at one of the guys: 'Pham – what is that? A woman's press-up or summin'?' Then he'd squat next to them and patiently and gently adjust their position.

'OK, mandem! Keepie-uppies on the bars, two at a time. The rest of you, squats!'

The prisoners were soon puffing and blowing.

Domingo appeared in the doorway. He saw me on

the bench and formed a gun with his hands. Then he aimed it at me and shot, before grinning and coming over to sit down next to me.

'No session with PT for you today, then, Domingo?'

He snorted. 'There ain't no need for me to get strong. I'm scrappy instead, innit! Besides, I always stay skinny, even when I'm in jail. Jus' smokin' weed all day, innit.'

A group of younger prisoners strolled out on to the yard looking dishevelled and yawning. They'd obviously been dragged out of bed by Walter and hurried out. They casually gravitated towards Domingo, and he touched knuckles with each of them. I nodded hello to some. Plenty of prisoners like to be friendly with officers, but a lot also choose to keep their distance, particularly the younger ones.

I saw a prisoner called Michaels approaching at the back of the group. I knew I'd get no acknowledgement from him. Whenever he was around officers, he fixed a look of distaste on his face, as though there was a bad smell in the air. His hands were thrust down the waist of his low-slung tracksuit, but he pulled one out for a moment to bump Domingo's knuckles. His icy-blue eyes fixed on mine maliciously and purposefully.

'Bro – how's the murder case going then?' one of the young prisoners asked Michaels, toying with an elastic band between his fingers as he spoke.

'Tsss, bro,' Michaels answered, in a tone of cool disapproval, 'it ain't no murder case. Dickhead's still alive.'

He shrugged his shoulders. 'He just can't walk or talk no more.'

A couple around him shook their heads but most of the group didn't even flinch. I hated seeing such young boys so apathetic about stabbings. But I also knew full well that none of them were strangers to knives. They knew plenty of perpetrators, but they knew plenty of victims too.

'The prosecutor, right?' Michaels went on, angrily kicking an empty can into the fence repeatedly. 'He's makin' 'im out to be some "innocent sixteen-year-old with a promising football career ahead of 'im".' He lifted his hands, forming ironic air quotes around his words.

'Tsss! Naaah . . .' His listeners understood. In their world, an enemy is an enemy, even if he's still only sixteen.

'They got his mum there,' Michaels added with a snarl, 'sobbin' every day for the jury. All of them pushin' for the maximum sentence.'

I felt my stomach turn over. But I noticed how some of these young guys winced when Michaels mentioned the mother of his victim. Some of them cast their eyes to the ground, looking nervous.

Michaels spat on the floor and rubbed the phlegm into the ground with his foot. 'Wish I'd finished 'im off properly now.'

I felt disgust take over me then and I couldn't keep quiet any more. I made sure my voice was level when I spoke.

'Michaels – just to check,' I said coolly. 'Have you tried showing remorse in court? Cos that's something the judge is looking out for, you know. I don't think you're doing yourself any favours by wishing that you'd killed him.'

'Tsss!' Michaels' cold eyes met mine. 'Likkle boy's a snitch, innit? I ain't gonna sit in that courtroom grovellin' to no one. Man's got more pride than that.'

Some of the prisoners around him hummed in agreement with this.

I knew he was trying to shock me, even scare me. But the most difficult thing for me was to see how the other boys were reacting. It never ceased to infuriate me how they valued pride over each other's lives.

I glanced at Domingo, who was listening to all this. His expression was blank. It struck me that he looked just like a therapist, letting the client speak.

Michaels was on a roll now, and added, 'That feelin' of stabbin' someone, you can't beat it.'

He looked at the group around him again, but most of them averted their eyes.

He's taken it too far.

'You know,' Michaels continued with relish, 'when you put the knife in, you don't usually feel anythin'. But when you rip it *out* and you feel that *tear* – oooff!'

Now a couple of the boys kissed their teeth. It only seemed to encourage Michaels.

'An' you know, when you rip it out? That sound it makes? An' then if they're screamin' – even better.'

That was when Domingo finally spoke up. 'Pham – this guy is crazy.' He spoke almost warmly, like a despairing older brother, shaking his head at Michaels. 'No one likes stabbin', you li'l psycho.'

I felt that he could have piped up slightly earlier, but I got the feeling he was weighing up his response before he said it. As though he felt that the important bit was telling the audience that they didn't have to pretend to play along, or even act like they admired Michaels. So, perhaps Domingo was a leader, just like Walter said.

Michaels sensed the change in atmosphere. 'Fuckin' pussios,' he said, stretching out his foot and slowly crushing a beetle that was crawling across the concrete of the yard.

That evening, after the officers on main shift had gone home, I sat in the office whiling away the time until the end of my shift at 9 p.m.

With very restricted internet access in the prison, the closest thing you could get to a time-wasting scroll through social media was scrolling through the NOMIS prison database to see what you could find out about each prisoner. I'd been instinctively searching for Johnson's name every time I opened NOMIS, just to check where he was. I had this horrible feeling he was going to turn up again out of nowhere, and it was reassuring to see that he was far away in HMP Isle of Wight. I was about to click on his notes yet again, just to see if anyone had written anything new on him, but as my mouse hovered over the button I paused, then gave myself a shake.

He's not worth the energy, I thought. *He's not even here any more. Enough. Stop letting this guy live in your head.*

Instead I typed in 'Gabriel Domingo'.

Domingo had spent enough time in prison that there were plenty of notes on him. I scrolled right back to the beginning. The first ten or so were from 2012 and were mainly automated notices with standard wording.

Awarded basic regime for fighting.

I soon came across one that made me chuckle: *Smelled cannabis on Mr Domingo, but when I asked him about it he said, 'Are you sure it isn't you, sir?'*

I kept on scrolling through. He was released, then four months later he was registered into another prison. Then more of the same – fighting and cannabis. As I got towards more recent years, though, the notices began to change character.

I awarded Mr Domingo a positive IEP because he helped a prisoner with learning difficulties to clean his cell.

Positive IEP for Gabriel for defusing a fight.

And they kept on coming – appreciative comments by officers, prison teachers and nurses. Domingo had calmly intervened when a prisoner had been rude to them. He'd shown himself to be a good role model to the people who looked up to him by encouraging others on the wing to go to education and gain qualifications. He was worshipped by his community – the five TVs he'd received for his birthday alone were testament to that. And when I thought more about what I'd seen and heard, I understood why. He was forever building his men up, or going to the defence of others. There was the birthday cake – he'd told me warmly about Baker's cooking business and praised the skills he had. He'd not liked what Michaels had said about enjoying stabbing, but he hadn't torn him down in front of the others. Instead, he'd let him talk and then encouraged him to tone it down. He gave guidance without making anyone look small. Those are the skills of a leader right there.

That's what he was, and in another world – where he wasn't in prison, and where he could use those qualities differently – how much more could he become?

14

The Strangest Place

Steve and Ellen were doing roll count upstairs together. I said I would take the lower landing to speed things up because *once again* it had taken twice as long as it should have for everyone to be locked in their cells before lunch break.

Roll count is carried out twice a day, at lunch and at the end of the day. Officers go round their wing to check that every door has been locked and count how many prisoners are in each cell. This is then recorded, and before anyone can go home, every prisoner in the jail has to be accounted for. It's meant to happen only when everyone is locked in their cells, but officers who had been there for a while often got it out of the way before the last couple of prisoners went behind their doors.

Ellen was definitely one of these short-cut types. She

had grown up in the local area and was forever making trips to the manager's office to ask to move wings for the day because she'd recognized a prisoner who'd just arrived. Today was no different. Yet another boy from her old school had come in that morning and he'd recognized her. It's prison policy for an officer to declare it if they know someone who comes in.

Kane Williams looked like a severely overgrown teenager and you could just tell he lived to piss people off. When we were handing out lunch, he had winked at Ellen and quoted her dad's address at her, loud enough for everyone around to overhear. She hadn't risen to it. She'd just turned her back and gone straight to the manager to complain again. But Kelly had told her there was nothing she could do because the prison was short-staffed. All Ellen could do, she told her, was try her best to avoid Kane.

Even from downstairs, I could hear the frustration in her voice as they moved around the landing above me, rattling the doors to check they were locked.

'Uncover your flap, uncover your flap, bro! We haven't got time for this tonight!' she yelled, thumping her fist on a door.

When she got to Kane's cell, predictably there was trouble.

'Open this fuckin' flap, mate! I ain't leavin' it, Kane! You've bin enough of a dick today, it's roll count, it happens every day, you need it uncovered. Kane!'

She thumped her fist on the door again. Then I heard

the click of a cell door being unlocked. It was quickly followed by a loud crash and then a sharp scream.

I hurtled to the top of the stairs. I was just in time to see Steve running towards me, away from the scene. I'd no time to consider what this meant. I raced past him towards the cell with the open door. Ellen was on her back on the floor, her hand pressed across Kane's face. He was straddling her, one hand on her head as she tried to throw a punch. He'd ripped her weave violently out of her hair and thrown it to one side. I grabbed him from behind, tugging at his shoulders to pull him off Ellen.

Seconds later, I saw someone over my shoulder charge through the cell door. They gave Kane a rough shove sideways, and I fell against the wall with him, still with my arms locked around his chest. I looked up to see that it was Domingo, who was now dragging Ellen out of the cell while I struggled to my feet. Kane grunted angrily but made no attempt to get up from the floor. I slammed his door locked behind me, noticing that my hands were still trembling, and saw Kelly running towards us down the landing.

'Fucking Steve, bro!' Ellen hissed, and spat a mouthful of blood on to the floor from her bleeding lip.

'Steve?' I was shaky and confused. 'What did Steve do?'

'It's what he *didn't* do! Kelly, mate, I ain't workin' with that *pussy* again!' Ellen snapped. 'Is he even a gov? I fuckin' look round an' he's legged it. Fuckin' dangerous, bro. How'd that man pass training?'

I suddenly clocked that I'd passed Steve running away from the incident as I'd headed towards the sound of Ellen's scream. When Kane had gone for her, Steve had clearly legged it.

Kelly was checking Ellen's split lip and calling for the nurses over her radio.

'Ellen, listen to me, lovey,' she said briskly. 'I hear what you're saying, and I'm gonna investigate this. But listen to this as well, love: you can't go cracking doors at roll count, yeah? The door's there to protect you. If you wanna have an argument, do it through the door. You hear me?'

Ellen was wiping away a tear now. I couldn't blame her. I felt disgusted, suddenly – absolutely outraged with Steve. How could an officer just run away when one of his colleagues was pinned to the floor? And *Steve*, of all people, who swaggered about the wing talking about which jobs were for male officers and which jobs were for female officers all day long, fled at the first sign of a physical struggle.

Once again, I'd seen a prisoner come to the defence of an officer – not another officer.

That day was a bit of a turning point for me. There were officers I knew I could rely on deeply. There were others I wouldn't rely on to tie their own shoelaces. There were prisoners I was sure would chop me up and put me in a suitcase if they ever got the chance. But there were also prisoners who'd opened my mind to new worlds and made me question everything society was built on.

So who should I trust? It was a hard pill to swallow but there could only be one answer. Myself.

My shift finished at one o'clock and I raced out of the prison, keen to catch some winter sun. When I picked up my phone from the locker on my way out, I looked at the date. I realized it was a year to the day since I'd applied for this job – a whole year.

As I walked back to my flat from the station along the market street I looked around me at the people bustling from store to store. I thought about this new world I had got to know and I began to understand something. While prison, as a place, is about as strange as you can get, the people in there aren't. They're the very same people who live alongside us, just getting on with their lives, whether that's working, or struggling, or thriving – or barely just surviving.

I saw a boy, no older than eighteen, edge out of a convenience store. A blue plastic bag swinging from the handlebars of his scooter contained three rolls of clingfilm and I could just make out a bottle with a label reading Overproof White Rum. Even if I couldn't read it, I'd have known what he had in there, and why. White rum is one of the main ingredients for cooking crack cocaine.

The boy looked left and right as he came out of the store, as you would if you were about to cross the road, except I knew he wasn't looking out for traffic. He was looking for police, or maybe for an op – a member of a rival gang from the nearby area. His face was deadpan, casual but alert.

I walked into the underpass. It was almost completely dark in there, and the stench of piss and weed immediately transported me back to the wings. A woman in a leather dress wearing only one sandal whooped loudly and threw her arms up in the air as she swayed her hips to the beat of the drum coming from a speaker in the bits and bobs shop around the corner. Then she laughed loudly and slumped into the wall before falling into a squat. Her friend, swaying just as badly, caught up with her and tried to pull her to her feet, but the two of them just ended up on the ground together.

Behind them, the wall was layered in years' worth of graffiti, the words 'mandem' and 'smack' prominent among the brightly coloured bubble writing. And on the only part of the wall where light reached, where the sun came pouring through a perspex roof overhead, I saw a mural of children playing, commissioned after the Rock Against Racism rally in the seventies, to depict racial harmony.

The two women slumped on the ground together were arguing light-heartedly over a piece of tinfoil containing some dark crumbs. As I walked past, I saw one of them emptying the contents of a cigarette butt she had found on the ground near by into her palm to try to make a rollie. A sad-looking man with a pile of plastic bags was hunched at the other entrance to the underpass.

His pale hands were thick with grime, clasped around a piece of cardboard that read 'HUNGRY'.

As I emerged on the other side, the vibrancy of the street came as a stark contrast to that scene in the half-light. A group of older men were standing under the concrete staircase where a convenience store had been neatly slotted, smoking cigarettes, sipping from tins and laughing. One of them – taller, his right eye slumped towards the bridge of his nose, and with a good-natured grin on his face – I recognized from prison. This had happened to me a couple of times before. The men housed on H-Wing came from the same borough I lived in, so it wasn't all that surprising that I'd bump into some of them on the high street.

Most of the time they'd just say something like, 'Eyyy – gov. H spur, innit! Oi, guys, this 'ere was my gov on the inside!'

It had taken me by surprise the first time it happened but I'd just replied with a 'You all right? Look after yourself, yeah? I don't wanna be seeing you back in again any time soon.' The men in question were friendly enough but I never got the feeling they wanted the conversation to go on any longer.

The market street was filled with men pushing carts packed with leather shoes, or wearing hairnets and aprons and standing behind polystyrene boxes shimmering with fish, or under striped awnings surrounded by purple aubergines piled high, crates of yams and vast bunches of herbs. Any one of these men could be the fathers, brothers, cousins or uncles of the men I spent my days with – the families they'd told me about in the stories of their lives before jail. The stories which very often had one thing in common: a normal life turned upside down by one wrong decision. Any one of these mothers, wheeling their bags, buying warmly coloured spices or greeting friendly faces at the steps to the church, could be the mothers who the men on H-Uppers told me about. The mothers who sobbed in the courtroom, who prayed with their sons over the phone late at night, whose hearts had been ripped out as each one of their boys was swept up by crime.

At the edges of the market, where stores were laden with mobile phones and electrical accessories, there were three boys wearing black balaclavas, but I could see school ties peeping out from underneath. They were exchanging something with the man behind the counter. They all looked nervous and ready to flee. I peered over, knowing full well what I was going to see, and sure enough they were buying stacks of little see-through ziplock bags. Under what pretence these bags were originally manufactured I didn't know, but their destination was certain. They would be filled with meticulously weighed powders or brown rocks, and sprung far and wide across the country by a network of drug dealers.

Yet life went on around them completely as normal. Everybody saw that it was happening, but the spotlight would only shine when one of them got caught. No one stopped them now. No one offered them a hand, or a chance at doing something else. No – we'd all wait for them to get caught and then throw them in a concrete cell and expect them to understand the connection between their actions and the consequences.

During the last few months on the wing, one of my favourite things to do had been scrolling through a news app which reeled off all the latest crime news, like 'The faces of the 42 murderers from London already locked up this year' or 'Serbian gang sentenced to a total of 43 years for sex trafficking and fraud'. I got a strange bittersweet sort of thrill just from seeing the name of someone I knew under a picture of them scowling into the camera, thick-necked, eyes watering with malice and a curl about their lips. While everyone else who saw this picture would just see another man to fear, another example of evil in this world, I was lucky enough to actually know the man. More than that, I actually liked him.

This man might have made me coffee every morning, or polished the floor of the wing and then asked me proudly what I thought of his work. He might have told me that he planned to buy his daughter a bike when he got out of prison.

To me, it felt like a privilege to know these men.

15

War Poets

'Well, if it ain't my Gen! I thought I saw a sparkle out the corner of my eye!' It was Domingo, swaggering down the wing towards me.

It was my first day back at work in the New Year.

'As I live and breathe – the Violence Reduction rep of H-Uppers *actually* helping out at the meds hatch?' I replied with maximum sarcasm.

'Man likes to keep busy. You know me, Gen, I just like to help, you feel me? So go on, then – tell me 'bout your New Year. I bin cooped up here, left to live off the govs' social lives, an' it's makin' me crazy. I bet you and your friends are them posh types that rent a table at the club and order them magnums of Grey Goose, innit?'

I laughed. 'Pha! Nope, 'fraid not, Domingo. We're more "lots of beers and a house party" kind of people.'

'Is iiiit?' He was nodding his head enthusiastically. 'Ahh, I can see that now, you know? I love a house party, I do. I miss them. All sorts of madness.'

'They're the best. All your family or friends in one place. Sometimes that's so much better than being all spread out with loads of strangers, especially on New Year's Eve.'

'That's the truth, ya know?' said Domingo thoughtfully. 'But my problem, see, is I got so many bros that don't see eye to eye. You get me? Like so many of the mandem can't be in the same area, let alone the same house – you get me? Sad that, innit, when we all grew up on the block together.'

'Yeah, Domingo. That is sad. I'm not gonna lie – your house parties sound kinda different from mine.'

'Word.' He looked suddenly despondent. 'It kills me, Gen, you know, what us mandem are doing. We're killin' our brothers. Them ones that look like us, talk like us and was brought up by their mamas just the same as us.'

I nodded. It was something I'd actually been thinking about a lot recently.

I'd learned from my mistakes out in the exercise yard. When I was on duty now, I went straight across to the window with its wire grid, leaning up against it to make it clear to everyone that nothing was getting through it under my nose.

The prisoners trickled down the stairs in little groups.

Some were sucking on their vape pens. Others were laying down towels for a workout. One group quickly caught my eye: they splayed out in a rough circle and started taking it in turns to rap. Domingo wandered over, an impressed look on his face.

I caught myself grinning at the sight before me. It was exactly the kind of romanticized scene you might see in a US prison drama. If I'd not known it was real, I'd have looked over my shoulder for the camera crew and the director.

Domingo, despite his infamous reputation, was taking a back seat in the circle, nodding along and encouraging, joining in with the boys who weren't rapping but tapping their feet and whipping their hands to the beat, some sporadically humming a melody.

I shuffled to the other end of the window so I could hear them better. They were really good. They were reeling off lines they had written themselves while in jail with an effortless poetic rhythm, their words filled with both anger and humour.

I hadn't really registered that the group was entirely made up of Black men until I saw a young white prisoner hesitantly making his way over. He had bad acne and his shoulders sloped down sharply from his long neck, giving him a look of awkward shyness. The boy who was currently freestyling took one look at him, then invited him to join in with a movement of his hand, finishing his bar with:

> – an dem shots they fire like brap! brap! brap!
>
> But I ain't never seen a white boy rap!

The white boy missed his first beat, drawing in a quivering, nervous breath. But he picked up the next beat, and suddenly his vocals were exploding into the cold air with lyrical fluency. Everyone around him dropped to the ground in appreciation of his talent, stamping their hands to the beat, cheering him on euphorically as he leaned into the pace. His lips seemed to dance around each rhyme. Suddenly he wasn't awkward any more. For the first time his body moved with a natural rhythm.

He finished with a line about shanking a police officer and the crowd closed around him, jubilantly clapping him on the back. I watched his head bobbing among the jostling crowd, a look of bemused bliss spreading across his face. I felt my heart warming as he basked in the feelings of respect and belonging, of the acknowledgement of his talents. When Domingo wrapped his arm around him and patted him on the back, the boy looked about ready to pass out.

Despite my novice status as a drill listener, the talent of those boys wasn't lost on me. Some of their lyrics were disturbingly vicious, but then again, every musician writes songs about what they know – about their boyfriends or girlfriends, their families or hometowns, the ups and downs of their lives – and that was true of drill music too. In between the bloodthirsty, trigger-happy rhymes, though, I was surprised to find that their lyrics were rich in history and politics, wrapped up in sharp satire and immaculate poetry. I felt disheartened hearing the passion in their words and knowing that instead of their music being widely celebrated, it was widely banned.

But as I watched the last men trail off the yard at the end of exercise, I had a thought. Perhaps, like a lot of great art, drill is deemed dangerous by the people of its time, but in years to come the songs will be admired by intellectuals and historians. Perhaps, one day, the politics in them will be unpacked by a class full of History students, or the pain in them dissected by an English Literature professor.

Maybe, just maybe, they'll be remembered as the war poets of our generation.

It was as I was returning from the yard that I was pulled into the office by my manager, Kelly.

'No need to take a seat, love,' she said briskly. 'I just need to let you know you've been moved across to your secondary wing.'

My nerve endings jangled with anxiety as I ran through everything I could have done wrong. *Could this decision be something to do with Johnson?* He'd left the wing weeks ago now . . . *surely it couldn't be him? Or could our interactions have left some kind of black mark against me?*

'OK, um – that's fine,' I said. Then, still trying to sound casual about it, I continued, 'How come?'

'Don't worry, lovey. You ain't done nothin' wrong. It's just it's January, isn't it? Everyone's quit cos they didn't get the day off they requested over Christmas and New Year, blah blah blah. It's the same every year. Anyway, so you're gonna go across to G-Wing cos they're seriously thin on the ground. You don't mind, do you?'

'Um, I, um—'

'It's just that, well, they turned down Steve when I offered him, and I'm not up for the argument with Ellen, and – look, it would be H-Wing straight down the shitter if I moved Walter.'

'Ha. Yeah, fair enough. I get that,' I said. 'Nah – I don't mind. It will be a different experience, I guess, on the vulnerable persons wing.'

'And foreign nationals, remember! It's a good wing – it's got some good officers. You'll like it. Plus it's only about two metres to the left of H-Wing, so you'll still see plenty of the old ugly faces you're used to. Anyway, as you were!'

As I left her office, I felt as though my feet had been swept out from under me.

I'd just got to grips with the job on H-Wing. I'd painstakingly learned what cell every one of the ninety prisoners occupied, down to exactly which bunk they slept in. It was mapped out in my brain: I could open a cell door one morning, see an empty bed and know exactly who had left it, and in the same moment mentally register that space and what type of man I might be able to slot in there when new prisoners arrived that afternoon. When a prisoner came to me to request a five-way cell swap, part of an elaborate plan he had negotiated with ten other prisoners so that he could eventually share a cell with his cousin, I could work it out like an equation in my head. I could calculate that the third move would result in an adult being paired in the same cell as a nineteen-year-old (illegal) and a recovering user being put in the same cell as a prisoner that takes methadone medication (neglectful). So in a matter of moments I could firmly tell him no – and, as is always vital when saying no to a prisoner, I could tell him exactly *why*.

But now I had to start all over again – and all because I was the most disposable officer on the wing. Still.

16

The G-Wing Cycle

On the first day of my new posting to G-Wing I sat in the office, glumly scrolling through NOMIS, hoping I could get a feel for the men on the wing before the day began.

G-Wing held vulnerable prisoners who mostly needed to be there for their own protection. Some had learning disabilities or psychotic disorders, and couldn't cope on other wings. Some had got themselves into debt with other prisoners, so weren't safe on their wing. Some were in for rape or child pornography, so they'd had the shit beaten out of them on other wings. But the largest category was made up of foreign nationals, which included both non-British citizens who had been charged with committing a crime and undocumented migrants for whom there wasn't enough room in immigration centres.

Pictures of characters with straggly grey hair and greasy moustaches swam before me on the screen. It was almost comical that sex offenders could have such a clichéd look about them. I peered with dismay at the names of some of the foreign national prisoners: Hoxha, Konaj, Botezatu, Ngo, Gabrielus, Duong, Silva, Stonkus. It's hard enough to remember ninety names when they're familiar to you, but learning to remember and then pronounce ninety names which you're quite unaccustomed to felt near impossible. I clicked on the profile of a particularly cross-eyed, greasy-looking man, guessing what I might find.

46 counts of sexual assault. 36 counts of penetration. Victim under 12 years old. Special notes: not to contact daughter, 8 years old.

I felt dejected. I thought of all the people who had ever said to me, 'That's a really noble career choice you've made.' I'd always tell them firmly that I wasn't getting up at 5 a.m. to be charitable. I'd made this career choice because I was fascinated by the people I knew I'd meet; I'd felt drawn to the challenges crime presents to society. But was I really going to come into work each day from now on just to make sure someone like this lowlife got his three meals a day and didn't get beaten up on the exercise yard?

I kept on scrolling through the images. A picture of a man with an eyebrow piercing, winking suggestively at the camera, made me laugh. The name underneath read

Andres, Felipe. Maybe the foreign nationals could be my focus instead. I thought longingly of the humour and brotherhood I'd experienced on H-Uppers – Tisdale, who would only get out of bed each morning to collect his seizure medication if I woke him up by drumming his mug and plate together to the tune of 'Stayin' Alive'; or Creighton, who needed to be taken to get his blood pressure tested four times a day or he risked having a heart attack, but always said he didn't want to bother the officers too much by asking them. Through getting to know these men, a scary, intimidating world had become familiar, even comforting to me.

I took the G-Wing prisoners out for medication on the core. I was secretly hoping I'd cross over with a couple of guys from H-Wing to check in on them. Right now, any familiar face would be a comfort.

As luck would have it, there were indeed some H-Upper faces out there. Domingo and Fingers were standing next to the meds hatch, covering their nose and mouth with bunches of tissues. There was an unmistakable stench of sewage.

'Gen! Was that you?' Domingo said with a snigger as I came closer, gesticulating towards the source of the horrible smell. 'Did you block the toilet?'

I laughed, reluctantly. I could see a murky puddle growing out from underneath the staff toilet on the landing.

'For real, though, these are the conditions they're keepin' us in now?' Fingers complained.

He had a point. 'Yeah,' I said, 'give me a minute, guys, I'll go and report it.'

I marched up to the office, poked my head round the door and saw Dimitra behind the desk. She had also been moved around in the New Year swap and she'd joined Kelly as a manager of the upper wings. She was a Greek woman nearing fifty, with sweeps of blue eyeshadow over each eyelid and lips permanently pursed.

'Dimitra, you know there's, like, actual sewage flowing out on to the landing?'

She didn't look up from the computer screen.

'How are we meant to do medication when there's sewage all over the floor?' I asked, reasonably.

Dimitra sighed. 'Everything is a problem, Gen, isn't it?'

'Not everything. But I certainly think this is.'

'I do not see how a bit of toilet water stops you from doing medication. It is not going to kill anyone, is it? Shut the door, will you? You're stinking out the office.'

Domingo and Fingers had made use of the time I'd had my back turned. When I got back to the meds hatch they were crouched down by the G-Wing door, passing through a torn-off piece of paper. I put my foot on it and kicked the paper into the growing puddle of sewage just beyond.

'Gen! What are you even doin'?'

'Honestly, look around you. Does it look like I've got time for you to be up to shit like that today? That's my wing now as well and they don't need any more spice on there, trust me.'

Domingo opened his mouth in mock outrage and

turned to another prisoner. 'Would you believe it? I'm VR, you know, and she don't even trust me!'

'Ha!' I said. 'Domingo, I *especially* don't trust you. We all know VRs are the most corrupt guys on the wing.'

'Can you believe she just said that?' he said to Fingers, shaking his head emphatically.

Fingers grinned. 'Phaaa!' he said. 'Miss, that's where you're wrong. It's *officers* that are the most corrupt on the wing.'

'Yeah, yeah, I've heard it all before,' I said to him.

Remarks about the behaviour of officers didn't get to me the way they used to. When I thought of Dimitra sitting smugly in the sewage-free office, or Steve legging it away down the wing while Ellen was being attacked, or Reffie, who was still moping around telling everyone about his plans to get laid off with permanent sick leave, I thought the prisoners' criticism was pretty accurate. I certainly wasn't going to get defensive about any of them.

But it didn't scare me any more that I was surrounded by officers I couldn't rely on. I'd worked out who I could trust. Best of all though, now I knew I could trust myself.

That day I was on duty with an older officer called Chris. He wasn't at all how I'd expected him to be. I knew he'd been an officer for thirty years and had spent the last five of those working on G-Uppers – so he knew his way around. But most old-timers like him looked as though the life had gone from behind their eyes – as though one more piece of backchat from a prisoner might be the straw that breaks the camel's back. Chris, though, still had a boyish twinkle in his eye and a sense of humour to match it.

He took me through the residents on the wing. 'I'll start with the worst – Dimitra. She ain't a prisoner, mind you, she's the manager, but she'll cause you more trouble than any one of them out there. Sometimes I think she feels like she was put on this earth to wind people up. Like she's got some degree in pissing people off.'

I laughed. After working with Steve enough times I could understand only too well the hatred Chris might harbour for an officer who only made his job harder.

'Anyways, you'll make your own mind up about her.'

'I think I already have,' I said, almost under my breath, recalling my conversation with her over the sewage spill.

'Then we got our lead servery worker, Rankin. He's serving eighteen years for rape, right – but he's an all right guy if you get past that. Then Radu helps him out, Albanian fella, hard worker. Silva is our wing cleaner, he ain't bad, and speaks a bunch of languages which is always helpful on this wing. Portuguese, Spanish and German, I think. Oh, an' all of 'em speak better English than I do!' Chris grinned.

'Wait, so, how does the sex offender thing go on this wing? People know if that's your offence and they're fine with it? Or the prisoners just aren't as nosey here?'

'It's a bit of both,' Chris said with a shrug. 'Sometimes things get around and we have a few black eyes. But mostly, these foreign national types, they've got more issues going on. They're worried about being extradited an' that.'

I nodded, but I still wasn't quite sure I understood. Everywhere else in the prison, at the slightest whisper of a sex offence people would get beaten to a pulp by their cellmate. It even happened if the cellmate was getting on with the prisoner OK. The other men on the wing would either pay him or force him to do it.

'Then there's Bert,' Chris continued. 'Bert and I go back a long way. We first met about seven years ago. I've given 'im a sort of unofficial role as odd-jobs man. He helps out wiv the painting round the wing since our head painter got shipped out. And he ain't bad at fixing fings either.' Chris's eyes twinkled. He was sounding almost affectionate now. 'Mainly, though, prison is pretty much the only home he's ever known and he don't do well behind his door. So I do like to get him out and about a bit. Watch 'im, though, cos he does like the spice. And the hooch, when he can get his hands on it.'

'So spice is a big thing on this wing?' I asked. 'I've seen it here and there, but never saw anyone really *on it* on H-Wing, I don't think.'

'That's cos the H-Wing lot can afford grass! It's the ones that can't afford the grass that go for the spice,' Chris explained darkly. 'The population on this wing goes in cycles, you see. It depends what kind of vulnerable prisoners get tossed our way at any time. At the moment, see, we've got all the self-harmers the rest of the prison can't deal with any more. But after a bit of time the other wings will be begging for their self-harmers back, asking to swap them with their most troublesome gangbanger YOs. When the gangbangers arrive, so does the next batch of spice. That's when all these nice friendly foreign nationals we got on here right now turn into angry, aggressive spice-heads. Then *everyone* starts self-harming.'

I nodded slowly. 'Right.'

'It's a cycle,' Chris went on, 'and it's been going on here as long as I have. Right now it's starting to peak – you mark my words. All the spice-heads on the wing were all over the place last night. Oh, talk of the devil . . .'

A middle-aged man wearing paint-spattered overalls and rubbing his eyes was approaching us along the landing. He had cracked teeth and a sagging pot belly which sat upon his little pin-like legs.

'What you sayin' about me now then, Chris?' the prisoner asked.

As soon as I heard his voice, I realized he was much younger than he looked.

'Bert,' he introduced himself, putting out his hand for me to shake. His fingertips were brown – a telltale sign that he had been shovelling something into the end of his hot vape to smoke. Faint scars criss-crossed his wrists.

'Hi, Bert. How you doin'?' I said, shaking his out-stretched hand.

'Where you at with that library book I asked you about?' Bert said, turning to Chris.

Chris chuckled. 'Ah yes. Have to say, Bert, *Pride and Prejudice* was a bit of a surprise. I weren't even sure you could read!' He said it with a cheeky grin, and gave Bert's arm a good-natured thump.

Bert looked uneasy. 'Well, I'm tryin' out sumfin' different, ain't I?' he said, before shuffling away.

Chris sighed. 'He's not usually one to take a joke badly. Wonder what's got into 'im!'

Over the next few days, I realized Chris had been right about the cycle of spice on the wing. And about Dimitra too. Never had the expression 'face like a smacked arse' been truer of anyone, and she had the attitude to go with it.

We were seeing more and more prisoners high on spice with each day that passed and Dimitra had taken to tearing around the wing demanding to sniff prisoners' vapes every time she thought she caught a whiff. Other than the fact that she really shouldn't be sniffing that stuff, she was seriously pissing prisoners off – it's offensive to be accused of smoking spice as it's considered a dirty drug. Unsurprisingly she had had little success, and probably a banging headache from inhaling a good deal of the stuff, so she had attempted to assert her powers in other ways, like enforcing pernickety health and safety rules.

Technically, prisoners could only vape in their cells with the door and obs flap closed – a rule left over from when prisoners could smoke real cigarettes. It's one of those battles, though, which just isn't worth fighting, and every officer in the jail was in agreement that it was a bit of freedom we could afford them. Dimitra, however, chose this point to crack down on them all, shouting at prisoners who couldn't even speak English to get back in their cells with their vapes, and sending prisoners back up from exercise for vaping on the yard.

'Let the men smoke in the fresh air!' Chris said, billowing clouds of vapour as he spoke (the same rule applied for officers: we were only allowed to vape in our offices). 'You can't just go enforcing some rule that no one's told 'em for years. You'll cause a riot with that attitude, Dimitra.'

'There is dangerous spice on the wing,' she replied, curtly. 'I will find out who is smoking and I will take them to be drug-tested myself.' She pursed her lips still tighter.

'Dimitra,' I interjected, emboldened by Chris's presence, 'you get someone drug-tested, they come up positive, then what? We confine them to a cell for two weeks where they smoke themselves into oblivion every day. That's the last thing they need! We need to find out where the source is, and to do that we just need to watch. And please, for God's sake, stop letting on to them that we know what's going on, they'll just tighten things up otherwise. Let's just watch, and wait, and find out where it's coming from, OK?'

I thought I'd made a pretty sensible argument. I even thought it might have sunk in. But she just turned on her heel and muttered, 'I am going to talk to Kelly.'

Dimitra was particularly hard on Bert about smoking, and I had a horrible feeling that he was just being used as a pawn in her battle with Chris. Although it didn't take a drug test to see that from about 4 p.m. every day Bert was wandering around with glazed, watery eyes. In the mornings, though, when he was sober, I was starting to see the man for whom Chris had so much affection.

It was as though he was twenty-seven going on fifty-seven. He was like some East London boozer you might have found sitting on the same barstool in a tavern in Whitechapel for the best part of the nineties. Most of the time you could find him in the office, reminiscing about *the good old days* when you could buy a pint for a couple of quid in the pub. Otherwise, you could be sure to find him somewhere down the other end of the wing, scuffing up skirting boards so he could ask to be unlocked to repaint them later.

It was frustrating to see him on spice. Not only because it was sad to see his usual cheery self so doped up, but also because I actually enjoyed his company when he was sober. He was funny, and oddly charming, but all that disappeared into a dull state of existence when he smoked.

Spice had a different effect on everyone. It can be made up of any number of different synthetic chemicals, so a couple of dazed, zombie-like prisoners walking about the wing was actually one of the better effects — as I would soon find out.

17

Spice and Prejudice

One morning I was handing out the post around the wing, slipping postcards and letters crammed full of photos under cell doors, when I saw a familiar face. Steve was striding up the stairs towards me, puffing on his vape.

I gave him a slight nod but carried on posting the mail.

'Ah,' he called out to me, 'they got you on the nonce wing then?'

'Hey Steve, good morning to you too. Yeah – I was transferred across cos of staff shortages or something.'

'Like long-term? Ah, peak, Gen, that's peak for you. I'm jus' covering for today. Yeah – Kelly told me they requested me on G-Wing full-time too but she said she didn't want to lose me off H-Wing. So – yeah.'

I remembered what Kelly had actually said, and a laugh crept out. I couldn't help it.

'What?' Steve said, chuckling defensively. 'What is it?'

I thought on my feet. 'Just this letter says S.W.A.L.K. on the back of it.' I held up the envelope to show him. 'Dread to think what the photos are of inside.' I had a fairly good idea, though: there is a rule for everything in prison, and when it came to nude photos it was 'top half only'. Any 'bottom half' photos would have been confiscated on their way in.

Steve looked relieved. 'Ah, yeah. Probs a nonce. They're all nonces on here.'

I had a feeling this was going to be a long day.

Just as I had finished handing out all of the letters, I heard the wing door opening. When I got to the bottom of the stairs I saw a tall, bulky prisoner appear through the door escorted by two officers. I could see a dark-coloured wig perched awkwardly on top of their head and I realized who it was immediately – Scarlet. Her huge frame was hugged by a pair of tight hot pants and a roughly stuffed sports bra. Deep purple welts criss-crossed her legs, arms and neck – but not at all like the scratch marks I was so used to seeing on most prisoners. These gashes were thick and savage. Her thighs looked like pieces of meat bound in tight string, flesh bulging out between bloody straps of carved-out tissue.

Kelly had warned me that one of the other wings had

been trying to get a transgender prisoner moved to G-Wing for some time now because they couldn't cope with her level of self-harming. Kelly had been adamantly opposed to the move. 'G-Wing's got too many self-harmers on it as it is,' she'd told me. 'It's dangerous. There aren't enough staff to do all the paperwork, and we've got enough vulnerable people on there at the moment. We don't have the capacity for someone with needs like Scarlet's.'

I reached the wing office just as Steve disappeared in there with the two escorting officers.

'Yeah,' Steve was saying, 'he'll fit right in on here.'

I quickly took over, and turned to the new prisoner. 'Scarlet, is it?'

'Oooh, you smell lovely, darlin'. What type of perfume are you wearing? Is that Ravishing by Ann Summers?'

'I don't wear perfume to work,' I said, 'there's no one I'm trying to smell nice for in here. Scarlet, would you mind just waiting outside a second while we talk in the office? We just need to sort out some paperwork. Is that all right, yeah?'

'No problem, darlin'. I'll be over there!' She went outside and leaned against a pool table with her legs crossed, as daintily as she could.

In the office, one of the officers escorting her explained what was happening. 'Yeah, your manager agreed to take her. She gets to come here for association and exercise cos she can't go out on other wings any more.'

'Pha! I'm not surprised, lookin' like that!' Steve blurted out.

The escorting officer shot him a glance. 'No, Steve, it's not because she's trans.'

I saw Steve recoil as he heard the word 'she'.

'It's because she's got herself into debt smoking spice she can't afford all day long. She owes some dodgy people money, and we need to make sure she stays away from them. And this is the VP wing, innit? She's vulnerable, so this is where she should've come first anyways.'

Steve looked put out. 'What's all this *she* stuff? That's an *it*. A *he* at best. C'mon, man!' he jibed, looking at the other escort officer for support.

The escort gave Steve a dismissive pat on the back. 'Steve, my little man, *she* could knock any one of us out cold with one punch. 'Specially you, mate.'

'Moving on!' I said, with a queasy look at Steve. 'The thing is, last time I spoke with Kelly, she said Scarlet definitely *couldn't* come on here. Kelly refused to authorize it. It was because we've got too many self-harmers at the moment. It's actually getting dangerous.'

'Listen, Gen,' the escort said, 'I promise, it's bin approved. I dunno – I guess call Kelly about it or something? Anyways, it's not like she's here overnight. It's just nine 'til twelve each morning, yeah? So she can get some time out of her cell without being bashed in. Then we'll come back to pick her up. Plus you'd be doing us a huge favour, and her.'

A fusillade of banging followed by a whoop came from outside the office. I stepped out to see Scarlet standing near the wing door, which was surrounded by an only partially frosted perspex window. She was lowering her hands with her bum in the air before performing one of the most expert slut drops I've ever seen and then swallowing an Evian water bottle halfway down her gullet.

Having Scarlet on the wing was going to be – at best – eventful.

Events moved even faster than I'd thought. First thing next morning, I woke up to a text from Kelly.

You'll never guess who was giving out blowjobs in return for spice on G-Uppers yesterday . . .

I laughed and texted back: *Steve!?*

Hahaha. No. That would solve a lot of problems, though. Still, we can't have Scarlet on G-Uppers now after that, so at least that's one problem off our hands!

A couple of weeks later, though, Kelly admitted that she'd lost the fight to keep Scarlet from joining us. 'I'm afraid there's simply nowhere else for her to go, guys,' she explained. 'But for Christ's sake, make sure she's on the lower landing. We don't want her hopping over those railings and threatening to jump every time she wants to throw 'er toys out the pram. She's strong and she can stay clutching on to them railings for bloody hours. Long as we keep the wing as spice-free as possible, she shouldn't be too bad.'

★

'But Miss Gen, I need my foundation, it's my human right!' Scarlet whined. She was leaning against the frame of the office door, fiddling with her bra strap.

It must have been the sixteenth time Scarlet and I had had the talk about foundation in the last fortnight. I had given up explaining to her that access to anything on the prison canteen list was a privilege, not a human right. Also, her habit of self-harming to get what she wanted was precisely the kind of thing that *wouldn't* earn her any privileges. But it was the only way she seemed to know to try to influence any situation. The worst possible outcome was to give her the idea that her self-harming would benefit her in any way. Because when she did it, she didn't mess about. She would cut right through muscle without even flinching.

'Scarlet! Good morning, how are you? I'm good, thanks, and how are you, Gen?' I sang back to her.

She giggled and put her hand over her mouth. 'Oops, sorry, Miss. Where are my manners? But I do need that foundation. It's my human right, remember, cos I'm trans?'

'Scarlet, make-up is not a human right. There's at least a four-step process for me to get you some foundation. Security needs to approve an unregistered item, canteen needs to order it, then someone has to deliver it to the prison, then you need to put the order through, then it has to be delivered to this wing on canteen day. You know I've put a request in and you know things take a long time in prison. You're going to have to be patient.'

She stuck out her bottom lip and started scratching at

her forearm. A deep gash held together by some stitches started to bleed.

'Scarlet, will you go grab your meds? And when you get back, I have a surprise for you.' I winked at her.

'Ooh, what is it, Miss? I like a surprise, I do!' She cheered up immediately and swept out of the office.

I'd suspected for a while that it wasn't the foundation at all that she was worried about. It was returning once again to a life of selling her body on the streets for drugs when she was released in a few months' time. However, today was going to be a good day for her. Jake was on duty on the wing.

I'd done my PO training with Jake. He was broad, muscly and tanned with never a hair out of place in his meticulously sculpted beard, and it was no secret that Scarlet had taken quite a fancy to him. He'd groaned as he'd been allocated to G-Wing this morning, knowing full well how his shift would go with Scarlet around.

Sure enough, the first chance she could get, Scarlet had Jake cornered in the office.

'You're a big boy, aren't you?' she purred at him seductively. Despite Jake's *Love Island*-esque appearance, he was really very humble and incredibly shy and I couldn't help but laugh at Scarlet's delight as he muttered a flustered thanks. 'Do you work out, then? You know what they say, don't you? I give the best blowjobs in the whole prison, I do. I can give you things you never dreamed of!'

I thought about intervening but Jake seemed to be

taking it well enough, and I was actually quite enjoying the show. There was a strange edge to Scarlet's voice today though which made me look at her more closely. I saw that her eyes were glazed, and a film of sweat coated her skin. Only one thing made her like this, and that was spice.

I watched Jake sitting there with the blood rising in his cheeks, gently letting Scarlet down with an earnest politeness.

Who could be bringing it in? I thought to myself, with the faces of likely suspects floating through my mind.

Then I remembered: *today is canteen day* – and canteen day was always full of clues.

Prisoners can purchase canteen items once a week on the online portal – the same way they book visits, sign up for education and work, and choose their meals for the week. They pay for it out of the account they have on the system which can be topped up by friends or family on the outside. They can choose from a range of items, from vape capsules and stamps to crisps and tins of mackerel.

It's when canteen arrives that prisoners have to pay their debts. That's when you can see who's been selling what to whom. So, today was the day when we were going to start working out where this spice was coming from.

The why at least we knew. There'd been a couple of Lithuanians with us until recently, but they'd been moved when Chris and I found an enormous supply of hooch under their beds. Hooch – prison-brewed alcohol – normally smells of the decaying bread and fruit that is used to make it, but this stuff smelled like pure ethanol. Chris took a whiff and was so impressed with their distilling skills that he laughed and shook their hands. They proudly offered us a taste, and looked slightly put out when we placed the bottles straight into evidence bags. When there's hooch about, I had come to learn, most of the prisoners are usually happy enough to wait until the evening when we've gone home before they drink it. Spice, though, is just too irresistible to wait. Which is why, once it's got on to a wing, the whole place pretty rapidly becomes like a scene from *The Walking Dead*.

When Jake arrived on the landing tugging the enormous trolley filled with canteen, I unlocked some of the workers to lug the bags to the correct cell doors. Each prisoner receives a heat-sealed, transparent plastic bag filled with the canteen they ordered, and their receipt. The rule is simple and strict: you can only claim something's missing before the bag has been opened.

Only once all the prisoners had received their canteen could they be unlocked for exercise – and this was the bit we had to watch. To the untrained eye it was a mad rush of men dipping in and out of each other's cells clutching armfuls of Pot Noodles and energy drinks, then coming back out empty-handed. But I'd been in the job long enough now to do the maths.

I saw a prisoner who'd arrived on the wing just the week before zip into Silva's cell with a handful of tinned mackerel – about the same amount as a tab of spice goes for. But, I reasoned, the most likely explanation here was that his money hadn't dropped into his account in time for him to order canteen when he'd arrived the previous week, so it was more than likely that he was repaying Silva with four mackerel tins in return for the three Silva must have ordered him last week – that was usually the deal. Technically, trading like that is not allowed – but it wasn't what I was looking for.

On the opposite side of the landing I did see something suspicious – a bit of congestion building outside the cell that was home to servery worker Radu and another Albanian man. I'd had my eye on them for a while because they often had an unusual amount of traffic coming in and out of their cell. What's more, Radu's cellmate Marku had been asking Chris and me for a job on the wing for weeks now. He had been offered a role in the kitchens but had turned it down, saying that he only wanted wing work. After this, Chris had put him straight to the bottom of the list for jobs on the wing, saying that he clearly didn't want the job and just wanted to be unlocked more, probably so he could pass contraband around.

I noticed that another Albanian prisoner had been going from cell to cell, collecting loot as he went. Now he'd ended up outside Radu's door too. *Could he be doing the drug running? Collecting payment so that the crowd outside that cell didn't get too noticeable?* He didn't seem like a spice-head. And he didn't need the money – he was Albanian, and Albanians look after their people in prison.

Keeping that door in my line of vision, I leaned over the railings so that I could see Scarlet downstairs, zigzagging between cells. Her hands were empty, as was her canteen bag each week, containing only a packet of vape capsules. It was all she could afford from the £1.82 statutory pay every prisoner received per day. She didn't have anyone on the outside to send money in for her, so her only currency was sexual favours and begging. That's what she'd be doing now, bouncing between cells asking prisoners for the dregs of their old vape capsules now their new ones had arrived.

I noticed her wandering into Bert's cell downstairs. This was strange, because Bert was another who didn't have any money coming in. In fact, the two of them were in direct competition – both scrounging old vape caps off the other prisoners. I crouched down so I could just about see into Bert's doorway. There was a buzz of activity there too. Prisoners were dipping in and out but I couldn't make out who it was from this far away. Then I saw Scarlet reappear at Bert's doorway, look both ways, shut the door and stand outside it like a guard. *That's strange*, I thought. If it had been on H-Wing I would have been sure that a prisoner was being beaten up in there, but that was unlikely on G-Wing.

'Miss Genny!'

My train of thought was interrupted and I looked up – it was Radu. None of the foreign nationals had got their heads around 'Gen' and had instead opted for 'Miss Genny', which made Chris giggle no end and made me feel like a nursery school teacher.

'Who are you spying on?' Radu said with a grin.

'Everyone!' I said firmly.

'So what's the progress with that job, Miss Genny? My friend has been waiting patiently, he is always a polite guy. How much longer will he have to wait?'

'Radu,' I said bluntly, 'I'm new to this wing, but not to this job. And I know what's going on in your cell. One, there are prisoners coming in and out all day long. Two, you have both been asking about this job for weeks now. Three, there's spice on this wing and we know that someone's bringing it in and moving it around. Four, there is an unholy amount of canteen being delivered to your cell today.'

Radu looked a bit taken aback, but then an amused smile spread across his face. 'You think cos we are Albanian we are selling drugs?'

'No, I think you're selling drugs because of all the reasons I just listed.'

He gave me another grin. 'Would you like to see what we really collect this canteen for?' he asked.

'I dunno. Is it going to give me paperwork to do? I've got a busy afternoon as it is.'

'Ha – I don't think so! Come, look.'

He took me to the windowsill in his cell and pulled back the curtain. Hung up along the top of the window was a series of bulging socks, tied tightly with elastic bands at the tops.

'Albanian cheese,' he announced proudly. 'We take the breakfast milk to make it. It's a little taste of home for us Albanians on the wing. Try some?'

He handed me a Tupperware box and used a plastic knife to cut some off for me. I drew the line at trying hooch, but when else in my life was I going to try Albanian cheese made in a sock in prison? And I was amazed. It tasted like a mixture between paneer and goat's cheese. It was tart, but it was really good.

'So, you see, people are exchanging canteen for our cheese. We are not dealing drugs. At least not in prison we aren't,' he added with a chuckle.

I had to laugh.

'I have absolutely no idea what the rules are on making cheese in prison,' I said to Radu and Marku, 'and I'm sure that there would be plenty of govs who would take it off you. But ten out of ten for creativity, guys. Just make sure Dimitra doesn't find it. Also, there's no trading allowed in prison either, so please just do that kind of thing behind my back, yeah?'

I suddenly remembered what I had seen happening in Bert's cell and hurried down the stairs, but by the time I got there it was empty – they'd all gone out to the yard. I couldn't see any signs of a scrap so I was about to close the door and lock it when something on Bert's bed caught my eye. It was the copy of *Pride and Prejudice* he'd asked about a few weeks ago.

I laughed and shook my head. So, he really was serious about reading it.

Late in the afternoon I was supervising the dinner queue while Radu and Silva were serving the hot meal from behind the servery window. Bert hobbled over with his plastic plate, his head at an odd tilt. I could tell immediately he was trying to hide half his face from me.

'Bert!' I said, beckoning him over.

He came closer, sheepishly, and I saw then that he had a shining bruise spreading across his left eye.

The final set of clues on canteen day came after exercise. The stairwell going down to the yard doesn't have any cameras in it – it's the prime spot for a threatening thump for those who haven't paid their debts that day.

That must have been why there was a crowd in Bert's cell earlier. They wouldn't have roughed him up in there, because his cell was right next to the office. But they would've been making sure he was going down to exercise so that they could do it there.

Someone isn't happy with Bert, I thought. But it seemed like it was a little more than a bit of debt.

When Jerry crept on to the wing the next morning, tailed by two officers from his security team, he wasn't his usual booming, energetic self. I knew then that Dimitra must have demanded a whole wing search. I also knew, just as well as she did, that all that would do was root out the men on the wing who had been forced to hold the spice, and they would take the fall. The big players behind the contraband were never the ones who held it – they made the vulnerable prisoners do that.

I stayed out on the wing. I always felt it was important at times like this to look prisoners in the eye, as one by one their belongings were taken apart and their cells were turned upside down. Dimitra, however, had disappeared off to the stores unit as soon as Jerry had arrived, claiming she needed to get herself some new shirts.

After only ten minutes Jerry called out to me and gestured towards the office. I'd never seen him look so serious before. It was then that I noticed he had something under his arm. He held it up to me. It was the copy of *Pride and Prejudice*.

'You ever seen this, Gen?' he asked.

I nodded. 'Yep, you must have found that in cell 8, Bert Harley's cell.'

'It's absolutely packed full of spice,' he said.

'How can you tell?' I asked. It looked totally ordinary to me.

He tapped his nose and held the book out to me to sniff. 'You smell that? Slightly petrol-like. An' if you look real close, the pages are slightly shinier than they should be.'

I sighed. I knew exactly what this was going to mean for Bert. He'd be put on basic and locked up in his cell for twenty-three and a half hours a day for the next couple of weeks. He would be broken by it.

'Honestly, Jerry, I thought it was weird that he was reading that book. But also, Bert hasn't got anyone on the outside, so I don't know who would've got that in here for him. He's holding it for someone, for sure.'

Jerry inhaled sharply. 'I'm afraid it don't really matter, Gen. Unless he wants to tell us who he was holding it for, not really much we can do. He's a grown man, he makes his own decisions.'

I nodded, grimly, even though I wasn't sure I totally agreed.

Grown man. It was an expression I was finding really hard to come to terms with in jail. Is getting older the same thing as becoming a *grown man*, or a *grown-up*? So many of the people I had met in prison never struck me as grown-ups. I'm not sure you can really be a grown-up if you skip childhood. If you're brought up on the streets like Bert, or by the streets like the men I'd met on H-Wing, you're hardly growing into being an adult, into a position of responsibility and maturity. You're really just learning how to get by, or how to survive.

I don't imagine Bert had much of a decision to make here, I thought glumly.

18

Night Shifts

Chanice was straddling a wheelie chair backwards, her chin resting on the back support, casually perusing a clipboard of papers.

'Good evening, everyone! For those of you who don't know me, I'm Chanice, and I'm your Oscar 1 for the week. Hope you're all feeling ready and alive for your week of nights!'

All officers did night shifts on rotation four times a year. On nights, we weren't based on our own wings, instead we covered the whole prison. Just one manager, a handful of operational support officers (OSOs) and five prison officers – one in the segregation unit, one in Healthcare and the remaining three covering the rest of the prison. It sounds daunting, but I had done enough night shifts by now to know what to expect. The whole prison is locked up and it's rare that a cell door gets opened, so most of the time you can find a quiet office to put your feet up in and watch a bit of Netflix for at least a few hours. Still, working seven shifts in a row and completely reversing your body clock takes its toll on you and I always felt a pit of dread in my stomach at the start of the week.

'Right. Caleb's late again, which is not a big surprise. So we'd better get started without him.' Chanice looked around the room. 'Don't think I've done nights with some of yous before, so I'll lay down my law of the land so there's no confusion. Get your work done, do your jobs, and we'll be best friends.'

She put both thumbs up in the air.

'There's not much to do on night shifts. Get your searches done early in the week. Make sure you do your four perimeter checks a night. Don't be lazy. Otherwise, you can do what you want. If you want to go for a sleep, for Christ's sake tell one of the others where you are and keep your radio on *loud*, cos if I need one of you and can't find you, I'll be really, really *pissed off*. Is that understood?'

We all nodded.

'OK . . . incidents from earlier today,' Chanice went on, reading from her clipboard matter-of-factly. 'Find on D-Lowers – brown substance wrapped in newspaper, Coke can filled with green substance and sixteen sheets of suspected spice paper. Substances tested by Security and confirmed to be eight grams of heroin, fourteen grams of marijuana and sixteen sheets of spice paper. Estimated prison value of eight grand so quite a serious amount there but by no means the most we've ever seen.'

She paused, then went on without looking up.

'Self-harm on G-Uppers – Mr Pine pressed his cell bell after making superficial cuts to his left arm, Healthcare attended, no further treatment was needed. Another self-harm on G-Uppers – Scarlet made cuts to, um, her right thigh using her tongue piercing. She was taken to hospital on escort and has since returned after receiving twelve stitches, so nothing new there. Everyone be vigilant with that tonight, please, because we don't want any hospital escorts this week.'

I could just imagine Chris hearing this news when he came in on shift tomorrow and joking: *I probably would've done the same if I was on G-Uppers with Dimitra all weekend!* And he would have had a point about that, except I also had a feeling that the spice which had suddenly flooded the wing might have had something to do with it as well. Another weekend spent in jail, on a hell of a comedown, with Dimitra. The perfect storm.

'Self-harm in Healthcare,' Chanice continued. 'Mr Filch has reportedly inserted three razor blades into his anus. He was taken to hospital and isn't due to return until the morning so we should be fine without him tonight. He's reported to have done it because he wants – yup, you're hearing this right – he wants the prison to give him a PS4.'

'Bruddah!' Sanjeet, one of the other officers, winced. 'Imagine putting blades up your arse for a PlayStation, man!'

'He's due back tomorrow, so everyone make the most of tonight because I have a feeling he's going to be giving us trouble all week. Then there was a staff assault in reception. Mr Hainhault refused to be searched and so was searched under restraint. During it he pulled out an improvised weapon and Officer Kenzy was slashed in the leg. Kenzy went to hospital but has since been discharged and I've heard he's on the mend. Mr Hainhault was relocated to the segregation unit.'

I looked around at everyone, listening to these incidents as though Chanice was reporting on an incoming mild weather front. *This isn't normal*, I thought to myself. But at the same time I felt a strange sort of pride swell in me for the level of madness we had become accustomed to, and coped with.

'Almost there, guys. Find on H-Uppers – one spliff. Not sure who thought it was legit to write the word "spliff" on a legal document, but oh well. This was found when the cell was searched after we received Security-led intel that a prisoner affiliated with the Wolves gang filmed a music video on a smartphone in their cell, uploaded it to YouTube and called it "Gangshit! Cummon then govs, see if yous can come find dis phone."'

We all burst out laughing. That one had Domingo written all over it. Of course he had managed to get his hands on a smartphone.

Caleb had appeared through the security gate just in time to hear the title of the video. 'Bruh,' he said, 'now that is gang shit. I'll give it to 'em – those guys are *funny*.'

'Caleb!' Chanice said with a tart smile. 'Good *evening*. The others will catch you up, but my main area of concern is Scarlet and the risk of her self-harming. And of course, as you have turned up twenty minutes late, you will now be top of my list to send out on escort if she does need to go to hospital.'

'Chanice! C'mon, don't do me dirty like that!' Caleb said through a grin.

'Any more questions?' Chanice asked without reacting. 'Nope? Good, thank you. Everybody get on with your work. I'll be on extension 213 if you need me. See you all here around eleven thirty to hand back keys, please. Sanjeet, you're in Healthcare tonight so will you pop your keys back now, and Malcolm, will you drop him off on your way to the seg? I'll rotate Healthcare duty every night so it's fair, all right? I fully understand why none of yous want to do it. On your bikes.'

We trudged along the tarmac walkway to the main houseblock, the clatter of each vast metal gate we passed through reverberating around us in the otherwise silent darkness.

'Bruddah, Hotel 1! How you doin', my friend?' Caleb said jovially as we walked into the bubble in the core of the prison.

He was greeting Aubrey, who was Hotel 1 – our duty

nurse for the night. Aubrey was one of those people who was *visibly* shy and always looked so terrified that I could never work out why he'd chosen to work in a prison. Our first task at the start of the night shift was to escort the nurses around the wings, giving prisoners their night medication at their cell doors. Aubrey always tried to avoid going with me – he'd much rather go with big strong Caleb, who made him feel safer. It was difficult not to take personally his obvious lack of faith in my ability to do my job.

'So, brother, you coming to pick up medication, yeah?' Aubrey said to Caleb.

Caleb chuckled. He knew what Aubrey was up to. Then he lightly flicked my baton with his fingers. 'You see this baton?' he said. 'Gen's an officer too, you know? Trust me, you'll be safer with Gen than you'll be with me!' He laughed again and swaggered off to accompany Hotel 2, an equally petrified female nurse who clearly didn't want to be escorted by me either.

As Aubrey and I climbed the stairs side by side, I signed in on my radio.

'Evening TS, PCO Glaister taking call sign Echo 14, work location Houseblock 1. Permission to sign on the net.'

I waited for the crackly voice to come back.

'Echo 14, that's received.'

'Echo 14 commencing medication on Delta Uppers,' I reported.

At night, when staffing levels are low, it's always

important to let the OSO watching the security cameras know where you are heading.

As we got nearer to the top of the stairs, I could see Aubrey getting paler and paler. He kept on looking nervously over his shoulder. It was getting more and more exasperating.

'You all right?' I asked him, fairly sharply.

'Yes. Er – fine. Er, Miss, don't you think we should wait for Caleb?'

'Aubrey,' I said, 'I'm good at my job, you know? I'm not gonna open any doors if I think someone looks like they're gonna give us any trouble, all right?'

I wasn't going to admit it, but this part of the job had always struck me as a bit risky. During the day, if I was ever left alone with prisoners unlocked it would be with prisoners I knew. Plus I could press the alarm on my radio and any number of the seventy other officers working in the prison would run to my aid. At night, though, there are only five people in the prison trained to come to your defence and two of those were locked in the healthcare and segregation units, on duty and unable to leave. So the general feeling on night shifts is – *things had better not go wrong*.

I peered through the hatch of our first cell. 'All right, mate, medication!' I said, knocking lightly on the cell door. I was always careful to keep it friendly at this time of the evening – it buys you a bit of time while you're deciding if it's safe to open the door or not.

One prisoner swung his feet out of bed and walked over to the door with a surly look on his face.

'How are you doing this evening, all right? Would you mind bringing your ID card to the door? Just gotta make sure we jump through all the hoops, you know?'

He gave a small smile at this, pulled his ID card from his sock and held it up to the glass panel. 'There you go, Miss. Apologies for the ugly photo.'

That was good enough for me, and I unlocked the door. Aubrey handed him the small paper cup with a quivering hand and the prisoner knocked the pills back before sticking his tongue out to show us they were all gone.

'Cheers for that, Miss. You 'ave a good night now, won't you?'

I locked the door behind him and tugged the handle firmly to check it was secure before moving on to the next cell on the medication list. When I went to look through the panel, I was met by another face right on the other side. I started a bit and Aubrey nearly jumped out of his skin. The bowl of pills he was carrying gave a loud rattle.

'I thought yous lot were never comin', bro!' came an angry voice from the other side of the door. 'I need my pills at nine p.m. on the dot! C'mon, man! What are you govs playing at?'

'No!' said Aubrey from behind me in a panicked voice. 'Do not unlock the door!'

I shot him a look and turned back to the shadowy face behind the door.

'Hey, Ahmed, is it?' I said, reading Aubrey's list upside down. 'You need your pills at nine every night, yeah?'

'Yes! Pham, these nurses know this. I got a serious medical condition, bruv. An' you guys don't actually care.'

'Ah, shit, Ahmed – I'm sorry about that. It's my first shift this week so I didn't know, but hear me out: I'm on all week now, so I can definitely make sure your meds get to you before nine every night. Does that sound OK?'

Ahmed looked a bit surprised but he nodded gratefully. 'Yeah, thanks Miss, thanks for that, yeah?'

I opened the cell door and Aubrey handed over the cup of pills sheepishly. Ahmed knocked them back with a carton of Ribena before putting his fist out to me.

'Respect, yeah? Night, Miss.'

When we stepped on to H-Wing, the stench of weed hit the back of my throat. Aubrey pinched his nose shut and I rolled my lips to suppress a grin. I could hear TVs playing loudly and as we got to the first cell the whole wing erupted with rattling doors and shouting. This time Aubrey jumped so much that he did drop the bowl of pills. I went to help him sweep them up, now unable to keep in a laugh.

'They're just watching *Love Island*, Aubrey. Don't worry about it! It'll just be someone getting voted out or something.'

He looked up at me uncertainly as I knocked on the first cell door.

'Mr Whittaker, good evening. How goes it?'

'Gen, you doin' all right? Ain't see you in a while!' came the response.

I could see Aubrey visibly relaxing as he realized that this prisoner knew my name.

'Gen, do me a favour, will you?' Whittaker said. 'Can you give Visits a call? They've blocked my visit again and Steve says he called 'em about it but I know he ain't.'

'Switch your brain on, Whittaker! I'm on night shifts for six more nights. All the Visits staff have gone home by the time I get in.'

'Ah shit, yeah, course. Silly me. Seven nights, is it? Man, they work you guys too hard, you know?'

'Listen, I can put an email into Visits for you,' I said to him. 'Can't promise they won't ignore it, but that's the best I can do, all right?'

'Gen, you're a star. Thanks, yeah?'

By the time we arrived on G-Wing, Caleb and the other nurse had got there too. I could hear Caleb teasing her on the landing below us. He was going from one door to the next, opening each with a dramatic warning. 'Careful of this one – he's a biter!' I heard, before he greeted a prisoner who sounded perfectly friendly and harmless. 'Don't look this one in the eye, yeah? Whoa, stand back, Auntie, stand back!'

Just when I thought the exasperated nurse was about to throttle Caleb for this, Chanice's voice came over the radio.

'Oscar 1 to all night-time officers. You need to finish up at the houseblock because I'll be locking up the prison in twenty. All night-time officers over at the entrance in twenty, please. Caleb, that includes you.'

Once the prison was locked up, that was pretty much our work done until 5 a.m. when we started waking up the prisoners who were due in court. The whole prison needed to be searched during the week of night duties, but none of us were in any rush to do this, despite what Chanice had said to us.

We were sitting in the C-Lowers wing office – purely because it had the comfiest chairs in the prison – and playing Caleb's favourite game, which was getting me to pronounce the West African names on the board in my accent, when the phone rang. I picked it up.

'Hello?'

It was Caleb's wife. I could've guessed. She rang every night when he was on night shifts.

I held the phone to my chest and looked at Caleb. 'Guess who?'

Vincent, another PO on shift that week, laughed and whipped the air. Caleb batted his hand away and took the phone.

'Hi, princess.'

Vincent turned to me and rolled his eyes. 'The real fun an' games is when she calls and he ain't on duty, but he's told her that he's workin' a night shift. I don't know what kind of lies to tell her!'

When I had first started I had been appalled by the brazen way officers, male and female, talked about cheating on their partners. I had been surprised to find that prison was such a sex-fuelled environment and that most of my colleagues, unbeknown to their partners, spent their evenings and weekends together in all sorts of overlapping love triangles. At first I thought that, like doctors and nurses, it was because of the unreasonable hours. But when I had floated this idea to Walter, he'd laughed.

'No, no, Gen. We are all animals, you know? This is what you get when you mix depravity and authority with keys and chains.'

As usual, I think Walter was probably right.

Either way, along with a lot of other principles I had held before prison, I'd stopped being bothered by infidelity a while ago. Besides, Caleb made me laugh, and I would take anything that made night shifts go a bit faster. So who was I to judge his private life?

By 11 p.m. I was already heating up a batch of my home-made soup – my first course of the night.

'This girl cooks up the maddest stuff on night shifts, ya know?' Caleb said to Vincent, nodding towards my home-cooked meal. 'What even is that, Gen? Not a Pot Noodle in sight, I swear!'

'I need something to look forward to!' I explained. 'Honestly, it's the only thing that keeps me going.'

Vincent shook his head disbelievingly as he tucked into a packet of dry-looking Bourbons.

The phone rang again, and Caleb answered. We didn't even have to put the call on speaker for all of us to hear Chanice's irritated voice.

'Who's been on this line the last twenty minutes? As if I can't guess. Literally one rule, guys – I need to be able to get hold of you. It's night one and you're not answering your radios and the phone line's engaged!'

Vincent and I checked our radios sheepishly. They had over-protruding volume knobs which had a terrible habit of switching the volume off if they got knocked even slightly.

'So Lindsey just called, guys,' Chanice continued, 'and she said D1-16 has been calling down on their cell bell saying they've been beat up by their cellmate. Will you go along and check him out? An' I mean *all* of you go along. I know I don't need to tell you – cracking that door is the last resort.'

We all looked at each other with the same expression. Lindsey was one of the support officers who worked night shifts answering the cell bells. She had a lot of time for the prisoners, which was refreshing compared to the other members of her team who would usually just make promises to be 'up in a minute' without any intention of getting off their arses. But she was constantly overreacting. Even worse, she also had the knack of giving prisoners that one inch they needed to take a mile. Too often I'd get a call from her saying something like, 'E4-19 wants toilet paper, so I said you'd bring it right up for 'em.'

'Lindsey,' I would say, 'that's an *emergency* cell bell. It's for emergencies, not toilet paper.'

'Yeah but, Gen, hear me out. He was really polite on the call. I think he just wanted toilet paper. He said only this once!'

Sometimes, though, Lindsey created much more serious problems. There was once a self-harming prisoner who was so desperate to do damage to himself that he'd used a carefully folded piece of paper when he didn't have anything else to do it with. After this we had stripped his cell of absolutely everything, leaving him only with anti-ligature clothing and bedding. This made it impossible for him to take any drastic action. But then he rang the cell bell to ask for toilet roll, and Lindsey felt so sorry for him that she snuck up there to give him some without us noticing. Thirty minutes later his cell was ablaze after he'd lit the entire roll up using the electrical socket.

Caleb and Vincent trooped off to D-Wing and returned ten minutes later telling a tale of a squabble over which TV channel the two cellmates were going to watch.

Half an hour after that, Lindsey called again.

'Uhh, Gen, can you come and look at something on D-Uppers for me, please?'

I hesitated. *She can't be doing this again.*

'Um, could you tell me what it is first, Lindsey?' I asked her.

'Well, I think it might be a code red.'

I told Lindsey to meet me up there and left the office heading for D-Uppers. When I got there, I found – unsurprisingly – that no code red was in progress. A young prisoner called Aaron Piper had scratched his arm a bit with his plastic knife, and it took me three minutes to discover that he had done it because he was feeling lonely. He was a pale twenty-something with the mental age of a boy. Never has 'he wouldn't hurt a fly' been truer of someone, although he was in because he'd set fire to his foster home. There was very little I could do about it at that time of night, so I pushed a few antiseptic wipes under his door and asked him if he'd like Lindsey to sit outside his cell for a while so he'd have some company. His face lit up and I turned on my heel without a backwards glance at her.

That would get her out of the way for a while. Plus, half an hour alone at night on the wing might just improve her judgement in the future.

19

Code Red

The blare of my alarm clock woke me up in the middle of the afternoon. It felt like I had only just closed my eyes. Sleep felt different in the daytime – not as deep and not as peaceful, as though my body knew I shouldn't be resting right now, and refused to cooperate with my best efforts to do so. I had an achy underslept feeling down my neck and back.

I tugged off my eye mask and saw daylight flooding through the gap in the curtains. Every inch of me wanted to stay right there in my bed, but I knew from experience that getting outdoors and seeing the sun – even through the clouds – was the first key to surviving night shifts.

The second key was to cook delicious food and pack it into Tupperwares so that I had something to look forward to throughout the night. So I sleepwalked into the kitchen to start my routine. Make 'breakfast', brisk walk, long bath. Then the third and final key to surviving night shifts: dance around the living room until I'd willed myself into a false state of euphoria which would last just long enough for me to bear pulling on my stiff uniform and making my way to the bus stop. The further through the week you go, the harder it becomes to reach this state. By the time I headed out of the flat to face the hour-long bus to work, it was dark.

When I arrived for my third night shift, Chanice already looked exhausted.

'So,' she began, 'a bit of good news, which is always a rarity. Mr Domingo finally got shipped out today. They've sent him to some prison up north in the hope that some time away from all his minions will bring him down a notch or two.' I smiled at this. I wasn't surprised. I knew his days would be numbered after his YouTube stunt. It was the idea of Domingo being taken down a notch or two that made me smile. I knew full well he would be up there thriving on the challenge of winning new people over, converting burly northerners to astronomy on the exercise yard.

'Of course it's never all good news,' Chanice went on. 'Mr Filch has been a pain in all of our arses, including his own. Healthcare staff found him bleeding from his backside all over his floor at about eight p.m., claiming he's now inserted *four* razor blades into his rectum. He'll be going out to hospital in the next thirty minutes. We don't want to do anything in a hurry for him, as you can imagine. And Caleb is late three nights running, but when he does grace us with his presence, I'll be delighted to inform him he'll be joining that escort as we've only been able to find one other officer to take the overtime. The rest of you, this is shaping up to be a week from hell, so I suggest you make a start on those searches that you didn't do last night. All right?'

'Right, yep,' we all muttered.

When I reached the houseblock, Aubrey was still sorting out the night's medication. I took a minute to browse my emails. It was mostly just spam and training opportunities, but I noticed I'd had a reply from Visits entitled 'Mr Whittaker'. It must be a response to the email I'd sent about his visit query, I thought, with the rest of the officers on H-Wing now copied in. Ah well – at least that was one problem I'd managed to sort out.

'FYI all H-Uppers staff,' the email read:

Most of you have now emailed me with the same request about visitors for Mr Whittaker. Mr Whittaker is very much aware that he has a one-month ban from visits after he ignored his third warning to remove his hand from his girlfriend's trousers on the last visit he had.

Please refrain from emailing us again on this subject. Please be sure to check the recent notes on a prisoner's

NOMIS before emailing us with requests in the future.

Or you could communicate with each other.

Best, Angel.

Later that night I wandered through the ghostly silent wings of the houseblock. Conducting a vague search, I ran my gloved finger around the rim of the pool table. I found half a cereal bar in one of the pockets, and then headed to the laundry room. I clipped off the plastic covering under the dryer door and pulled out the dust collector – always a classic spot for hiding things. I checked the back of the machines and found a plastic spoon melted out of shape with two razor blades stuck into it in parallel.

I'd seen a lot of these before. They're called 'marzbars' and they're nasty because you don't just slice someone open when you use one, you slice a strip out of their skin, which makes it much harder to sew the wound back together. I tugged the marzbar from the bundle of cables it was concealed in and found a sock on the floor to slip it into.

Everything was quiet as I made my way up D-Wing. I had almost finished the search and reckoned there might even be a chance for a bit of shut-eye in the C-Lowers office – the one with those temptingly comfy chairs. But I jumped when I heard a tapping at a door just behind me, and someone whispering, 'Gen, Gen!'

It was Aaron Piper.

'I've swallowed the batteries from my TV remote

control,' he informed me, matter-of-factly, before adding, 'Because I want to die.'

He looked utterly forlorn as he said it. I felt bad for him every time I laid eyes on him. He'd never received any support with his autism and he struggled to understand why he had ended up here. Prison life was never going to be kind to him. I called over my radio for Vincent to come upstairs. I just didn't have the energy to deal with Aaron on my own.

Vincent arrived moments later and winked at me, then turned to the hatch. 'Whoa!' he said, shielding his eyes. 'Aaron, mate, did you know you're glowing?'

Aaron stopped pacing up and down his cell for a moment.

'Gen, can you see this? It's those batteries!'

I noticed Aaron had come very close to smiling, then he very quickly tried to cover up the smile with a frown. There was a time when I probably would have found Vincent's lack of seriousness at the situation frustrating, careless even. But I knew he was trying to strike a balance: trying to cheer Aaron up so that he didn't do it again while also not giving him the sort of attention he was aiming for.

'This is serious, Vin, so take it seriously,' Aaron said indignantly. 'I really want to die.' He started to pace again, then picked up his radio and started fiddling with it.

Aubrey arrived, looking flustered, as ever. 'What is the emergency?'

'I want to die!' wailed Aaron, and with a flourish he produced the screws from his radio. Slowly, staring at me through the hatch, he swallowed each one with a gulp.

Aubrey went pale and started rummaging around in his bag. I groaned. Aubrey was beginning to undo everything Vincent and I had set up: he was rising to it, and Aaron would act up to him. This was exactly why we were trained to be calm.

He popped out a few laxatives from their casings and I placed them on a bit of paper and slid them under Aaron's door.

'I'm not taking them!' Aaron cried like a child, kicking the pills back under the door.

'Mate,' Vincent said to him, 'I can see you really mean it. I think, if you're serious about this, we're going to have to plan your funeral.'

I could tell by the twinkle in Vincent's eye where he was going with this. And who knew? It just might work. Nothing else we'd tried so far had made a difference. I decided to join in.

'Yep, for sure,' I said to Aaron. 'It has to be held here, doesn't it? D-Wing – where could be better?'

'You up for the sermon, Gen?'

'Absolutely I am! I have *always* wanted to preach a sermon! We'll have to bury you in the exercise yard, though, Aaron.'

By now, Aaron was trying not to smile.

'Yes!' exclaimed Vincent. 'We'll need a gravestone

for you too. How about "Aaron Piper, haunting D-Wing since 2018 – the glow-in-the-dark ghost"?'

It went on and on and by the time Vincent and I had got to Aaron's eulogy we were aching with the exhaustion of performance but Aaron was rolling about the floor laughing.

'Right then, young Aaron,' Vincent said. 'Give us a call on the cell bell when those screws come out, should be a couple of hours tops.'

'Code red on G-Wing, code red in Houseblock 1!'

Aaron had barely swallowed the laxatives when the siren came over the radio, and my heart sank. I heard Chanice's immediate response: 'Almost on the scene.'

Vincent and I dashed for the wing door, but as I was unlocking it, Chanice's voice came over the radio again.

'Vincent, Gen, I need you to meet me in reception ASAP.'

Chanice rarely sounded anything but calm, but there was an edge to her voice which made me hurry.

When we arrived, Scarlet was standing under the flickering lights in Reception. Bits of blood-soaked toilet paper were hanging down her thighs and off her wrists, and blood was trickling thickly down her calves.

'Morning, Gen,' she said as I approached, giving me a bright smile and a childlike wave.

'Bit early for good mornings, don't you think, Scarlet?' Chanice pointed out. Then she turned to me. 'Gen, you and me need to do the full search for her top half. Vince can do the bottom.'

Before a prisoner is taken out to hospital, they are full-searched to check if they have anything in their possession that they could use to escape. I'd never done a full search before because the prisoners I worked with were male and only male officers are allowed to full-search them. A transgender prisoner, however, can request that their top half be searched by female officers. Then two male officers would search Scarlet's bottom half, with trousers – or in this case, hot pants – off.

'Did you hear that, Gen?' said Scarlet to me seductively. 'I requested you specially. Come on then, ladies, let's get this orgy started!'

'What's this about then, Scarlet?' I said, brushing over her salacious comments as Chanice ushered her into the search room.

She was silent for a moment, and I looked up just in time to see her bottom lip wobble. When she saw me looking she tightened her lip quickly.

'Sometimes I'm not even sure, Gen,' she said, removing her top and then her bra before holding her arms out to the side. 'You know, sometimes I just feel sad or angry or trapped and the next thing I know I'm bleeding like this. Doesn't even hurt me no more, can't feel anything really.'

I realized that I hadn't expected such a coherent and honest answer, and the sudden humility I saw in her as she stood before us topless and vulnerable made my heart plummet. The stench of her festering scars was soon starting to make the back of my throat sting. Again, I wondered how I would have fared six months earlier, standing inches away from seeping wounds and talking to someone candidly about why they decided to rip themselves open so regularly. I felt that strange feeling of satisfaction swell within me again, a strange sense of achievement that I could do it.

'That's fine, Scarlet, pop your T-shirt back on and we'll get you cleaned up in hospital, all right?' I said, wearily but kindly.

She nodded and smiled, but a tear rolled down her cheek before dropping heavily on to the floor, into the pool of blood that was forming under her feet.

20

Staying Alive

The night shift week from hell continued, one thing after the other, disaster after disaster. It was relentless, as though something was in the air.

It was my turn to be on duty in Healthcare. It was a miserable place, especially in the dark, and given the week we'd already had I didn't have a good feeling about it.

The whole unit felt like a location from a nineties psychological thriller. It was a quarter of the size of other wings and laid out in a square. It had a big office (with the second comfiest chairs in the prison) but someone had put the reflective film on the wrong side of the observation window that looks from the office out over the wing. So instead of the officers being able to watch the cell doors before them, the office was a fishbowl – an enormous reality TV screen for all of the prisoners to look in on. And unlike the main wings, where everyone is asleep or at least quiet for most of the night, in Health-care there was a constant deafening racket.

Mr Xaba appeared not to sleep for the whole night, and staff on the day shift said they never once saw him asleep then either. He'd constantly recite story after story in an impossibly monotonous tone, speaking to no one in particular.

'My name is Amy Williams, but I have a penis,' he would say. 'I need to speak to the Newcastle Chief of Police. I have evidence in this very cell that five girls, aged twelve and under, have been raped and murdered tonight on the River Tyne. I am the only person who can identify the man that did this. You must release me from this cell so that I can take you to the location immediately.'

Then he'd move seamlessly into yet another mono-logue.

'I am Hamish Grant of 14 Pricer Street, New Jersey, New York, except I talk with an English accent. I have the cure for cancer and all you need to do is ask the Brit-ish Prime Minister to put four million dollars of taxpayers' money into my bank account. My account details are sort code 04-96-30 and my account number is 6554890. Once the money is in there, you shall let me free and we can go on to cure cancer together.'

Every speech he made always finished with the con-dition that he was set free. But there was something compelling about the precision of these stories – the names, the addresses, even the bank account numbers. Could he *really* be inventing all of this? He could go on talking for so long and so fluently that I started to question if I was in some fantasy horror film where he was actually telling the truth, or something based in truth. I even googled a couple of the addresses he mentioned to see if they existed. They didn't.

Then there was Adams. He saw himself as a wannabe troublemaker, pushing open the flap on his door and sticking his head half out to encourage the others.

'Come on, lads! When are we gonna have a riot in this place then? Oi, Punter, I'll stick fifty quid in your account if you start shitting up in that cell. Come on, lads, let's fuck this place up a little!'

There were moments when he sounded like a pretty convincing revolutionary, but then the next time I walked past his cell he wouldn't say a word. He'd just be standing there, silently masturbating. Then an hour after that he'd be strutting round and round, lost in his own little world, theatrically reciting verses from the Bible word for word, like a preacher.

At the start of my second night in Healthcare, Chanice handed me a crumpled wad of paper.

'Found under Mr Adams's door this morning,' she said. 'Looks like you've got an admirer. Anyway, I thought you'd want to see this before I handed it over to Security.'

I peered down at the sheets. They were pages of Scripture, clearly given to him by the chaplain, but in between the lines, in tiny but immaculate handwriting and all in capitals, Adams had added his own thoughts.

For the first few lines, I couldn't see how what he'd written was anything to do with me: 'The suffering and the glory of the servant, Our Father, up in heaven . . . All you Jews are shallow bitches . . .' But then one section caught my eye, and the nausea started to rise in me.

And my sister Jen is who I address now, who defends the right to dress like a slag without unwanted male attention. Jen is the one I dreamt of, screaming in my dreams. I have waited too long to kindle my passions to fire.

Allah made me King because he gave me you, Jen. You're off with all these other men but I don't even know the beating you will get when they find out you're a whore.

I looked up at Chanice, to gauge her reaction. She looked apologetic – a look I realized I had never actually seen on her face before. I cleared my throat, kept my face expressionless, and carried on reading.

You are the key, Jen, the final piece to my puzzle proving that I am the return of Christ. Jen, come back to me. I'm not a threat to you. I love you more than you realize. I dream of you crying over me.

I looked back at Chanice again. 'I mean – uh – I

literally don't know what this is about,' I said to her, stumbling over my words. 'I don't – um – I don't even think I told him my name.'

'Listen, Gen, don't worry about it. He's just crackers. He's getting shipped out tomorrow, but I still wanted to tell you, cos he's in here for rape an' all.'

I nodded, swallowing hard. 'It's OK. Cool. It's fine, honestly.' My throat had grown so dry that it was difficult to speak.

Have I done something to give him the wrong idea? Have I even said anything to him?

I felt as though everything was creeping up on me. I was underslept. I was underfed because I'd hardly had a moment to eat every night. I hadn't spoken to, let alone seen, any of my friends and family for almost a week. And now a rapist had sent me a creepy love letter.

By the final night no one had a sense of humour left. There were no games, there were no jokes, we all just sat in the bubble with dark circles under our eyes, staring at the floor. The minutes crawled along and the clock had hardly struck midnight when Lindsey shaky voice came over the radio calling an 'urgent' code blue.

We all walked slowly over to the wing she had called from, imagining it was just another one of her overreactions. Caleb and I were making our way up the stairs when we heard Chanice's voice on the radio, calm but firm.

'Gen, Caleb, I need you here now.'

I started to jog, and even Caleb picked up the pace.

As soon as we got to the door, Chanice cracked it open. I saw a large prisoner lying next to the bunk at an awkward angle. His head was tilted back towards the door and his face was blue.

Chanice quickly knelt down and put her hand around his wrist.

'Caleb, will you pull him away from the bed so we can get to him properly?' she instructed us calmly. 'Gen, get ready to start on the chest compressions, yeah?'

Caleb dragged the prisoner under the arms as though he was a sack of sand, manoeuvring him into the middle of the floor. I'd had training in CPR of course, but doing it for real was very different. I felt my mind go blank as I knelt down next to him.

Do I straddle him while I do it? That can't be right. Perhaps I just lean over.

I heard Chanice raise her voice ever so slightly on the radio: 'Hotel 1, where are you? We need you here now.'

I placed my hands on the prisoner's chest, and as I did this, my training immediately came back to me. The Bee Gees' song 'Stayin' Alive' – that's how we'd been taught to do it. With my whole weight I pressed down on his chest, over and over again, all the while singing rhythmically in my head: *uh uh uh uh, stayin' alive, stayin' alive . . .*

Chanice spoke into her radio again: 'Sanjeet, you need to call an ambulance, please. Hotel 1, where the *fuck* are you?'

I heard Aubrey's voice responding shakily: 'One moment, please.'

Chanice grabbed the pillow from the prisoner's bed and shoved it firmly under his lolling head. My arms were beginning to feel like jelly now with the effort I was making. As I tired, I knew I wasn't putting enough weight behind my compressions. I paused to lower my ear to his mouth to listen to his breathing for a moment. I knew you were meant to do this at some point – I had no idea when that point was, but my arms couldn't go any longer. Luckily at that very moment Aubrey arrived in the doorway looking flustered.

'I don't think he's got a pulse, and he's definitely not breathing,' I told him.

Aubrey moved quickly, pulling out the defibrillator as I tugged the prisoner's T-shirt up so he could stick the pads on his chest.

After the third shock the prisoner jolted awake and the rattle of his breath filled the room.

Chanice raised her eyebrows and lifted the radio to her lips.

'Get that ambulance to Houseblock 2. Now, please.'

Several hours later I was sitting on the bus. The sun was pouring in. It was the moment I'd been waiting for all week, the end of my run of seven nights, and I was on my way home for my week off.

But my mind was flitting between visions of the prisoner's lifeless body which had been under my hands earlier that morning and grating images of Adams writing his letter. I imagined him, sitting there in his filthy cell, thinking about me, writing about me. I felt as if the filth of the prison was clinging to my skin and my hair. I felt dirty and I felt sick.

A man dressed in chinos came bounding up the stairs on to the top deck of the bus and saw me sitting there, lost in my thoughts. He bent down to look me in the eye and said to me: 'Smile, darlin' – it's only a Monday morning!'

21

A Study in Scarlet

'Happy release day, Scarlet!' Steve cried. 'Back to the brothel tonight then, is it?'

'Sorry, Steve, not tellin', you ain't my type!' she replied with a mischievous chuckle. Even Dimitra laughed at the look on Steve's blushing face. Scarlet had practically skipped out for morning medication, telling every nurse and prisoner she saw that she was being released today.

In her three months on the wing, Scarlet had self-harmed on twenty-three occasions. She'd been taken out to hospital on eight of those occasions. Her problems and crises had generated a mountain of paperwork. But all of it was nothing compared to the amount of spice paper she had smoked in that time.

Although I had turned down the opportunity to

learn the dance moves to 'Single Ladies' with her, she had taught me all the words to it, along with some orgy-related slang which I would rather have remained innocent of. She'd made me laugh at least as many times as she had made me want to scream, but ultimately, what she had taught me was that there was no limit to the amount of pain a human being could feel. The only conclusion I could come to was that she carved up her body in that way in a desperate attempt to create something physical out of the roaring pain she felt inside. The worst part, though, was that I knew there was no way out for her. This would be her life until the day her actions killed her.

It was a swelteringly hot day, unusually warm for May, and the sun was beating down through the perspex roof. The air in prison isn't like air anywhere else – it doesn't flow around you coolly as you move. It stays exactly still, sticking to you like mud. My dark, rigid trousers had trapped hot, wet air around my legs and every step felt as though I was wading through water. The thick utility belt hung heavily around my waist, rubbing on the welts that were forming where the folds of my coarse shirt grated against the soft skin of my stomach. I hadn't been to the toilet yet that day, partly because I had sweated out anything I had consumed, but also because I didn't think I would be able to pull my trousers back up again over my sticky thighs.

At the morning meeting, the duty manager had casually informed us that the temperature could well reach

35°C on the upper landings today. 'Drink plenty of water, and try not to move around too much,' he had added, by way of safety advice. All the same, I was glad that I was on shift for the day, because a week earlier Scarlet had asked if I could be the officer to bring her to reception for her release. I was less thrilled, however, when I learned that I was sharing this shift with Steve.

Opening each cell door on days like this was like opening an oven. At lunchtime I was met first by a stifling gust of hot, stinking air and then by a wearily protesting prisoner: 'You can't! You can't keep us in here, please!' It felt criminal as I proffered sagging sandwiches then closed the door in each of their faces with meaningless apologies.

Scarlet, however, cheerfully turned down her lunch, reminding me she was getting out in good time for summer so she needed to start working on her 'bikini bod'. 'Models' diet for me, Gen. Fags, coffee and crack!'

I offered her a couple of apples instead, which she took apprehensively. Then she handed me a handful of torn-up pieces of paper.

'Got my number on 'em. Pass 'em round, will you? Case anyone wants to get hold of me!' she added with a wink.

I nodded, suppressing a grin. 'Sure, Scarlet.'

Desperate for a breeze I wasn't sure I would find, I headed for the prison gates on my lunch break. I passed the manager's office where the door was ajar, and saw a large plastic tube protruding from it. It was piping hot air out on to the core. In disbelief, I swung the door open to see Dimitra and Kelly sitting there in front of an air conditioning unit attached to the fire-breathing tube.

'All right, Gen?' Kelly said, looking up at me guiltily.

'Do you know how hot that thing's making it out there?' I said to them bluntly.

Kelly bit her lip. 'Any time today you feel like comin' in here for a li'l cool down, just come on in, Gen!'

'Right. Well, I'm gonna go and get lunch. Scarlet's going this afternoon though, remember?' I said.

'Trust me, I have been countin' down the days,' Kelly responded brightly.

I trudged towards the gates, thinking of the faces of the men I had just locked in furnaces while those two sat there like smug coal-mine masters in their cool office.

On my way back to the wing, a reception officer told me they were ready for me to bring Scarlet down for release. I got back to the office, scrabbled together a few packets of biscuits from the drawer and threw them into a bin liner before heading towards Scarlet's cell with it so she could pack up her few possessions. What else would she have to eat tonight?

But when I opened the door, she was just standing there. I didn't think she'd even noticed me come in. The floor was glimmering with blood, some of it spattered on the walls, some smeared on the bed, some forming in small pools at her feet. Her figure was silhouetted against the window, and I could see heavy drops falling from both her arms to the floor.

'Scarlet? What d'you want first, a mop or a nurse?' I asked her.

She turned around with an almighty sniff. She wiped her nose with her arm and smeared dark clotting blood across her face. 'Mop first, nurse second, Gen.'

I nodded and went to leave.

'Gen?' she croaked. 'Please don't lock it behind you.'

I looked at her, towering and haggard but so forlorn. I couldn't bring myself to lock her in. So I left the door ajar.

No sooner had I turned left on the landing than I felt a gush of wind behind me. She had leapt through the door and passed me, running for the stairs to the upper landing.

I knew exactly where she was going. When a prisoner really wants to make a point, they jump over the railings on the upper landing and cling there for as long as they can. When a prisoner is 'at height', the whole wing comes to a standstill until they can be negotiated down. And Scarlet was well-versed on this tactic.

Please, not today, Scarlet – it's too hot, I pleaded under my breath.

Steve was on the top landing, carrying two large containers of floor cleaner to the store room, lifting them like weights as he went. In a stroke of genius I didn't know he possessed, he dropped them both in an instant and leapt sideways on to the staircase with his arms spread to block Scarlet from coming up any further.

Now we had her cornered, Steve at the top of the staircase and me at the bottom. I knew it wasn't a good idea to make her feel trapped, so I stood slightly to the side as if I was just there to talk to her.

'Scarlet, it's over thirty degrees in here. Please don't leave on this note, not today,' I begged.

'You're mugging me off! Leave me alone!' she cried.

'No one ain't mugging no one off,' Steve reasoned.

'You are! You're mugging me off cos you're a transphobe!'

She was glaring at Steve as she said this, and she had a point on that one. I knew I had to take over if we were going to have any chance of keeping her off the railings.

'Scarlet, listen to me for a moment, yeah? Come on now – we've had good times together. Can we chat about this properly? Like both of us, sat across from each other, over a coffee, at ground level?'

'I'm not leaving wivout my foundation, Gen! Why ain't you got it for me yet? Cos you're all transphobic, the lot of you! Transphobic *sluts*!'

As she said this she latched on to her forearm with her mouth and before I could even grasp what she was about to do, she spat at me, spraying me with her blood, then turned to take aim at Steve. He darted towards her, but with surprising agility Scarlet leapt over the railing halfway down the stairs, leaving splatters of fresh blood as she went. She swerved past me and lunged for one of the wing tables. She pulled herself up on to it but she kept on slipping in her own blood. I reached her first and grabbed the back of her T-shirt to try to pull her back down. The smell of decaying flesh hit me and I tasted sour saliva welling up in my mouth. Steve came running over and also grabbed her T-shirt. Neither of us could bring ourselves to touch her arms, or get any closer to the oozing source of the unbearable stench where fresh wounds sagged open across old ones. I felt like if I touched them her flesh would just come away in my hand in gory chunks.

But we have to grab her arms. If we don't, we'll never hold her.

Steve and I must have had the same thought. We both grabbed on and I twisted her arm behind her back. It was a reflex – a way that I'd been taught to apply restraint. This time, though, as I tried to get a grip, I could feel Scarlet's flesh tearing. I clenched my jaw in an effort to suppress my surging gag reflex.

I half expected Scarlet to scream out in pain. But she didn't – she just smiled, and then she laughed. Her laugh became a cackle and then a howl before her whole body sagged and her shoulders began to heave with deep, gasping sobs.

We all stayed still for a moment, half on, half off the tabletop, panting but not willing to loosen our grip. Then, silently, all three of us unable to speak, we gently walked her back to her cell.

Bert appeared in the doorway, holding his paint-spattered radio. He quietly squatted down to plug it in and turned the knob to Magic FM. Strains of Cyndi Lauper singing 'Girls Just Want to Have Fun' drifted down the hallway. Bert nodded at Scarlet kindly and walked away from the cell.

Steve and I slumped into the office chairs. Kelly was talking but I wasn't listening. My ears were ringing and my spine was still tingling. Kelly pulled out six forms from the drawer and pushed them across the desktop towards us. Neither of us reached out to take them. Our hands were shaking far too much to write.

'OK, guys,' Kelly said, 'I'll write for you. One at a time, just tell me what you want me to put, OK?'

'Thanks,' I mumbled.

'Not to worry – we all get the shakes after a wrap-up. It's the adrenalin coursing through yer veins!'

'Yeah,' said Steve, 'it's that, coupled wiv the heat and the feeling I'm about to puke. That was somethin' else, that was.'

Steve was right: it wasn't just adrenalin, it was pure revulsion – there was no other word for it – over the state of the human body I had just been so close to. It was as though I'd touched a corpse. I could taste death in my mouth. I suddenly felt haunted by a dread of the future: one day, I was absolutely certain, Scarlet was destined to quite literally rot to death in a prison cell.

Walter brought over a couple of new uniform shirts,

since our old ones were blood-streaked. He gave me a kind squeeze on the shoulder and I leaned into his touch, feeling comforted by his warm, living hand. Then Bert arrived with two cups of steaming tea. Even though the heat was still stifling, I cupped my hands gratefully around my cup in the hope that I could scorch away what they had touched.

'Right!' said Kelly brusquely. 'That's enough pampering for you guys. We don't want anyone going soft. You've got association for the afternoon so it's back to work for you both – all right?'

22

The Man Who Hated Carrots

I saw more suffering and more trauma in prison than I
ever thought was possible. And then – I got used to it.
By the time I'd been in the job for a year, I could tell I
was accustomed. Even numbed. What terrified me,
though, was that one day I might stop feeling compassion entirely.

One morning, G-Wing was reverberating with
crashing thumps which were coming from the landing
above. As I headed up the stairs towards the noise, I saw
a folding screen outside a cell door. This wasn't an
uncommon sight in prison. The screens are used when
a prisoner is doing a 'dirty protest', which means they
have smashed their observation panels and they are
throwing anything they can get their hands on out on
to the landing. Their own shit is a popular choice, but

when that runs out they tend to get quite creative, opting instead for things that *look* like shit, such as bits of soaked brown bread or the contents of teabags.

I crept up to the cell so that the person behind it couldn't prepare something to throw at me, and peered tentatively around the screen. To my surprise, there were no foul-smelling lumps of brown mush there, but instead a dismantled coleslaw sandwich lying in a sad heap on the floor.

Feeling reassured that the worst I could get was a dodgy sarnie in the face, I crept a bit closer to squint through the smashed panel which was trembling in the door as the man behind it repeatedly pummelled the metal.

'Hey, everything OK in there?' I said loudly over the noise.

His face appeared at the door. His unwashed hair curled uncontrollably around it and his lips were wet and trembling. His expression was manic, but there was something unusual about his eyes – quite different from the hysteria I was used to seeing in prisoners who had fallen into a state like this. They were soft, filled with tears and defeat.

The prisoner looked at me; then, as though he was going for the jugular of his prey, he lurched, open-mouthed, and let out a desperate roar. He hit the door in between us with a thud, his howling lips now framed by the panel, empty but for a few shattered shards. Instead of shock or fright, I felt that familiar pleasing adrenalin surge within me. I knew it was a lack of compassion threatening to raise its head. But at the same time I felt satisfied that I could now let the adrenalin course through me and still feel in control.

'You let me know if I can do anything, OK?' I tried to say as kindly as I could, suspecting that the prisoner might not speak English.

As I turned my back to go downstairs, the pummelling stopped. I smiled to myself a little: perhaps he'd recognized the kindness in my voice. I'd made a difference.

I logged into the computer in the office to see if I could find out anything more about my new friend on his NOMIS profile, feeling a sense of renewed energy and motivation. No sooner had I clicked on his photo than the banging resumed, louder and more ferocious than before. My intervention hadn't helped him after all. I shrugged and laughed at my moment of egotistical naivety.

His file told me that he was Mr Dawar, from Pakistan, date of birth 1 January 1992. His crime was the cultivation of cannabis on a large scale. That date of birth was familiar: back in my early days on G-Wing, three young men from Iraq had arrived on the wing, and when I looked them up on the system all of their birthdays were on the first of January.

'What are the chances? All of you born on the same day,' I'd said to them, trying to make friendly conversation.

One of them shook his head and laughed. 'Miss, when we arrive in this country, they strip us of our identity. When we go to the office to claim asylum, we have no documents, so they put our birthday down for the first of January. It's the same for everyone I know. Sometimes they don't even put down our real names.'

'Wow, I didn't know that. I'm sorry. So what *is* your real birthday?' I said, trying to say something – anything – meaningful.

The young man laughed again, shrugging. 'When you grow up with your cousins and siblings being blown up around you, no one celebrates a birthday, Miss.'

I just smiled back at him apologetically.

So, Mr Dawar must have come here to seek asylum. The NOMIS system said he was from Pakistan, but the language box was empty. I racked my brains for ways I could find someone who could speak with him. An idea came to me: I could search for other prisoners with the same surname as his, as they would be most likely to share his nationality.

That has to be a good place to start.

Later that afternoon, I headed over to H-Wing to speak to a Mr Dawar there.

I knocked on the cell door. 'Hiya, Mr Dawar?'

A prisoner came to the door.

'Do you speak English, Mr Dawar?' I said, and he nodded back at me.

Great, I thought.

'I was wondering if you could come to my wing and help me translate?' He looked a bit confused but I went on. 'There's a prisoner on the wing and he's not doing so good. Thing is, there's no one on the wing that can speak Urdu so we can't communicate with him at all.'

A smile spread across his face now. 'Miss, I'm from Birmingham, you know?' He spoke in a thick Brummie accent. 'Haven't been back to Pakistan since I was six months old, then it was straight to foster care for me. I'd love to help but can't speak a damn word.'

I gave a guilty laugh. 'Sorry, mate. It's just – it said Pakistan on the system.'

'Not to worry, Miss. But if yous need anyone to translate Brummie for ya then I'm yer man!'

Three days later when I arrived on shift I was immediately met with cries of 'Gen, can't you get this man moved? We're desperate! None of us have slept for three nights now!'

I completely understood why: days had gone by, and Mr Dawar was still banging and screaming in his cell. Radu was helping me hand out lunch, taking the trolley cell to cell, with Bert in tow attempting to help. I unlocked each door in turn and Radu passed in the sandwiches, and at each door I was met with the same plea from every prisoner on the wing.

'Please – can't you get him moved?'

I felt awful. It's torture when something is stopping you from sleeping.

'Konaj, I promise I am trying. Healthcare says there's a long wait list to get him in there. I've spoken to managers, I've done everything I can. So has Chris. I can't just move him – I don't have that kind of power.'

Konaj muttered something else despondently.

I always looked through the panel before opening each door. But I'd been focusing on Konaj, trying to work out what he was saying over the din Dawar was making, so when I opened the next door I was taken by surprise. The prisoner in the cell fell forward, landing on my shoulder before sliding to the ground. He was lying there at my feet, shaking uncontrollably, violently fitting. Epileptic fits are common in prison, like lots of health problems which are commonly rooted in intergenerational deprivation, so I knew exactly what to do. I bent down and put one hand under his thrashing head and opened his mouth to check his airways. I saw that his mouth was filling with blood.

'Someone chuck me his pillow!'

I lifted him and rolled him on his side, and as I did so I saw something dark red fall from the front of my shirt and land on the floor. I looked down at the lump in puzzlement for a second until I realized it was half of the man's tongue. He must have spat it out on my chest as he toppled into me. The piece of tongue had left a smear of dark blood down my front.

When did it get to the point where I can casually assess where a chunk of human flesh on the floor in front of me came from?

I reached for the radio in my belt. 'Code red and code blue on G-Uppers. That's a code red and a code blue on G-Uppers landing four.'

It was a code blue because that was procedure for a seizure, and it was a code red because of the blood. I thought back to the first time I had called a code blue and how helpless and panicked I had felt as I waited for backup. And now here I was, performing first aid with one hand and holding the radio with the other as if it was as natural to me as crossing the road.

Dimitra was on the scene very quickly – she always loved to get involved in a bit of drama. The nurses hurried in behind her. She took one look at the man, whose lolling head I was still holding in both my hands.

'Loud in here, isn't it?' she said, clearly talking about the racket Dawar was making. 'All right, Gen, you get on with lunch. We can take this over.'

I looked at her with my lip curled and pointed to the blood on my shirt. 'A man just bit half his tongue off and spat it on my shirt, Dimitra. Can't I even go and change?'

'Plenty of time to change on your lunch break, no? If G-Wing get their feed done in time of course.'

I noticed Bert and Radu looking at me sympathetically. It was bad enough when Dimitra spoke to me like that in private, but when she did it in front of prisoners I just wanted to smack her.

With the patch of blood slowly spreading across my shirt, I went on delivering lunches with Radu and Bert.

By the time we were outside Mr Dawar's cell, I could feel the bangs and thumps sending vibrations through the floor.

'Let me do it – 'e likes me!' Bert said cheerily.

I looked at Radu and he nodded in agreement and read out: 'Vegetarian. Salad wrap, orange juice, apple.'

Bert gave Mr Dawar a friendly wave and then handed him the food and drink. To my surprise, he stopped banging to reach out and take it. He inspected it and smiled, before giving a thumbs up to Bert.

'See, I told yous!' said Bert, gleefully.

He went to pass the apple too, but the panels are narrow and even the measly prison-issue apple wouldn't fit through. I knew I needed to take my moment while Mr Dawar was calm. I cracked the door and passed him the apple. He kissed it.

'Mr Dawar,' I said, miming and gesturing as I spoke, 'I want to help you. Come to the office and we can use the computer to talk, yes?'

He nodded his head emphatically and hurried out of the cell after me.

I pulled up Google Translate on the computer, selected English and Urdu, and typed: 'I would like to help you. Tell me what you need.'

My heart sank as Urdu script appeared in the other box. I'd forgotten that it didn't use the Roman alphabet. He wasn't going to be able to respond on the keyboard. Then I noticed the microphone button on Google

Translate. I clicked on it, and Dawar started talking. To my relief, words began appearing on the screen.

'I need the doctor.' And then: 'And I don't like carrots.'

Then, as though the word 'carrots' had set him off, he suddenly burst into tears.

I was stumped by this, but I wanted to keep him talking, so I typed on.

'Carrots? Can you tell me why?'

He spoke, for a long time now, occasionally stopping to take a deep breath, or to press his fingers to his temples.

'I left Pakistan just over a year ago. Before my father died in a flood, I had worked for his shop. Now my family had no income and my mother developed a brain tumour. We had no money for her treatment, so when a man passed through our village offering to take me to Europe to get a job in a factory, I left straight away, without thinking about it. I promised my mother I would send money back to her for treatment.'

I looked up from the screen at Mr Dawar. His eyes fixed urgently on my face. Then he carried on talking.

'I was transported in the back of a lorry. It was so packed with people that I could only crouch. For three days, I remained in that position, crouching ankle-deep in human waste. But when we were finally unloaded from the truck, I knew I wasn't in Europe.'

I looked up at him again, nodding, trying to communicate to him that I understood.

'We were made to put bags over our heads. Then they made us walk into a warehouse. We were forced to work there for the next six months.'

I was starting to feel sick. *How long had this man been crying out for help in his cell?*

'We worked for sixteen hours per day, sewing labels into garments. I slept in a room with a hundred other men, and we were given just two meals each day. One carrot in the morning and one carrot in the evening.'

'I'm so sorry, Mr Dawar,' I said to him, shaking my head.

He put his palms together and nodded.

I heard Dimitra's voice, barking at someone outside on the landing, and quickly typed: 'How did you get here?'

'The first chance I got, I ran away. I jumped into the back of a van and didn't get out until I heard the sounds of a city. I met a woman who said she worked for a charity and they took me to England. They said if I didn't have any money, I could pay them back by working for them. I was taken to another place where they grow marijuana. They were nice people there, and we ate good. I was so hungry – I hadn't had a real meal in months. They carried guns, though, and if anyone tried to escape they would be shot, so we lived in fear. Then one day, the police came and they arrested all of us. I was afraid, because they had guns too, and at first we didn't know they were police. I was afraid for my life.'

Oh my God, I thought. *That's what he's been charged with. He's in prison for growing cannabis, but he'd been trafficked and forced to do it.*

Dimitra was standing in the office door now, palms turned up to the ceiling as if to say *What the hell is going on?*

'Lock the workers up, will you, Dimitra?' I said to her. 'The lunches are all done, and I need a few more minutes here.'

She protested, but I ignored her and turned back to the computer. I needed to ask Mr Dawar one more question.

'While you wait to see the doctor, what can we do to make you happier?'

He thought for a moment.

'A friend for my cell, please. I have spent too much time alone.'

And then: 'And please, no more carrot. I cannot bear carrots.'

Kelly told me to submit a police report to say I had identified a person in the prison who might be a victim of human trafficking and/or modern slavery. 'But I warn you, Gen, it's not a quick process. He's in prison because he's been accused of a crime. He's in the care of the government now. He just won't be anyone's top priority.'

This made me furious. This man was in prison

because of the UK's own failure to protect him. It didn't feel right that he should spend another day here.

At home that evening I typed into Google 'How to find help for a victim of modern slavery'. It sent me down a research rabbit hole. Numbers online ranged from 100,000 to 150,000 victims of modern slavery living in the UK today; worldwide that number's estimated at more than twenty million. I had heard about forced labour in the UK, typically in prostitution and nail bars, or selling illegal drugs in county lines. But until now I had never considered that restaurants or construction sites were prone to it as well.

Then I remembered Avaro. Kind, gentle, funny Avaro – who was also a brutal, calculating human trafficker. I felt my stomach clench at the thought of Dawar, in desperation, meeting who he thought was going to be his family's saviour when they walked through his village that day. How the traffickers were charming, full of hope and promises. How must Dawar have felt when he was locked in the back of that lorry for days? Or when he ran away from his captors? Was he terrified? Was he angry? Or did it reach the point where he was just desperate to stay alive?

And what must he have felt when the British police arrived in full riot gear and he came face to face with the barrel of a semi-automatic rifle?

I resolved that all I could do was make sure he got as much support in prison as he could. No more carrot – that was easy. But a cellmate? My heart sank. Surely no one would agree to go in a cell with him now? What if it all got too much for him and he started banging again?

The calmness of mornings in prison before prisoners were unlocked often made me feel slightly sentimental. On this morning in particular, the sun was streaming in and the wing looked sort of beautiful in a brutalist architecture sort of way. I wandered slowly up to the window at the end of the wing thinking to myself, *There's no place I'd rather be.*

I loved this job. I loved that sometimes it entailed just sitting around with prisoners and having a laugh. I loved that I could walk in through those prison gates and forget anything that was troubling me in my life outside. I loved the way I felt when I heard an alarm come over my radio and I would run to another wing having no idea what I might find there. I loved getting to know people from all over the world and learning about so many different cultures and customs. I felt so *lucky* to be here. On the right side of the door.

I heard someone call my name and I spun round. It was coming from Bert's cell. I peered through his hatch.

'Morning, Bert, what's up?'

He looked pleased to see me. He was standing in his paint-spattered overalls, like he was ready for work for the day. I was confused. He'd been caught again recently harbouring spice in his cell after staying clean for a good few months. He would have spent the past fortnight on basic regime. And he clearly thought it was time for him to get his job back again.

'My two weeks of basic is up today, Gen! Ask Chris, I rode it like a champ again. Good as gold I was. Anyway, two weeks is up so I got some painting to do!'

I winced. 'Bert, you know what I'm gonna say.'

He shook his head, but colour rose in his cheeks.

'Chris has put his neck on the line twice for you now, Bert. I know you know that. He gives you that odd-jobs work cos he's trying to give you a bit of responsibility, a bit of trust. Cos he cares, yeah? But he can't keep giving you more chances. And you know you don't just automatically get a job back after losing it for something like that.'

Bert was now looking down at the floor, wringing his fingers, his mouth moving furiously but silently.

'Do you know how much harder it makes our jobs when the wing's filled with spice, Bert? Do you know how many vulnerable people there are on this wing? That if one of them does overdose, or kills themselves, it's me and Chris that end up in court? Do you know that?'

Bert let out a cry and started tearing at his hair, his knuckles turning white. I decided to try joking with him. Maybe I could lighten the mood.

'Look, Bert, I don't want you behind your door either. You're a fecking nuisance when you're behind your door. I've never known someone that's spent so much time in jail and still can't ride their bang up.'

He looked up at me with bloodshot eyes. 'This mean I'm losing my job then, Gen?'

'What would you do if you were me, Bert?'

'I'd give the man one last chance, Gen.'

'Bert, look. You're not a young man any more. No one else in this world is going to keep giving you chances. The next judge you're up in front of isn't going to suddenly start letting you off. What kind of message would I be giving if I didn't act on this? It's hardly like it's the first time, is it, Bert?'

He flopped on to his bed, face down, not speaking. I was starting to lose my patience now. I had never seen him take responsibility for anything he had ever done. But then again, why would he? It's not like he had ever had someone who cared enough about him to teach him that. Still, it was definitely one of those moments where you had to be cruel to be kind. Besides, Dimitra would never stand for him resuming his job.

'Bert, I'm gonna go, but can I offer you one bit of advice?'

He put his hands over his ears.

I raised my voice a notch. 'Can you think about what advice *you* would give to yourself? Cos I just can't help but feel when you're talking to other prisoners, you give them real respect. But I have never, even once, seen you treat yourself like that.'

I waited until Chris came in a bit later to speak to Bert again. We went to his cell together, and saw through the hatch that he was sat on his bed with a razor blade in his hand. I could tell he'd been waiting for us. He cut some angry scratches into his upper arm as we unlocked the door. Chris just silently walked over to him, wrapped his hand in a wad of toilet paper and put it out to Bert, as if to ask for the blade.

Bert paused for a moment, then placed it carefully in Chris's paper-covered palm.

'So it's true, yeah? I'm losing me job?'

'Course it's bloody true, ya silly bugger!' Chris exclaimed. 'Not that we don't want you all tickety-boo an' all that, but we got standards, 'aven't we?'

Bert suddenly looked hopeful. 'So can you do me one favour then?'

Chris and I shared a suspicious look.

'If I'm gonna be behind my door all day, then can I get a cellmate?'

'Be my guest!' Chris said. 'Only reason you're not sharing at the moment is cos you had a hissy fit with the last one we put in here.'

'In that case, can I bang up with Dawar upstairs?' Bert said, hopefully.

Ah, the perfect solution! Dawar would finally have a friend, and Bert would have someone to aimlessly chat to all day. I knew that Bert needed to feel like we were doing him a favour though: as long as he thought that he would feel cared about.

'We'll think about it,' I said firmly.

Of course we had nothing to think about, and Dawar

looked wild with excitement when Bert and I went up to tell him later that day. He started frantically clearing away the very minimal mess about the cell, and pointed emphatically at the top and bottom bunks, apparently offering up either one to Bert.

At roll count that evening, Chris opened the observation flap and beckoned me over. The two of them were sitting at the desk with mugs of tea in hand playing rock, paper, scissors.

I practically skipped into work the following afternoon, feeling well rested and excited to talk to Dawar about the charity I had found which supported victims of modern slavery while they were in prison.

But when I got to G-Wing, I was disappointed to see Steve and an officer called Hannah there. Hannah was arguably worse to work with than Steve. The only thing she loved more than a good scrap with a prisoner was telling everyone about it afterwards, so she was always provoking prisoners into fights. She and Steve were bent over some forms they were filling out at the desk.

'Mad morning on G-Uppers, Gen!' Steve announced, not even looking up at me.

'What? What do you mean, Steve?' I asked curtly.

In my mind, I immediately blamed the two of them. What had they mishandled? Who had they wound up? *Of course those two had managed to wring some drama out of the wing!*

Hannah spoke up before Steve could reply. 'It was mad, you've got some real crazies on this wing, you know? Don't know how you do it with nonces and crackheads all day – respect.' She said it not with concern but with contempt. 'One of your servery workers, yeah? He takes the lunch up. The two guys sharing on the top floor, the South Asian guy and small British man?'

Steve took over. 'He gives this guy his lunch, and he starts buggin' out over some dumb sandwich. Really losin' his shit.'

I felt a sense of dread come over me. I looked at the forms they were writing out.

'Are those Use of Force forms?' I asked, more urgently now. 'You didn't wrap anyone up on here, did you?'

There was rarely a reason to restrain someone on G-Uppers. Any decent officer could talk these prisoners down without having to lay hands on them.

Hannah drew in an excited breath. 'Yeah anyways, me an' Steve were talking to 'im, like "Chill out, you wasteman", but bro was buggin' out! So anyways, one thing leads to another an' Steve grabs one arm an' I take the other. But this man is strong!'

I was biting my lip hard to keep my anger under control.

'Was it Dawar? Is that his name?'

'Dawar! That's the one,' Steve exclaimed. 'Swear down, Gen, this man saw red. He was spazzin' out! We're tryna get him to the floor but we can't with just the two of us. He's like some animal, man, like he was on spice or sumfin'. He was buggin'!'

I shook my head slowly.

Hannah took over again. 'So I grab 'im by the neck and finally we get 'im to the floor. Now he's tryna bite Steve though so I'm smackin' 'im with my radio, like anywhere I can get 'im. Smackin' 'im in the balls, smackin' 'im in the knees. I had to, though. He was tryna bite us!'

I felt my stomach turning to knots and my jaw clenching. 'I'm gonna go talk to him,' I said, walking out.

'Nah,' Steve said, 'he ain't up there no more.'

'He's gone to seg – fuckin' prick,' Hannah added.

My stomach knotted still more. 'What sort of sandwich was it, Steve?'

He looked at me and laughed. 'What d'you mean? What's it matter what was in the sandwich? Guy's a space case.'

'Can you just try and remember? *Steve?* It's important!'

I knew I was speaking too intensely. Steve and Hannah were staring at me.

'Fuck knows, Gen. I dunno. Maybe coleslaw?'

23

Gangbangers

Two new names had started to dominate staff briefing in the mornings: Kamal Aziz and Connor Paynter. Every single day, an alarm would sound on E-Uppers. You could be sure that you would run there to find Aziz and Paynter, bloody-nosed, their skinny arms pounding into another prisoner or wielding swinging socks filled with tuna cans. They were only nineteen, and they were gang-affiliated up to their necks. Of course, because of this there were plenty of people who wanted to get to them – and it certainly didn't help that they both loved a good scrap.

One day, one of the senior governors came to talk to Chris and me in the office. Chris was vaping as usual, and flapped his hand at the swirling cloud he'd just exhaled to create a pathway for her to walk through.

'Welcome to the G-Uppers sauna!' he croaked.

The governor grinned. 'Well, I hope you'll all be keeping your clothes on at least! Now, I imagine you've heard of Connor Paynter and Kamal Aziz by now? You'd be living under a rock if you hadn't. They're coming on here this afternoon, I'm afraid. We're striking a deal with them: if they can keep their noses clean for two weeks on this wing, they can go back to E-Uppers with all their mates.'

Chris and I exchanged glances.

'What they don't know,' she went on, 'is that they actually *have* to come on here for two weeks cos it's gonna take us at least that long to get rid of all their little enemies on E-Uppers.'

'Right,' said Chris resignedly. He sounded as fed up about this development as I felt.

'One thing though, guys,' she added. 'If those two leave the wing to go anywhere, doctors or anything, you need to call Security to check the route first. They've got over two hundred conflicts each, so really, if they know what's good for them, they won't leave the wing unless it's for a visit. Any problems, ring me directly on 633, yeah?'

After she'd left, Chris turned to me. 'An' here we go, Gen. I told ya! In come the gangbangers. This'll be the start of it, mark my words.'

Aziz and Paynter were pretty much dragged kicking and screaming to G-Uppers that afternoon. They arrived looking like ferociously grumpy teenagers, sluggish and hostile, their knuckles black and blue. They informed us dismissively that they were only here for two weeks and that they would be going back to E-Uppers to 'rejoin the mandem' as soon as it was over with.

'Absolutely fine by me,' I responded. 'Your cell is upstairs – let's go.'

It was only at that moment that I noticed another man standing behind them, facing away from me. This had happened before – the induction officers had a terrible habit of just dropping new prisoners on your wing without bothering to inform the officers on duty. He looked like he could've been a child. His physique was slight and boyish and although I couldn't see his face, the way he was gazing around made me think of an infant riding a train for the first time.

'Oh, hey, I didn't see you there,' I said to him. 'You'll be needing a cell too, I guess?'

He turned around slowly and gazed at me dreamily. He had a thick beard with a large scar running through it from his earlobe to his chin, but still his eyes had a look of childlike wonder about them.

''Ello, Miss,' he said with a smile, then went on staring at me disconcertingly.

I don't think he's on drugs. His pupils aren't dilated – they look normal. But if he's not on drugs then he's really not well. And either way, we aren't Healthcare and we aren't the addiction unit, so why do they keep treating us like a specialized wing?

'Single cell for you, I think,' I said, under my breath. 'All of you come in the office a second while I find a cell for . . .?'

There was silence. Then Paynter nudged him. 'Bro! Brother! She's askin' for your name.'

'My name?' He looked honoured by the interest for a moment. 'Oh, I'm sorry, Miss, it's Hamza. Yusuf Hamza.' Then, in a curious and innocent tone, he added, 'Miss, do you know where I can buy some crack around here?'

Chris and I both dropped our heads into our hands at the same time. Paynter and Aziz were sniggering too.

'Bruddah, bruddah – what you sayin'?' said Aziz. 'You can't ask that to a gov! Bro, this guy is funny, you know? I like him, still.'

Paynter put his long arm around Hamza's neck affectionately. 'Come to me, brother. I can hook you up.'

I rolled my eyes, looking at my watch. 'That took you less than five minutes on the wing, Paynter – well done!'

He put his hands up. 'I'm jokin', Miss, I'm jokin', I swear! Swear I won't give you no trouble. I want off this nonce wing asap – trus' me.'

Bert appeared pushing a broom around aimlessly. He'd served his time on basic and he'd been really torn up after Dawar's departure so we'd all agreed – including Dimitra – to let him take up his caretaking duties once again. He would always try to assert himself when new prisoners came on the wing, although it didn't always have the desired effect. He bumped fists with Paynter and Aziz and gave Hamza a friendly pat on the arm, before saying to me behind the back of his hand: 'Looks like you're gonna have your work cut out while I'm gone!'

'*When* you're gone, Bert,' I said sternly, but also with a smile, '*when* you're gone. If *you* don't even believe you're gonna stay out of prison, how are you ever gonna do it?'

Bert's release date was coming up in a few weeks' time. This was usually an exciting prospect and most prisoners would be counting down the days, but it was hard to feel positive when it was Bert's turn. We all knew, and so did he, that he was being released to a sleeping bag under a bridge. Chances were that he would be back inside before too long.

'That's what I meant, Gen, sorry. Just force of habit. I feel good about it though this time, really I do. Soon I start my new life!'

Paynter and Aziz were staring at Bert distastefully. It was the general assumption, by process of elimination, that anyone on G-Uppers who was not a foreign national was a sex offender. I wasn't often in the habit of addressing these assumptions – it was always safer to just claim ignorance. But as I watched Bert scrabble for respect from the new boys on the wing, I had to say something in his defence. If I could drop in the crime Bert *did* commit, at least it would clear up any misunderstandings.

'Well, Bert, like I said – get yourself registered with that GP. And try and get yourself off the booze and drugs. You won't have a reason to rob people then.'

While we were talking, I noticed Hamza casually picking up a whiteboard pen from the desk in the office. He popped the lid off and started to sniff it dreamily.

'Right, let's go to your new cells then, everybody!' I said, swiping the pen out of his hand.

Chris followed behind to keep them moving and I heard Hamza ask him hopefully: 'Gov, can I have one of your caps, please? One of your vape caps please, gov?'

'Certainly bloody not, son. I'd sooner give you back our board pen!'

Upstairs, Hamza skipped into his new cell happily. 'Thank you, gov, thank you!' he said to Chris as he tested out the bed, grinning.

Meanwhile, I was next door with Aziz and Paynter who were checking over their cell like two property surveyors. There were complaints about the limescale in the kettle and the light flickering. I'd heard it all before.

'Right, well, a new kettle I can sort tomorrow,' I said briskly, 'and I'll tell Works that you need a new bulb. Don't expect it to come before the end of the week, though.'

'What are you gonna do about my mattress?' grunted Paynter.

'Don't take the piss, Paynter. This isn't a hotel. I've seen bad mattresses and that one's perfectly fine.'

Chris bustled in past me. 'So how do you two like the honeymoon suite, then?'

They scowled at him, which only encouraged him.

'You've got the best views of the building! It's state of the art, ain't it? Here you've got your en suite shower. It has one temperature only and I think you'll find it's a perfectly pleasant lukewarm. Pick of the beds is totally up to you two, pick any one you want, as long as the other one don't want it. Here you've got your twelve-inch plasma TV – it's got all six channels on it. Although you two look like you've done enough jail to jimmy the wire out the window and get 'em all. We really hope you'll enjoy your stay with us here at G-Wing Resorts!'

By the time he'd finished, the two of them couldn't help but let out a little snort of laughter.

Aziz shook his head at Chris. 'You're a madman, ya know?'

'I certainly am!' Chris replied. 'Done more time in prison than I hope either of you will 'ave to do an' all. So, if that's all, make yourselves comfortable and ride ya bang up!'

Aziz and Paynter largely kept to the terms of their deal – two weeks of good behaviour and then back to E-Wing. Ten days had passed and there had been only one minor incident when a poor old Bangladeshi man accidentally walked into Paynter while he was carrying his dinner. Paynter had slammed his plate down on a nearby table and rolled up his sleeves, towering at least a foot over this very confused man. But Aziz quickly brought him to his senses with a firm tap on the back of his head.

'This guy's an uncle, bro! Leave the man alone. It weren't on purpose! This ain't E-Uppers, pham,' he said to him, kissing his teeth at Paynter before patting him on the back.

The real change I had noticed in both of them was that generally they'd started to relax. The tough, grumpy teenager exterior they had both displayed on their first day on the wing was gradually breaking down and they were even starting to enjoy Chris's sense of humour.

Today, Aziz and Paynter were scheduled for a legal visit together. Legal visits, from solicitors or other professionals discussing a prisoner's case, usually happened in the same hall as social visits, although there were side rooms for more confidential meetings. I could only hope that the Visits staff had done their homework and had booked those two into a private room. Aziz and Paynter's conflicts within the prison were serious enough, but in the Visits Hall, other gang-affiliated men who happened to be visiting their friends or family inside could be added to the mix.

First, though, it was my job to walk them over to the Visits Hall without bumping into any of the other prisoners in the jail they had beef with – just as the governor had warned me.

I swung their door open. Unsurprisingly it was pitch black and they were both fast asleep.

'Good morning!' I called into the darkness. 'You two've got a legal visit this morning so get yourself ready and looking sharp. You need to be ready to go at any moment over the next hour because I need to wait for Security to tell me that the route's been cleared of all your little friends. OK?'

As I turned to leave, I heard Paynter's voice.

'Gen, hang on a sec.' He was sitting up in bed, rubbing his eyes. 'Did you get laid over the weekend or something? You're really glowing this morning. Ain't she, Aziz?'

There was a time when I would have shrunk at a question like this. But if working in a prison teaches you anything, it's how to brush off a heckle.

'Always a pleasure talking to you, Paynter. Both of you – ready in five, please,' I said briskly, but with a good-humoured smile.

As I closed the door behind me I heard Aziz give him a telling off and laughed to myself.

'Yep, yep – route's clear, it should be fine,' said the voice on the other end of the phone, distractedly. The comms staff sit in front of a bank of security cameras so they can see where everyone in the prison is, and before you move any prisoners you are meant to get their permission over your radio.

'There's no one on our route, yeah?' I asked again. I wasn't convinced.

'Yep. You should be all good. Get moving quick, though, cos they'll be starting doctor's visits in the next ten,' the comms officer instructed.

I called up to the landing above. 'Aziz, Paynter – let's go!'

I could see Paynter plodding along from the laundry room to his cell, carrying a bunch of clothes. He was topless.

'Paynter! Put a T-shirt on, now!'

'Sorry, Gen!' he shouted back to me, pulling a T-shirt over his head.

Three minutes later, they were both still nowhere to be seen. I headed back up the stairs to hurry them down. Paynter was chatting to another prisoner through the hinges of the cell door. Somehow he was once again topless.

'Paynter!' I shouted. 'How have you taken your top off *again*?' I was shaking my head, but I was laughing. I was sure he was doing it to wind me up now. '*Put one on* and let's go!'

Five minutes later they were trailing behind me towards the wing door. I called over the radio: 'Beta 2-3. Moving two from G-Uppers to Visits. Can you confirm the route is clear?'

'Beta 2-3 – that's confirmed,' came the voice of the comms officer over the net.

Aziz and Paynter plodded down the stairs behind me,
making jokes to each other about their solicitor's 'dog-
breath'. At the bottom of the stairs I let them out of the
door of the houseblock on to the tarmac route which
wound through the prison to the Visits Hall, turning
around only for a moment to lock it behind me.

I heard silence fall between Aziz and Paynter and I
looked around to see their fists clenched and their
mouths twitching. Then I saw what was beyond them.
The route wasn't clear at all – a group of prisoners were
playing football on the pitch ahead of us.

'Bro, that's the Tottenham boys,' Paynter muttered,
not taking his twinkling eyes off them.

On the pitch, as though they'd picked up something
in the air, the players stiffened and turned to face us one
by one. I groaned. I knew what was about to happen,
but in the split second before anyone moved, I saw an
expression flicker over Aziz's face. There was no doubt
in my mind – it was reluctance.

He doesn't want to fight.

'Not worth it, guys,' I murmured, defeatedly, certain
it was already too late. The men on the pitch had reached
the waist-high fence and some of them were about to
jump over.

Paynter flashed past me, closely followed by Aziz. I
slammed the alarm button on my radio and took off
after them.

I got there just as the fists started to fly. I plunged

into the middle and grabbed an arm. I wasn't sure whose it was but I just pushed it as hard as I could to create some distance between the men. Someone else's elbow sank into my ribcage, and I winced, trying to make sense of the limbs which were jabbing and kicking all around me, alert for anything that looked like a weapon. It was only me and the football coach with at least eight prisoners. There was no use in us trying to restrain anyone, it was a case of just managing the damage before backup arrived.

Paynter's fist crashed into the face of a prisoner beside me. He toppled into me with a thud and I flew backwards into three other brawling prisoners, one of whom was Aziz. I took my chance. Twisting round, I drove him backwards with my forearms held against his chest. It took him by surprise and he started to lose balance, so I kept going until he landed against a wall, hard, a good few metres away from the melee. Then I heard a cry come from behind me and I turned to see a flurry of white shirts arriving – and also the weapon I had been looking out for. One of the prisoners was wielding a bulging sock above his head which I knew would be stuffed with cans of tuna – a classic makeshift weapon. He swung the sock twice and I heard it crack into a prisoner's head.

'Fuckkk!' he cried out.

The smell of tuna hit my nose – the blow had split the can open. I ducked as I ran back in, the prisoner still

wielding the sock menacingly but now with two officers trying to get his arms down behind his back. I
jumped to grab his head but just as I did so the sock
swung inches past my face and smacked into the cheek
of one of the other officers, opening a gash and shower-
ing us all in tuna brine.

'Fuckkk!'

This time it was an officer crying out, and the energy
changed in an instant. We needed to get this under control. Everyone was wrestling to keep hold of limbs and
legs. I could see arms twisted at awkward angles and
prisoners crying out and the stench of tuna was hot in
our noses but we kept on going, panting and gasping,
until finally all movement stopped. I looked around:
some prisoners were pinned up against the wall, some
were being restrained on the floor, and some were
already being handcuffed by the managers who had
arrived. I had Paynter's skinny arm twisted tightly
behind his back, my hand holding his fist locked into
place. My colleague who'd been hit was slumped
against the fence, the nurse holding a reddening gauze
up to the gash in his cheek where the tuna tin had
sliced it.

'He's on G-Wing,' I said to the two officers who
came to help me with Paynter. 'So's he,' I added to the
officer who had Aziz on the ground.

Back on the wing, I called the Visits Hall to let them
know Aziz and Paynter wouldn't be showing up. Then

I brought Aziz into the office to talk to first. He walked in holding a towel to his bleeding lip.

'What was that about, then?' I asked him.

'Nothing, Gen.' He stared hard at the floor. 'You know how it is.'

'You guys have been doing so well, and now you've thrown that all away by fighting. Over what? Picking on some guys you don't even really know?'

Aziz shrugged.

'I've got a theory,' I said. 'You wanna hear it?'

Aziz shrugged again.

'OK. So, I think that you didn't actually wanna get in that fight. You just did it cos you had to have Paynter's back. Am I close?'

He looked thoughtful for a moment. 'Yeah, Gen. To be fair, you've been good to us, still. Not that I weren't up for the fight – I just didn't want you gettin' caught up in it, that's all.'

'Nope, Aziz, I don't buy it. I think it was more than that. I think you've actually enjoyed keeping your nose clean for a change and you didn't want to throw all that away.'

'Nah – I don't even care about that, still.' Aziz puckered his lips and crossed his arms.

I raised my eyebrows. 'OK, well, I'll just give you something to think about. If you ride your basic on this wing with no problems – and I mean no problems at all – in two weeks we can start working to get you a job on the wing. What do you reckon?'

He laughed. 'Pha, Miss – you mean stay on this wing? I don't see that happenin'.'

'OK, that's fine. Just think about it – yeah?'

Aziz curled the corners of his lips down indifferently. I sensed it was the end of the conversation.

24

Comings and Goings

As part of their punishment for fighting, Aziz and Paynter were separated. Paynter didn't like it — he became even moodier than usual and stopped cleaning his cell completely. The place was always pitch black and acrid whenever I opened his door. He didn't cause any real problems, but he wasn't enjoyable to be around. If I made any effort to lighten his mood, he'd shrug and say, 'Well I'll be back on E-Wing soon, so whatever, yeah?' The only time I saw him smile was when he was leaning against the hinges of Aziz's door, trying to steal a moment to chat to him after being unlocked for his daily solo exercise.

Aziz, though, took the separation very differently. It happened quickly — he calmed down as though he'd matured a few years in only a couple of days. I could only assume that he was taking his conditions seriously, and really was just keeping his head down until the grand return to E-Wing.

The day of his departure finally arrived. I went to Aziz's cell to tell him to pack his stuff up.

'They're clearing up a cell on E-Wing for you and Paynter now, so get your things together.'

He looked at me sheepishly. 'One sec, Gen. Can you just come in for a minute?'

I shot the bolt in the lock and stepped into his cell, pushing his door shut behind me.

'Gen – I bin thinkin' about what you said. You think you can keep your word on that?'

'I always keep my word, Aziz,' I told him, trying to suppress a smile.

'So if I stay on this wing, no issues, I can get a job – yeah?'

'More than just no issues, Aziz. You gotta be helpful, you gotta be polite and you gotta make our lives easier.'

'I'm always polite!' He grinned at me. 'Thing is, though, Gen, I can't be saying that I don't want to get back to the wing, you know? I don't want the mandem talkin' that I like it on the nonce wing now, you get me?'

I thought for a second. 'That's fine, leave that to me, I'll make it like you have to stay on here.'

'Yeah?' he said, with a hint of excitement. 'What you gonna say?'

'Aziz, I'm an excellent liar. That's what makes me so good at this job. But don't make me regret it, yeah?'

He put his hand out for me to shake, and I took it.

Just before I left, I turned back to him. 'Why the change of heart?'

Aziz looked down at the floor. 'My girl called me this morning. She's pregnant, innit.'

I rolled my eyes, but I was smiling. 'Aziz, you've only been out of jail for like two months since you turned sixteen! How'd ya manage that?'

'Only takes one time, dunnit!' he chuckled.

'OK, well, that's the first sensible decision I've ever seen you make, so let's keep this up, yeah? *Especially* given the circumstances.'

I felt something close to hope bubble within me. I knew better than to think that having a baby was enough to turn these guys away from crime. But maybe, just maybe, I was going to be able to help him turn things around.

A week later, after I'd had a few days off, there was more encouraging news. I went to unlock Bert for his morning medication, and just before I opened the door I heard another voice in his cell. I couldn't quite work it out because the shower was running and it sounded like there were two people in there – singing, appallingly. I pushed open the door, confused. *Bert hadn't had a cellmate since Dawar was sent to seg—*

There he was. Dawar. Standing by the window, singing into a carton of milk while Bert belted out a totally different tune from behind the shower curtain. Dawar grinned at me, then leapt over to his shelves and started fumbling about, eventually fishing out what he was looking for and thrusting it into my hands. It was a letter, and its printed letterhead was familiar . . .

It's the charity I reported his case to!

'Thank you, thank you, thank you!' Dawar was saying, dancing around the cell now.

I had assumed he'd been shipped out to another facility after the segregation unit, and had worried that the charity was never going to be able to track him down, but he'd come back, and they had. Why had no one told me? I suddenly felt quite overcome with emotion. My eyes stung slightly. I couldn't remember the last time I'd felt this way in prison.

I grinned back at him and passed his precious letter back.

Aziz noticeably began to pay attention to the prisoners around him. He was observant, and he picked up on when people were in trouble. One day he came to find me in the wing's laundry room, with a worried expression on his face.

'Gen, come look at Habibi's cell. I fink he needs you.'

'Habibi? Who's Habibi, Aziz?'

'The small bearded brother – the one always asking for caps.'

'Oh, you mean Hamza?' I said. 'Right, OK, yep, I'll go take a look. Just let me sort this washing machine first.'

The door on it was locked shut. A wing without a functioning washing machine was going to cause a whole lot of trouble, and we didn't have the weeks I knew Works would take to come and fix it. I thought there was a chance I could sort it out myself.

'Nah, Gen,' Radu, who was with me, said discouragingly, watching me crouching by the machine, fiddling. He was shaking his head. 'I tried that already.'

Aziz went on fidgeting behind me. 'Gen,' he said, 'Habibi, he—'

'Just one second!' I said to both of them. 'One of you get me a pen, will you?'

Aziz passed me a pen, and I stabbed it into the toggle I was trying to reach. There was a satisfying click, and the washing machine door opened.

'Damn, Gen, that's impressive!' said Radu with a laugh. 'I've never seen a woman do something like that! I'll be real!'

Aziz kissed his teeth. 'Radu, bro, you know Gen's a feminist, bruv? Course she can do shit like that.'

I decided that discussing what the actual definition of a feminist was could wait for another time.

'Right, Aziz, now I'm coming to see Hamza.'

Hamza was sitting on his bed, rhythmically flicking his chin with his thumb. He stared, as if in a trance, at the wall before him. His room was in a total state. Cereal packs had been torn open and thrown everywhere, his bed sheets were ripped and lying all around the floor, and his empty, beloved vape caps were scattered everywhere. The ground crunched beneath me as I made my way over to him. I put one hand on his shoulder and squatted down to look in his eyes. His pupils were wide and he didn't seem to register that I was there.

'Hamza, what have you been smoking? Do you know what it was, mate?'

He didn't react, but he started breathing more heavily. I grabbed a cup of water from the tap and handed it to him. He clasped his hands around it and then in one sudden movement threw the whole cup into his face.

I realized that Aziz had crept into the cell.

'Do you know what he might have smoked, cos it doesn't look like spice?'

Aziz bent down next to Hamza. 'Habibi, bro, you all good, bruddah?' Then he looked at me. 'This ain't drugs, Miss. This is his mental health. It's cos he's schizophrenic – that's it.'

I looked back into Hamza's eyes. They weren't bloodshot and glazed like they would be if he was on spice, they were fixed and staring. I remembered from training that this could be a sign of psychosis. I nodded, thinking Aziz was probably right. 'That makes sense, Aziz, yeah.'

It's possibly something I should have picked up on earlier; it's definitely something I should have known about. The thing is, doctor–patient confidentiality exists in prison too, and unless a prisoner has told me what his medical condition is, there's no reason I would know.

'Come on then, Habibi,' Aziz said to him gently,

'let's get this shit cleaned up, no? Wallahi you can't live like this, brother.' Aziz tugged Hamza up on a bent arm and grabbed a bin liner from the corner. 'Listen, Habibi, I'll hold this an' you put all this nonsense in here, OK? You listenin', bro?'

Hamza nodded slightly. He seemed to be able to hear and understand a little now. He smiled at Aziz with glassy eyes.

'There we go, bruddah, there we are!'

By the time they were done tidying up in Hamza's cell, Hamza was almost back to full consciousness.

'Are you gonna say thank you to Aziz then?' I said, immediately aware of how much I sounded like I was talking to a child.

Hamza nodded, airily. 'Thanks, bruddah.'

Aziz nodded too. I waited for him to leave before I spoke to Hamza.

'I'm gonna give the nurse a call, OK?' I told him. 'Do you normally take medication?'

He nodded again.

'And have you been diagnosed with schizophrenia before?'

At this he looked suddenly very pleased. 'Yes, Gen! That's the one, that's the one I take pills for normally!' Then he added with a puzzled look on his face, 'They haven't bin givin' them to me here.'

Hamza was unlike all the other addicts I had ever met in jail, who were often charismatic and friendly but

readily capable of vicious deceit just beneath the surface. Before Hamza opened his mouth, the only clue to
his habit was his dirty fingers, their blackened tips the
telltale sign that he had repeatedly singed them while
shovelling embers into a scalding crack pipe. He was
always cleanly dressed, he kept his cell immaculate most
of the time, and he wandered around with an expression of ethereal honesty which was both infuriating and
captivating. Discouraged by nothing, he would bounce
from group to group on the exercise yard asking anyone
and everyone for a vape capsule. Some prisoners were
irritated by his persistence and would throw their empty
cans at him like they might at a stray dog, but he just
kept on going, never once erring from his polite 'Scuse
me, bruddah, could I get the rest of your cap, please?' I
don't know whether it was his childlike demeanour or
the way his face lit up when he saw me, but I'd started
to feel slightly protective towards him.

Unsurprisingly, Hamza took quite a liking to Aziz
after the cell clean-up. Aziz didn't seem to mind his
company and would often hand me a half-empty vape
capsule to pass on to him. I asked him about it one day.

'Have you ever considered a career in a rehab centre,
Aziz? You're a natural!'

'Tsss — leave it out, Gen. I hope for everyone's sake I
wouldn't get through their risk assessments — wiv a
criminal history like mine! Besides, I'd know half the
crackheads in there. Bin supplyin' 'em almost half my
life.'

'Well, yeah, but now you're helping them clean their rooms and get their acts together – looks like a bit of a career U-turn,' I joked to him.

'I got customer service skills too, you know? I weren't just handing the drugs to 'em and taking the money and leaving. People don't realize how hard you work as a drug dealer, you know? I built proper rapport with them guys. They don't always have the money, you know, so sometimes I walk past one of 'em begging and I just slip them twenty quid. Gonna come back to my pocket some time anyways.'

I laughed. 'To be fair, I've never really thought about it like that, Aziz!'

'You know how it is, Gen. You get paid to hang out with crackheads, same as me!'

25

The Hearing

By the time Paynter had been gone from the wing for two weeks, Aziz was unrecognizable. He was hanging around the office as much as he could, asking Chris and me what we thought about various issues in the news, and quizzing Dimitra on what it was like to be able to speak three languages.

His mind is leaving his former world behind, I thought as I watched him. He was looking, for the first time since I'd met him – and maybe for the first time in his life – beyond gang mentality and culture. Chris even told me how Aziz had broken up a fight on the exercise yard before anyone else had walked the ten yards to intervene.

Kelly too had been monitoring his progress closely. Apart from the fact that it looked good for her if her wing was able to look after one of the toughest prisoners in the jail, everyone loved a good-news story.

Rankin had been moved to a sex offenders jail to serve the rest of his sentence, so the head of servery job was up for grabs. We took a vote on it. The result was unanimous: all the staff on the wing voted for Aziz, apart from Dimitra, who insisted that she 'just didn't trust him'. To which Kelly responded: 'It's prison, Dimitra – you shouldn't trust any of them!'

The job was Aziz's, and I had a good feeling about it.

When I arrived on Monday morning for the new week I scoured the whiteboard for any signs of the weekend's action. I immediately saw an ADJ in red next to Aziz's name. My heart plummeted. ADJ stands for 'adjudication', which meant he was down to see the governor. What could he possibly have got up to in two days while I was away? The answer to that, as I reminded myself, was quite a lot.

I rummaged through the wing book to see if any incidents had been recorded. There had been a self-harming incident and by the look of things a small scrap on the exercise yard involving Hamza and a man called Silvio regarding a vape capsule. Nothing new there. I couldn't see Aziz's name anywhere.

It was early, and I knew he'd still be sleeping. I marched off to his cell, swung his door open and sang, purposefully loudly, 'Morning!'

He rolled over in bed, squinting. 'Gen, the fuck, what time is it?'

'Eight fifteen, which means I have been up and about for a few hours already so don't come to me complaining it's early. More importantly, what *on earth* have you got yourself into in the forty-eight hours I've been away from this place?'

'Tsss, Gen. It ain't anything. It's some bullshit thing.'

'Aziz, when I said you needed to keep your nose clean, I didn't mean only when I'm around. And I'm not just gonna keep bailing you out of stuff to keep you on the right track either.'

'Listen – this is the thing, Gen. They called me in for a piss test. You know they're out for me, or summin. Anyways, it come back positive, you get me?'

I sat down on his desk opposite him. 'This is exactly the kind of thing I meant, though, Aziz. You know as well as I do that that wasn't a random test. They've got your name down on that list because you make trouble. Just because you've got a few officers on this wing vouching for you doesn't mean you're invincible, you know?'

'Ah, Gen, sometimes man just needs a smoke ...' Aziz groaned, falling back on to his pillow.

'And sometimes he needs to grow the fuck up and take some responsibility for himself, Aziz. Get up, get dressed and be in the office in five minutes if you want me to help you with this situation. Five minutes, Aziz. I have other stuff to do today too.'

Seven minutes later, he was slumped in the chair in the office, yawning.

'So what's the plan, then?' I asked him frankly.

He looked a bit surprised. 'Gen, I thought it was you that had a plan. Thought that's why I'm here.'

'Well, yes, obviously I have a plan. But I want to see if the seasoned criminal in front of me fancies coming up with anything in his own defence.'

Aziz laughed at this, then ran the heels of his hands down his face despairingly. 'Well, I smoked, innit. An' they know that, so I'm just gonna plead guilty. No point me going to see the governor. I'll just ride the basic.'

A prisoner who wants to appeal against an adjudication can do so. It means asking the governor for a hearing during which he can put his case in person.

'So you're just gonna let it happen to you?' I said to him in exasperation. 'You're gonna take the punishment without even speaking up for yourself?'

'Well, I dunno, Gen. What do you think?'

'Aziz, I think that seeing as you have got the *right* to a hearing over this, in honour of all the people around the world who *don't* have that right, you should get out of bed and fucking do it. Don't you?'

'Yeah.' He stared at the floor despondently. 'I mean – I guess, Gen.'

He sounded so uncertain.

'Aziz, you need to start taking some responsibility, you know? You're a smart boy, so stop letting other people make decisions about your life. It's demeaning.'

'Tsss – what d'you even mean? Other people makin' decisions 'bout my life?'

'Aziz, there are people in this jail that you can look at and think "Well, at least they've got three meals a day and a roof over their heads." Because, frankly, what would happen to them outside? Could they cope out there? Could they get something to eat or a place to sleep? No way. Now, do you think you fall into that category?'

He shook his head, adamantly.

'Right! So what are you gonna do about it? Cos if you're not careful you'll be an old man one day and you'll still be in and out of this place, and *that's* when people are gonna look at you and think "He'd better stay here, cos where else can he go? He's spent most of his life here, where else is he good for?" You must realize that, Aziz?'

He rubbed his temples now and looked up to the ceiling. 'Shit. I never thought about it before like that, you know, Gen? Still, why you always gotta be so brutal 'bout fings? Jeez!'

'Aziz, I mentioned your name the other day in the staffroom and one of the governors overheard, yeah? You know what he said to me? "What's that shit-bag done now?" I told him that you were doing really well at the moment, that you'd just bagged yourself the servery job, and had actually been good as gold. What did he say back? "It won't last long."'

Aziz grinned, as though he had known that was coming.

'But d'you get what I'm saying, Aziz? When people hear your name, they assume you've done something bad. They don't believe in you. Doesn't that bother you?'

'Um, like, I guess. But it's kind of annoyin' that I've kept it down all these weeks and still people don't really think I can do it.'

'Right. So, guess which governor is doing adjudications this morning?'

He smiled again. 'Da shit-bag one?'

'Yep! So how about instead of wasting away in your shitty little cell and not even turning up to receive your punishment, you go down there, and you show this governor who you really are, you take your punishment on the chin and you apologize to him?'

'But what would I even say?'

'Aziz, I'm not gonna spell it out for you. Go down there, be humble, be polite, tell them you messed up *again*. Tell them that you've really enjoyed being out of trouble and that having a job on the wing is really going to improve your mentality. Tell them you understand if they don't want to give you a second chance, but that you really want the opportunity to show that you've changed, and you'll be seizing it with both hands.'

He chuckled. 'Gen, you should talk to my solicitor, you know? He could learn a thing or two from you!'

'So, what? You gonna do it?'

He looked down at the floor, nodded pensively, then

looked back up and said in a small voice: 'Gen, will you come with me?'

I took my seat next to Imam Abdi – a member of the chaplaincy who often sat in on adjudications as impartial support. Aziz sat at the opposite end of the table to the governor, sandwiched in between two officers from the segregation unit. This is always how adjudications are set up: if the prisoner kicks off, they are most likely to go for the governor, so the two officers flank the prisoner so they can respond quickly if they need to.

I stifled a laugh as Aziz opened the hearing in a voice I had never heard him use: 'Good morning, guv'nor. Thank you for taking the time to see me today.'

The governor looked up at him, unimpressed. 'So we are here at 11.04 a.m. on the eleventh of October. Can you confirm that your name is Kamal Aziz?'

'Yes, sir,' Aziz replied, nodding.

'It is alleged that on the ninth of October you were subjected to a random drugs test where they took a sample of your urine. I have it in front of me here that your result came back positive for cannabis. Do you plead guilty or not guilty to this offence?'

I saw Aziz's lips flinch at the word 'random' and prayed he didn't rise to it.

'Guilty, sir,' he replied.

'Good. You would be wasting everyone's time trying to plead not guilty to that one, young man,' replied the governor. 'Is there anything you would like to say in your defence, to either myself or any of the officers present?'

'Thank you, sir. I, er, I want to say that I actually feel like I've done a lot of thinkin' and a lot of growin' these past few weeks. Like I'm startin' to think I actually like the quiet life — I think it kinda suits me.' He smiled shyly. 'So yeah, the govs on G-Wing, they been good to me still and they've got me the servery job, and it's, like, satisfyin', and I think I'll be good at it, you know?' He paused for a moment and looked down at his lap. 'I feel like I've let people down with this, and to be honest I'm a bit embarrassed. So, yeah, I don't expect any second chances, I don't think I deserve them, but I just want to say that the G-Wing govs, Gen and stuff, were right to take a chance on me and give me the job in the first place cos, yeah, it's really affecting me in a good way. I'm grateful, even if it all ends here.'

The governor nodded, but looked unmoved, as if he'd heard it all before. He turned to me and asked, 'So, what do you think then? Are you here to vouch for him?'

'I am this time,' I said firmly, looking Aziz in the eye.

The governor turned back to Aziz and paused.

'If Gen's fighting your corner, Mr Aziz, then you must be doing something right. I'm writing you off with a caution. You won't have access to Visits or pay for the next two weeks. You do, however, get to keep your job. Don't be a prick and let her down, Kamal.'

As soon as we left the hearing, Aziz turned to me and

shook his head in disbelief. I was struck by a sudden, painful thought.

'Aziz, have you ever had anyone fight your corner before? I mean, like, an adult. Someone to stick up for you?'

He was pensive for a moment before looking at me sadly and shaking his head. 'Gen, I'm not sure I've ever given anyone any reason to, you know?'

A few days later Aziz, Radu, Chris and I were handing lunch around the wing. Bert was meant to be helping us but instead he had been darting about saying his good-byes to people I'd never even seen him talk to before. He was due for release that afternoon. He seemed to be over the moon about it, but I couldn't help but have an uncomfortable feeling. Partly because it was bittersweet watching him leave Dawar behind. Dawar was beaming with happiness for Bert while they busily exchanged numbers and addresses of relatives so that they could find each other on the outside. As we watched them from the landing above, I turned to Chris.

'In so many ways, prison is the best place for him, you know?' I said. 'He's got this community around him here. Outside, he has nothing. I just feel like he needs to be in here. I know how bad that sounds.'

Chris nodded. 'Always bin the same with him, Gen. Breaks yer heart, dunnit? There ain't nuffin' for him out there. They bring him in 'ere – we're the only ones who ever look after him. He ain't given no mental help, no education, no training. But then he meets some arsehole who gets him hooked on spice again and introduces him to the other crackheads. And then off he goes, back out into the big wide world. What's the point in that?'

We had an excellent rhythm going with lunch now that Aziz was used to the job. Aziz would read the name and the meal out on the list, I would open the cell, Radu would hand it into the cell, and Chris would lock the cell as I moved on to the next one. Aziz and Radu had been getting on like a house on fire and it was truly heartwarming to see. Radu had been teaching Aziz Albanian, and in return Aziz had been teaching him to speak 'roadman'.

'Uncle, who you on da blower to?' Radu said in a superb roadman drawl as I swung the door open to two middle-aged Albanian men.

I laughed. 'Very good, Radu. Except you let yourself down on the "blower" bit!'

The Albanian man who wasn't on the phone laughed too. 'What are you, roadman or cockney, Radu?' Before adding, 'He's on the phone to his solicitor!' At exactly the same time the man on the phone said: 'It's my boss, my friend! Shh.'

'Well, which one is it – his solicitor, his friend or his boss?' I asked, curious about their differing answers.

Radu and the Albanian man at the door looked at each other and laughed before the Albanian man explained, 'Gen, we do it properly in Albania, you know? We are all friends, we all get on – until it comes on to the subject of football of course. But when we come over here, we do it as a team. His friend is his boss first and then his lawyer. If we come here to sell drugs as a team, the rest of the team looks after us if we get caught and come inside. They defend us in court, they send us money in prison. It is a package deal!'

'An all-inclusive!' chuckled Radu.

I turned to Aziz who was shaking his head in disbelief. 'Aziz, your lot could learn a thing or two from these guys, instead of losing parts of your team to prison and then forgetting they ever lived — it's a bad business model, that.'

'Word, Gen, I was finking the exact same fing, you know? I should pitch it to the mandem still.'

We moved on, leaving the man to his phone call with his friend slash lawyer slash next-door neighbour.

'Well, that's a wrap,' said Chris as we closed the last door.

Bert was skipping up the landing towards us. He ground to a halt just in front of us and saluted me. Then, without warning, he wrapped his arms around me tightly, squeezing the air out of my lungs.

I laughed, keeping my arms firmly out to the side. 'OK, OK, Bert.' I patted him on the back. 'That's enough. You know how that looks for me on the cameras?'

Chris chuckled and gently pulled him off by the scruff of his collar.

Bert looked up at me with watery eyes. 'Thanks for the patience, both of yous. An' the laughs.'

I realized then just how much he was going to miss us.

26

Counting Straws

Despite the creeping sensation I had that I was getting far too used to casual violence, open wounds and appalling crimes, one day something sickened me to the pit of my stomach to a greater extent than I thought possible.

A dummy made up of pillows and clothing had been found in a prisoner's cell on G-Wing. Security had quickly escalated it as an escape risk, assuming it had been constructed to look like the prisoner was in bed at roll count. But as soon as they told Chris and me which cell it was in, we knew that it would be something far more gruesome.

When we first clapped eyes on the dummy, slumped up against the wall in the office, we saw that it was infant-sized, with a smiling face drawn on in pen, and we knew immediately what Mr Rains had been doing with it – exactly what he had been doing with his tiny victims before he came to prison.

It left the mood on the wing sombre and edgy. Of course I had been around many convicted paedophiles since I'd been on G-Wing, but the reality of crouching down in the office helping Jerry stuff a used child-sized sex doll into an evidence bag felt different. It left me with a bad taste in my mouth which I couldn't get rid of.

We were all still mired in a harrowing silence when a new prisoner was dropped on the wing late that afternoon.

'I am Angelos, I am Greek,' he announced as I was checking the system for a cell for him. 'You won't get no problem with me!'

I found his profile. *Domestic abuser. Attacked victim (partner) with scaffolding pole.*

'Is that right?' I said tartly.

'Ooh – I am Greek too!' Dimitra squealed. The two of them exchanged a quick flurry of words in their own language.

'Right, Angelos,' I said when they were finished, 'do you take medication at the moment?'

'Yes, Miss, three times per day,' he replied, as if he had just answered a quiz question correctly.

'OK – and you speak English. That's all we need from you, then.'

'Yes, Miss, I can even help translate for you on the wing. I am very good cleaner also, so I can be cleaner on your wing!'

'We already have a cleaner,' I replied without looking up from the computer.

But there was no stopping him. 'No problem, you can put me with anyone, I don't mind. I just want you to have easy and good job, Miss.'

The man's obsequiousness was blatantly insincere. And after what had gone on this morning, I wasn't in the mood.

'Well, it's prison, so yeah, I'll put you where I want to put you,' I responded bluntly.

'Except one small favour.' He was looking at me coyly, holding his thumb and forefinger an inch apart to indicate just how small this favour really was. 'Please put me with European. I want to be with European. Oh, and no Black person, I don't want Black person neither.'

There it was – the ugliness his obsequiousness was hiding.

'Well, as it happens, Mr . . .' I looked at his ID card in my hand – it read *Giorgos Angela*. 'Mr Angela, I've got a spot in a cell with a Romanian man – it's your lucky day,' I said dryly.

'Oooh – thank you, thank you, Miss. And also, my name is Angelos, not Angela. The officers in reception, they were not very nice, they make my name like girl's name and put it on my card. But it's Angelos, please, Miss.'

'I'm afraid what it says on the card is what we have to call you, Angela,' I lied. I knew it was small-minded and petty, but in that moment it felt like a tiny act of vengeance. Besides, I was finding it more and more satisfying to exert my power in small ways these days. I knew it was an unattractive trait, but in this place it helped. Especially on days like this, when I felt like the walls I had spent so long building were starting to crack. It helped me feel in control again.

It took less than an hour for roaring and pummelling to kick off behind the door of Angelos's new cell. I made my way over in no real hurry and looked in through the hatch. His Romanian cellmate was huddled at the foot of the door clutching a bin bag filled with what I assumed were his belongings. Angelos was marching up and down the cell, yelling and shouting. When he saw me, he thumped a fist on the door and demanded that I open it.

'Angelos, I don't crack doors when the prisoner on the other side is yelling at me,' I told him nonchalantly. 'Kind of rule number one we are taught in training.'

He puffed himself up. 'This man! He is disgusting. Disgusting, disgusting gypsy! I no share with him. Take him out now! Get him out of my cell!'

'He's European, Angelos. That's what you asked for. Now, calm yourself down, then I'll open the door and we'll sort this out, OK?'

He stayed silent, so I opened the door, partly because the poor young Romanian looked petrified and partly because I didn't feel that Angelos posed any real physical threat to me. As soon as it was open, Angelos moved forward and started bustling the other prisoner out.

I grabbed the prisoner's shoulders. 'Go and sit on the bed, mate,' I said, trying to sound reassuring. 'Don't worry, I'll get this sorted. Angelos – come take a seat on the wing.'

'Thank you, thank you, Miss! I could not stay in that cell! I swear any other cell you put me in—'

'Angelos! Listen to me, yeah?' I made sure to say the next part loud enough for at least half the wing to hear. 'I've got ninety other prisoners on this wing to watch out for, OK? So I haven't got time to be running around finding you a cell that suits your racist bullshit. Do you understand?'

Angelos looked nervously over my shoulder at a group of prisoners, three of whom were Black. All three were chuckling at my purposeful lack of discretion.

'Now, I'm taking you out of that cell cos I don't want that poor man to have to put up with your disgusting behaviour for a moment longer. I've got an empty cell upstairs where the toilet flush doesn't work so you can go in there for now until I find a better option.'

He opened his mouth but I'd already turned to walk away from him.

'That's it for today, Angelos. I'm not interested in anything else you have to say.'

Not long after that incident I was off sick for a few days, and when I returned I was feeling slightly out of touch with everything. I flicked through the incidents book which sat on the desk to see what I needed to catch up on. One note written by Dimitra jumped out at me – *Mr Aziz was wearing inappropriate footwear which he refused to change so was not allowed to do servery on Saturday*. I rolled my eyes. I'd known it would only be a matter of time before she started coming down on him.

The rest, still in Dimitra's perfectly round handwriting, concerned Angelos. The first one was a *positive IEP for Mr Angelos helping to clean the wing on Saturday*. Which wasn't him doing anyone a favour, it was Dimitra unlocking him over other prisoners. A second one read: *Mr Angelos self-harmed because the night officer wouldn't give him any toilet roll, ACCT opened*. The third one made me want to rip the page out: *Mr Angelos was given a positive IEP for informing me that a group of Colombians on the wing were selling spice*. For starters, prisoners should not be rewarded for informing on other prisoners like that, particularly before their claim is investigated, and secondly, that's really sensitive information and shouldn't be written up like that. I couldn't help but feel Dimitra was building a paper trail, a case to get her fellow Greek a job on the wing.

I put the kettle on to make myself a much-needed coffee, and just as it broke into a boil I saw Imam Abdi step on to the wing. He was a kind man with a mischievous sense of humour, always good for a well-told tale, and I immediately brightened at the sight of him.

His best stories revolved around being mistaken for a prisoner. There are some restrictions on the clothes prisoners can wear. One reason for that is preventing them from dressing too similarly to staff, which might present them with opportunities to disguise themselves and escape – a white shirt, black trousers and so on. But thobes were an exception to this because they are religious attire.

What's more, if an Imam wore a jacket over his thobe, it was hard to see the belt and key chain which differentiated him from a prisoner wearing a thobe. Imam Abdi would admit, giggling as he said it, that sometimes he made an extra effort to hide his belt just so he could see the embarrassment on someone's face when they realized they had mistaken him for a prisoner. Chris and I would always howl with laughter at these stories of profusely apologetic prison inspectors.

Today, though, his expression was sombre and earnest. He explained to me that Hamza's father had passed away in the night. He asked if I wanted him to break the news or whether it would be better coming from me as someone he knew better. I thought for a moment and said, 'Would you mind if we did it together?' Imam Abdi nodded appreciatively.

Hamza was sleeping when we opened his door.

'Hamza, can we talk to you for a minute?' I asked tentatively.

He sat up in bed. 'Course, Gen. What is it? Oh, Assalamu alaikum, Imam!'

I went to sit on the desk opposite, and leaned towards him. Imam Abdi looked at me to speak first. I'd no idea how Hamza would react.

'Hamza, Imam Abdi has come to let us know some news. Your father passed away last night. I am so sorry for your loss, Hamza.'

Hamza just stared back at me blankly.

'So,' I went on, 'I'm not sure you have any phone credit left, but do you want to come and call your mum from the—'

'Maybe later,' he said, cutting me short. 'Thanks, Gen.' Then, just as if it were any other day, he smiled at me distantly and said, 'D'you think you could sort me a cap?'

We closed his door to let him process the news in peace. I wondered for a moment if he'd even heard us, or if he'd have any memory of what we'd told him.

Down on the exercise yard that afternoon, I watched Hamza begin his usual meander from group to group. 'Bruddah, bruddah, you got a cap for me?' A group of Colombians shooed him away but he kept on going: 'Bruddah, bruddah, can I get the rest of that cap? Just the last bit?' And then, without missing a beat, he added, 'My dad died today, bruddah. Give me that cap, will you?'

As I watched him, a sense of hopeless frustration rolled over me. I felt a sort of empty sadness for him, as though his story had ended already and this was just a video I was watching, some tale of disaster that was rolling inevitably towards a sad and pointless ending. The utter waste of his young life.

Maybe the loss of his father hadn't yet sunk in. Maybe

it didn't seem real to him. Maybe he just couldn't feel it yet, after being in prison for who knows how long without seeing his family. Maybe he just felt too far away from it. I wondered what his father had thought about the struggles his son had in his life. Had he been disappointed in Hamza? Had he been angry with him? Or had he blamed himself? Had the two of them even been close?

I caught myself, surprised at how sentimental Hamza made me. He wasn't the first prisoner I had felt sorry for, but I'd never felt such a need to protect another prisoner before.

'Hamza!' I called out to him. 'Hamza – come sit over here.'

'Yeah – one second, Gen,' he called back, vaguely, without even looking at me. 'Bro, my dad died today. Yeah, it's really sad. Have you got a cap I can get, please, bruddah?'

A week or so later, back out on the yard, I noticed that the largest group of prisoners on the wing, which was made up of Albanians, was bunched together, talking urgently. Something must be up.

It was normal for groups from the same country to hang out together on the exercise yard. Apart from that, some of the older men often gravitated towards men of a similar age, even if they didn't have a language in common. Mr Chan and Mr Borgonsoni, for example, couldn't say a single word to each other but every day they would take up the same position and do their very gentle squats and press-ups together in unison. Usually, though, there were three separate groups of Albanians. I'd learned early on that they were mostly divided up based on which town they were from and therefore (and most importantly) the football team they supported.

Today, though, they looked more like one oversized football squad having a team meeting at half-time than a group of prisoners soaking up a bit of autumn sun. Another strange thing was that none of them had come to talk to me yet. Normally at least five or six would have come over to where I was sitting to say hello and ask how I was, or at the very least ask me for something. But today – absolutely nothing from any of them.

I wandered over as casually as I could. A few of them noticed and hushed the others, which also seemed strange, because presumably they were talking to each other in Albanian anyway. As I got closer I noticed that it wasn't just Albanians grouped together. Standing in the middle of them was Angelos.

'Anything I should be worried about happening over here?' I enquired. 'None of you even saying hello to me today, then?'

Two of them stepped forward – Radu and his cell-mate Marku, the cheesemaker.

'Miss Genny, we would like ten minutes of time with the director.'

I was starting to get a bad feeling about this. They looked like they meant business.

'We have decided that if a director doesn't come out here then we are going to use our right to protest peacefully. We will not return to the wing until a director will speak with us.'

I was quite caught off guard by their diplomacy. With the skills I'd gained in prison, I was actually better equipped to deal with an angry mob that might turn violent than a polite group of lobbyists. I didn't know whether I wanted to laugh, or whether what I was feeling in my chest was a calm-before-the-storm type of anxiety. But there was something about their tone that made me put off pressing my alarm. If I pressed it the yard would immediately be flooded with officers all ready to use force, and the entire group would quickly be restrained. But I believed them when they said they wanted to do this peacefully.

'Right, I see. Well, here's what I'm going to do. I'm going to get the rest of the prisoners off the yard, and I'm going to ask a manager to be sent down here. Can you let me do that first, before any sort of protest starts? Cos I'm sure you'll understand that I don't want to be down here alone with twenty protesting men.'

I made sure to put some sarcasm in my voice as I made this final point. It made me feel a bit more in control of the situation.

'Of course, Miss Genny, you do what you need to do first,' Radu said, nodding his head politely.

I walked away from the group and asked over the radio for Kelly to attend G-Wing exercise yard before calling the end of exercise for the rest of the prisoners.

Kelly arrived just as the last few prisoners were heading up the stairs. I spoke to her quietly for a moment and she nodded and turned to address the group. She hardly batted an eyelid, but I could tell she was glad I had called her before it escalated.

'Who am I negotiatin' with here?' Kelly asked them firmly. 'Who's the translator? Who's the boss?'

Radu and Marku stepped forward again. There was silence.

'Right – you've got two options,' she said to them briskly. 'I can bring fifteen officers down here kitted up in riot gear with the dogs. Or all twenty-two of you can walk back to your cells and I'll come and talk to you again at a time that suits me. It will be this afternoon – you have my word on that.'

Angelos was shaking his head and grumbling, as if to say 'no deal', but Radu translated what Kelly had said to the rest of the group and they nodded in agreement and strolled up the stairs back to the wing just like any other day of the week, leaving a distinctly disappointed-looking Angelos behind. I hadn't expected them to give in so easily – and I don't think Kelly had either.

Still, it struck me how well they had handled the situation – how calm they were, and how supportive to each other. I imagined how differently this same scenario would have gone down on H-Wing, and how much more effective British gangs would be if they stopped driving around and trying to stab each other and actually had each other's backs for a moment.

We locked them up behind their doors one by one. When it was just Radu and Marku left, Kelly called them into the office with us.

They took their seats looking grateful but tenacious.

'Now,' Kelly said to them, 'I'm talking to you now *not* because of the protest, but because of the way you ended it when I asked you to. This is your chance to tell us what you would like to say. If we think it is appropriate for a director to hear, then we will pass it on.'

Radu opened. 'Miss Genny, Miss Kelly, thank you. Albanians, we are proud people and we are patriotic people. We do not ask to be unlocked all the time. We only ask that we are employed fairly. We are the biggest nationality group on the wing, and this is not something we are proud of, but we are polite to officers and we are hard-working people.'

Kelly nodded as they spoke, more as if to say she was listening than to say she agreed.

'However, other prisoners have been promoted over us, even above many of us who have earned it. Aziz – he was given the head of servery job. Why? Why not one of us who has been on the wing for longer?'

I raised my hand, wanting to reply, and Kelly nodded again. I appreciated her letting me handle the situation.

'I just wanted to say, you're absolutely right. We have prioritized Aziz's progression over your right to a job.

Sometimes we do need to manage people's needs on this wing, but this should have been communicated with you in some way, so I'm really sorry about that.'

Radu put his hands up as if to stop me. 'We are glad of what you have done for Aziz. We have seen his improvement and we are happy to see his progress. But I think perhaps a conversation with us about it may have been nice.'

'I totally hear you, guys,' I told him. 'Of course we can't always discuss our decisions with you, but I think you're right, so thanks for pointing it out to us, Radu.'

'And I am meant to be helping with the cleaning, but on the weekends only Angelos is let out to clean,' Marku added.

'Sorry?' Kelly and I said at the same time.

Marku looked slightly guilty now and put his hands up. 'I do not want to snitch, but it is hard for us if we prepare in our minds to be unlocked for work and then Angelos is unlocked instead.'

'So, who is unlocking Angelos?' Kelly asked. 'What officer is on?'

'It's the weekend with Dimitra and the small man that comes to help,' Radu replied.

Kelly muttered to me under her breath: 'And now they've practically started a riot. Thanks for that, Dimitra and Steve.'

I blew a sigh out between my lips. *This job is like trying to catch a cloud*, I thought. No matter how hard you tried to hold on to some certainty or some order, it just kept on slipping through your fingers. You could sort out one problem, but more just kept rolling in. Increasingly, when confronted by problems, I found that my first thought now was *Oh God, I haven't got the strength for this.* It was exhausting. I was exhausted.

27

The Infinite Threshold of Shock

I'd been off sick, again.

It was the third time in two months – yet another bout of tonsillitis. It felt as though I was in a never-ending revolving door of bacterial infections and antibiotics. I was starting to see what prisoners had complained to me about so many times before: with no sunlight, a nutrition-poor diet and people piled in on top of each other, prison slowly destroys your health.

'Gen?' Aziz said that morning when I opened his door for him to clean the servery. 'Um – I wanted to tell ya somethin'.'

'OK, so what is it, Aziz?'

'So – um. The E-Wing manager come over here today. And anyways I spoke to him, Gen, and I think I'm gonna go back over there, you know?'

My heart sank to the pit of my stomach. *Back to E-Wing? Back to the gang life I've seen him trying so hard to leave behind? Why would he do this? After how hard he's tried to change?*

'Aziz,' I said, 'you know what's gonna happen if you go back there.'

He nodded. 'Thing is, Gen – and I'ma be honest with you, yeah, cos you always been honest with me. It's been cool on here, an' I learnt stuff. I learnt stuff about myself and that's been *mad* for me. But I ain't ready to leave the road life. I got someone to provide for now, yeah? And selling is what I know how to do, you get me? Like I see in my future now a way out of that life, and I got that from what you did for me. But at the same time I ain't done with it yet, you get me?'

With every word he spoke, I grew more despondent.

'Aziz, look,' I said. 'I don't get you actually. I don't think I *can* get you. I haven't come from your life. But I've said it before and this is the last time I'll say it – you're really smart. You can do whatever you want with your life, but to do it you need to surround yourself with the right people.'

I paused then. I could see he had already made up his mind.

'So, you want to go back to E-Wing, and do all that stuff,' I went on. 'I can't stop you, obviously. But I'll be so pissed off, Aziz, if I see a picture of your smiling face under another headline about a teenage stabbing one day. Some young guy dead. Dead for what? And that's what's gonna happen to you, you know.'

He gave a sad little half-smile. 'See, Gen, that's what I mean about you bein' too honest.'

What I wanted to say to him was – *please, Aziz, please don't.* But it was pointless. I had no more words that would do any good.

'Still, though,' Aziz finished, with a shrug and what I thought was an apologetic smile, 'thanks for it all, yeah, Gen?'

As we handed lunch out later, I was met with angry cries of 'Gen! Where you bin? Why do only crackheads get jobs now?'

From the top landing I saw Angelos burst back on to the wing after his medication. I could see him striding pluckily and grinning from ear to ear, his arms swinging back and forth like two pendulums.

I know that walk, it's the universal 'I've got my hands on something to smoke' walk.

He grabbed a mop and a bucket and started scrubbing the floor. I headed along the landing to Marku's cell to hand him a parcel of photos he had been sent. Marku was sitting on his bed, quivering with rage. I had never seen him like this before – he was always so laid back and cheerful.

'I can't fucking believe it, you know, Miss Genny!' he cried. 'I'm so mad I really want to do something stupid!'

'Marku, I've literally just got back in this morning.

I've been off, so I've got no idea what you're talking about. Start from the beginning.'

I had an inkling, but I didn't mind hearing it from the horse's mouth.

'I'm never a problem, am I?' Marku blurted out indignantly. 'I've minded my own business all this time. I got that cleaning job, you said I had it officially. But I'm still locked up in here all day! I'm going fucking crazy, Miss Genny! I don't know what to do!'

There were tears in his eyes and his fists were tightly clenched.

'Marku, I know it's frustrating, but you have to be patient. You are next and I don't think it will be very much longer.' It was only an attempt at reassurance – I could tell there wasn't much point.

'But you've given that crackhead Angelos a job, haven't you? You know he deals spice on the wing?' Marku burst out.

I rolled my eyes, silently cursing Dimitra. 'He hasn't got a proper job, Marku, I can promise you that. I know some officers let him out on the weekend just to give themselves a break from his whining, but trust me, he's not being let out to work. And he's going back behind his door right now.'

But my words had little effect. Marku had worked himself into a state of agitation that any person could have succumbed to when they were locked up for hours in a five-metre-square room with only their own frustration for company.

'What the fuck do I have to do?' he wailed, a look of desperation on his face. 'Start fucking cutting my arms up?'

With that, Marku stood up, reached for an empty tin of mackerel from the canteen which was sitting on his desk, wrenched the lid off and started slashing at his wrist with the sharp edge.

I switched into assess-the-situation mode. The cuts he was making weren't deep. He was just angry; he'd most likely stop if I left. And there was nothing I could do to appease him here.

'Marku, leave this with me. I agree, it isn't fair. I'll see what I can do. I promise, OK?'

I closed the door behind me and headed downstairs towards Angelos.

He beamed at me. 'Morning, Miss Genny! I sweep the floor.'

The smarmy look on his face alone was enough to make me want to smack the broom over his head.

'No, you bloody don't!' I ripped the mop from his hands. 'Let's go. You don't have a job and you need to bang up. Now!'

The blood rushed to his face and he started hopping up and down on the spot. 'Dimitra – she tell me I have job! And now you come back and you take job away from me! You bitch! You fucking *bitch*! I wish that you die and you never come back!'

He grabbed the mop back from me and wielded it threateningly. I caught it just in front of my face and tugged it back off him with a shove on his shoulder, holding it above my head and out of his reach.

'Angelos! There are plenty of other men waiting for jobs. And they're doing it far more patiently than you.'

He then shoved me back in a bid to get me to lower the mop, and it worked, but I didn't let go. Now we were holding either end of it, trying to twist it out of the other's grip.

'But the other officer, on the weekend they let me—'

'I don't care what the other officer did!' I told him sharply. 'You think every other grown man on this wing doesn't want to cry? Doesn't want to stamp their feet and get what they want? They all want to be unlocked – it's not just *you*!'

I gave a final tug which pulled the mop from his grasp, then locked my hand around his forearm to drag him back to his cell. He was struggling and fighting, and only then did Dimitra turn up to gingerly take his other arm and walk him back into his cell with me. I glared at her pointedly but she avoided my gaze.

Predictably, a few minutes later the red light of the cell bell started to flash outside his door. I carried on with my day, ignoring him. Then I waited until I thought he wasn't looking, and peered through his hatch. He appeared on the other side almost immediately, cocked his head and started slashing at the side of his neck with his snapped prison ID card.

I opened the door and stood there watching with my hand on my hip.

'Look what you do to me, Miss Genny!' he shrieked. 'I do this because of you! And I keep on doing this until you give me job!'

I could hear the taut skin of his neck ripping with each slash – but nothing stirred in me like it used to. No horror, no revulsion – just a kind of numbness. I could feel that the expression on my face had remained unmoved, deadpan.

'So, Angelos. Let's say I give you a job because you cut yourself. What do you think happens next? Suddenly I've got ninety other men slashing their wrists to try and get out of their cells. Is that what you want?'

He looked at me sulkily, and tried another half-hearted slash.

'Angelos, all that's gonna get you is a nurse, at best. You cutting up will not get you what you want. Not when I'm on the wing.'

Clearly unsatisfied with my reaction, he tugged down his trousers, angrily kicking them off to one side. Then he grabbed hold of his penis and started hacking away at it with the edge of the broken card.

I held my hand below my eyes to shield his crotch from view. I knew I should be shocked, but I wasn't. In fact, the only thing calmly ticking through my mind was *I really don't want an image of Angelos's prick and balls taking up space in my brain*. I knew he was doing it for the audience now, so I decided it would be wisest to leave him to it before he did some irreversible damage.

I checked on him every now and then, peeping

through the door hinge. The first couple of times he didn't spot me; I could see him sitting there watching TV while chewing angrily on a plastic fork. The third time, though, I tried to get a better look through the hatch. He saw me, and promptly grabbed the card and resumed hacking, on his arm this time. Then he bustled over towards the door and began filling his obs panel with drenched toilet paper until I couldn't see inside any more.

On my next inspection through the hinge, I could see he had placed his desk chair on the top bunk and was tying a sheet to its outstretched legs. I swung the door open.

'What's this, then, Angelos?'

'I tie noose around my neck. I want kill myself so you go to prison!'

'I see.'

I took a seat on Angelos's desk, watching him with interest. He was moving with theatrical exaggeration and struggling to tie the crucial knot at the other end of the sheet.

I knew I had a few options here. *I can do what he thinks I'm going to do, which is beg him not to do it and then call a nurse and a manager in to talk him down. That way he has got what he wants. Or, I can do the exact opposite of what he wants me to do.*

'So, where does this bit go?' I asked him, pointing towards the knot he was trying to tie.

'It goes around my neck!' He gestured dramatically towards his throat.

'Ah, of course.'

The knot came undone again and he grunted with frustration.

'Here, let me help you,' I offered, putting my finger over the knot to hold it still.

He looked instantly taken aback. Just as I'd hoped, the absurdity of the situation was beginning to dawn on him.

'So what's the plan?' I asked.

He scowled up at me. 'I hang myself and then I die and it's your fault.'

'OK, and what do you think you're gonna think about? You know, when you're dying?'

I kept my voice light and inquisitive. He just shrugged.

'Are you gonna think about your mum? I know you're close with your mum – you speak to her on the phone a lot. You gonna think about your girlfriend? You know, the one you smacked over the head with a scaffolding pole, who still sends you money, who still writes you letters?'

He dropped the knot without taking his eyes off it and his arms fell to his side, his fists clenching.

''Cos the thing is, Angelos, you've got a temper, and when you're not taking it out on your missus, you're taking it out on yourself.'

Tears started rolling down his face, which I hadn't quite expected. I spoke to him more gently, but still firmly.

'I am not gonna start giving you special treatment when you start slashing up, or tying nooses. Cos one of these days, Angelos, you might just cut a bit too deep, or you might slip with this round your neck. And it won't be because you wanted to kill yourself. It will be because you wanted to get your own way. And wouldn't that just be a giant fuck-up?'

Angelos began sobbing bitterly. His shoulders shook. 'Ahhh, Miss Genny, I'm sorry! I don't know why I do this . . .'

I suddenly felt a little out of my depth, a bit awkward. It hadn't been my intention to break him down and have him begging for my forgiveness. I'd really just wanted him to pull himself together and stop wasting everyone's time. But he was now heaving with sobs, and after my little righteous outburst I felt the need to clear the air a bit.

'Listen, Angelos, just promise me one thing, yeah? Never, ever show me your penis again.'

He nodded sheepishly at me.

'Well then, I think we're about done here.'

I walked straight from his cell to Kelly's office to have a good moan about Dimitra. I slumped on the chair opposite her desk and blurted out the whole story. It was only when I got to the part with Angelos and his noose that I paused. At the time I'd felt sure I was doing the right thing, but as I heard myself recount it out loud, a sense of dread dawned on me.

What had I done?

I trailed off after I told her that he burst into tears – I just couldn't keep listening to myself. But Kelly's expression was not one of judgement, or of disappointment. Instead, she gave me a measured look.

'Gen, let me start by saying that what you did was not actually as unorthodox as you are making it out to be. We were all taught in training that if someone expresses that they want to kill themselves, you need to ask them explicitly how they plan to do it. You must have done that plenty of times already in the job. Now, this doesn't mean that you should necessarily go around helping prisoners to tie their own nooses, but what you did was effective. You made it real for him. You de-escalated it. You can't learn how to do this job from a textbook. It's unpredictable, so sometimes you need to be unpredictable.'

Kelly's words had reassured me, but all the way home that evening the same questions whirled about in my head.

At what point have I reached the stage where I'm not compassionate enough?

At what point am I too tough for my own good?

How do I know when that moment has come?

Lost in thought, I wandered down the tube carriage looking for somewhere to sit. I eventually flopped into a free seat, and my eyes fell on the man sitting opposite me. His face was pasty white, he had a plastic bin bag between his legs and was wearing a grey tracksuit. He had clearly just been released from another prison in the area. He looked broken. Almost without thinking I conducted my usual check: unwashed hair, large pupils set in wide eyes, prison-issue clothing. And before I even looked, I knew what I'd find next: criss-crossed scars of self-harm along his forearms.

I saw the woman next to him staring at him uneasily, her eyes running from his arms to his eyes and back to his arms again. I watched her feelings of compassion for a human being who was obviously in need, battling with her caution and nervousness at being close to him. I wondered if she realized he'd just been released from prison. After a few minutes, looking upset and confused, she got to her feet and moved away.

I didn't move. What I'd just watched, I thought, was probably a very normal way to react. Pity. Fear. Shock. Shouldn't seeing someone in that state at least make me uneasy? Should I feel sad? I turned different reactions over in my head, but none of them remotely resembled what I actually felt. I kept arriving back at the same sensation: a sort of neutral nothingness.

I understood what had happened: after everything I had seen and experienced, my parameters for shock and repulsion had shifted, just as I'd suspected they would. I remembered that first night shift during training, when I had seen a man shove a toilet brush into his arse. That was where I'd first explored that dark desire within me to discover what shocked me, what *really* shocked me.

With every gruesome scene since then, each one

more stomach-churning than the last, I'd had the sensation that I must be drawing closer to finding my limit. With one more grisly thrust, I would be there. But instead I'd found it to be forever slipping out of my grasp like a saviour's hand in a dream. It was as though, after each one of these encounters, I was never quite returning to my baseline. Rather than bringing me closer to that limit, what I was seeing and hearing was pushing that limit further and further out, recalibrating my senses at a molecular level.

It struck me that nothing about the way I had responded that entire day, to all the shocking and distressing things I'd witnessed, was normal. So, staring nervelessly at yet another pair of scarred and bloody wrists, as if they suddenly looked different under the rattling lights of the Victoria Line, I made the decision to hand in my notice.

28

Recycling

At home, while I made myself dinner, I had the distinct feeling in my gut that I had failed. I poured my chicken and lentil soup into the pan, then stood looking at the perfectly recyclable empty pot. All I needed to do was give it a quick rinse and then pop it in the recycling. Except, I didn't. Instead, feeling exhausted and discouraged, I thought *sod it*, and tossed it straight in the bin.

In that moment, something occurred to me about Aziz's decision.

If you're like me – privileged in a middle-class life, moderately hopeful and fairly confident in your self-efficacy – then recycling is probably fairly high on your list of priorities. That's why I'm usually a pretty diligent recycler. I read articles on it, I follow a load of Instagram accounts about it, I very rarely buy plastic bottles, and when I do I feel guilty about it. I know what does and doesn't go in the recycling bin – and if I'm not sure, I google it. I pick non-recyclable sticky labels off recyclable materials. I do the whole recycling dance. And even though I know that the system is very far from perfect, and I've seen all those pictures of all our recycling piled up in Indonesian rainforests and floating on the Pacific Ocean, I still do it. I still try. It's partly in the hope that the materials I'm using actually might be recycled sometimes, and partly because it makes me feel like a good and valuable person on this planet.

But not today. Today I felt like shit. It seemed that nothing I could do could make a difference in the world. I felt inadequate, powerless and small – hopeless and frustrated, crap about myself. And when I'm in that state, if the recycling bin needs emptying, or that carton needs washing out, or the recycling information is in an annoyingly small font and I have to squint to read it – it's going straight in the general waste. I haven't got the energy. I haven't got the will.

Many of us do things because when we do them, we know that we're contributing to society – and that makes us feel good. We're polite to the person at the checkout, we use a bin when we're walking down the street, we say sorry when someone bumps into us. It makes us feel a part of something we are proud of.

So now imagine, I thought, if that same society had repeatedly let me down, repeatedly shut me out, hung me out to dry. Imagine if the only society I could see around me, or ever had seen, was a filthy, overcrowded prison wing filled with other people just like me. People who had been churned up and spat out.

Or imagine if I'd grown up, not on a tree-lined street of nice houses with gardens, but in a block of flats with peeling, leaking ceilings and stairwells that stank of piss and weed. Imagine if I'd had barely enough money to buy my favourite packet of sweets while all day long I'd watched adverts on TV for Action Men and Barbies clutched by children laughing and smiling in a way I'd never seen in my own home. Imagine being told to work hard at school just so that I could get the same ball-busting job I'd seen my mum do her whole life – and still I'd know that however hard I worked there was no way at all, no chance in hell, that I'd manage to escape from this concrete jungle where people sit slumped against walls and inject God knows what into every vein they can find.

Imagine I'd heard people talking about how the police are there to protect me and should be praised and hailed as heroes when all I'd seen was them making my mum cry when they arrested my dad in front of our family, or arrested my cousin, who'd done nothing wrong, when he was on his way to work at TK Maxx.

And imagine if this society I lived in existed in parallel with another society, where hedges are trimmed into the shapes of exotic animals and £10 natural Botox smoothies are lapped up by smiling women having their nails painted, and kids wear smart school uniforms that are new and actually fit them. Imagine if I saw this parallel place everywhere around me, and advertised incessantly on TV and online. But all the time I knew that there was no way – ever – to cross over from one world – my world – to the other.

And what if someone had removed almost everything that gave me any kind of pride in myself and in my life? Where could I find that motivation to stay on the right track? Where could I find the enthusiasm to give anything at all to a society that I had been told every day of my life, in every way, I wasn't even part of? Where would I find the motivation to *do better*?

Let alone recycle.

It was a well-known phenomenon among officers. Once you have handed in your notice, you've signed out. You don't think or act like you used to. During my final four weeks as a prison officer I swung between feelings of regret and nostalgia and that floaty sensation of relief you get when you take off a heavy backpack.

Today, though, was the day before my sister's wedding. My whole family was already gathered together, arranging flowers on rows of tables in the sun. In between my unforgiving shift patterns and catching every bug which went around the wing, I had hardly seen them and I was desperate to make it to the dinner that night to spend the evening with my sister. But I was on shift until 6.30, then I would have to leg it across London to King's Cross in my uniform and jump on a train to Royston in Hertfordshire. There was no way I would make it until nine – unless I could find a way to leave early.

In the afternoon I knocked on the door of the manager's office and I was disappointed to see Dimitra in Kelly's usual seat.

'Kelly's not in today,' she said to me sharply, before I'd even asked anything.

'Um – OK. Well, Dimitra, can I ask a favour?'

'You can try.'

'My sister's getting married tomorrow. All my family's there already, getting things ready, and we've got a dinner tonight with all of us and her friends – it was kind of a last-minute thing which is why I didn't take the day off. But anyway, I was just wondering, can I leave at five thirty today so that I can get there in time for the dinner?'

I was suddenly regretting all the times I'd talked back to her and I was fully expecting her to be the last person who'd agree to do me a rule-bending favour, but to my surprise she nodded. 'Sure you can, Gen.'

I couldn't believe what I was hearing.

'But if,' she added, 'and *only* if, you can get every prisoner on your wing fed, medicated and locked up by then.'

She might as well just have told me, 'No, Gen, you can't leave early.' She knew as well as I did that this was a near impossible task. I skulked back to the G-Wing office and told Chris about the ridiculous ultimatum I'd just been given.

Chris looked furious and shook his head in disbelief. 'Not gonna be the same round here without you, ya know, Gen? Listen, we'll get you on that train, yeah? Don't you worry about it.'

It was a nice sentiment, but I couldn't imagine how he thought he was going to manage it.

'Gen, this ain't gonna cheer you up neither, I'm afraid,' Chris added. 'Walter just called – he's asked if you can take some prisoner from H-Wing to get his methadone at the controlled-meds hatch.'

I was hardly concentrating as the prisoner tipped the methadone powder into his mouth. As is procedure with heroin treatment, he was meant to sit down where he was for a couple of minutes before opening his mouth so that I could check that all the medication had dissolved. Instead, he strode back to the wing immediately.

Suddenly catching on to what had just happened I followed him back to H-Wing. When he got there, he bent down in order to pass something under a locked cell door. Then he saw me hot on his heels. He legged it back to his cell and passed it to his cellmate instead. Feeling substantially mugged off by this point, I lunged for the tiny wrap and attempted to wrestle it from the cellmate's grasp.

'I'm not an idiot, mate. You're not having that!'

I grappled with his fist to open it, trying to peel his fingers back, but nothing is stronger than an addict and their craving.

He shoved me hard over his bed, and I caught my shin on the frame with a crack. I pushed myself back up but I felt my leg go weak, and when he shoved me again, I fell to the floor below the sink. But I hadn't let go of his fist and I was still trying to force his palm open, with both of my hands, while he lay across my torso. I felt his other hand take a handful of my hair and push my head over what I now realized was the toilet. The smell of stale piss filled my nostrils, but it didn't occur to me to call for help. I didn't feel threatened – I felt indignant. The only thing going through my head was getting my hands on that powder.

I was trying with all my might to lift my knee into a position where I could push back, hard, to get him off me. But his quivering hand was pushing my face closer and closer to the piss-soaked stainless steel of the toilet basin.

Suddenly, I felt my belt tighten around my waist. There was a very firm pull and I was on my feet again. Walter, still gripping me by the back of my belt, was dragging me out of the cell away from the prisoner.

'You!' he barked to the prisoner behind me. 'I am coming back for you later.'

Just before Walter closed the door I saw the look on the prisoner's face. He was mortified. I don't think he had meant to hurt me at all – he just wasn't going to let anything get between him and that precious powder.

'Gen,' Walter sighed, letting go of my belt as he locked the door shut with his other hand, 'no need to risk your life going after some nitty. You know that!'

He was right. I was under zero obligation to go in there alone, and an intelligence report would have more than sufficed.

He patted me on the shoulder kindly and added, 'I know you might have run out of shits to give because you've got your release date coming up, but no one's asking you to chase after no one by yourself, mind.'

'Ha! I forgot how fast news travels in this place! Sorry, though, Walter – I wanted to come and tell you in person.'

He chuckled. 'You know how it is in this place – word of mouth is quicker than an email. It will be a sad day for me though, Gen. An' I mean that.'

I smiled back at him and said, 'Thanks for everything, Walter.' I could've said, 'Thanks for showing me the way when no one else would: I don't think I would have survived those early days without you.' But you don't say that kind of thing in this environment, in the same way that no more words were uttered about the fact he had just pulled me from underneath a man who was trying to shove my head down a toilet. Besides,

I knew Walter understood what I meant. He put his hand on my shoulder and walked me the short distance back to G-Wing.

'I'm gonna miss that adrenalin,' I said, as he opened the G-Wing door for me.

He chuckled again, loudly. 'Gen, you know I don't doubt it! Whoa, G-Wing going for some kind of record? Almost served dinner and it's not even five o'clock!'

I looked at the servery, and he was right. Aziz was standing there, piling the remnants of some tepid-looking oxtail stew on to a dwindling line of blue plates held by outstretched arms.

'Aziz! What's going on? What is this?' I asked in disbelief.

Aziz shrugged, like he always did. 'Gen, you got your sister's wedding, innit? We just tryna pattern you up!'

I looked at Chris, who had rolled up his sleeves and was handing out doughnuts to the men in the queue.

'You told them!' I said.

He laughed. 'I told them!'

Then I heard Radu bellowing from the other end of the landing: 'Gen's gotta get to her sister's wedding! Banging up early today everyone! Come on, off you go!'

All around me was a buzz of activity. Aziz, Mr Chan, Marku, Dawar and even Angelos started bustling prisoners into their cells. Suddenly the wing was empty, and it was only 5.13 p.m. At 5.15, Angelos was standing at his door gesturing towards the lock on it.

'Gen, will you do the honours? I wish your sister all the best at her wedding.'

I couldn't believe what I was seeing.

'Thank you, Angelos,' I said to him sincerely.

Finally, I got to Aziz's cell. Once crammed full of neatly stacked canteen and fresh white trainers, it was now stark and empty. He stood among bin bags filled with his belongings. Only his bedding remained in place.

I smiled at him gratefully, but inside I felt helpless.

'Thanks, Aziz, it means a lot, you helping me with that.'

'Gen, family is family. Don't say nuthin'.'

'See? You can achieve so much when you put your mind to it! Just remember that when you're back on E-Wing. And wherever else you end up after that.'

'E-Wing's the closest thing to family I've got in here. But I'll never forget what you've done for me, Gen.'

He put his hand out earnestly, and I shook it.

Then he grinned. 'Now get goin' else you're gonna miss your train!'

My last day came around sooner than I ever could have expected.

With each door I locked at the end of the day I felt more sentimental.

Dawar was sat cross-legged on his bed, reading an English dictionary and chewing on a cereal bar. The charity was sending him money and books on a weekly basis now. He waved goodbye to me and then flicked through his dictionary for a moment before looking up triumphantly.

'I wish you all the best on your travel!'

When I got to Hamza's door, he was hunched over the plug socket where his vape was charging, trying to suck on it without unplugging it.

'Hamza!' I called to him. 'Just came to say goodbye!'

He looked up at me with a gormless smile. 'Gen! I'm gonna miss you!'

I pulled a full vape capsule I'd found earlier out of my pocket. 'My parting gift to you, Hamza.'

His eyes widened and he took it from me, holding it in his hands, transfixed by it. Without looking up, he just said in his childlike sing-song voice, 'Thanks, Gen, see you tomorrow then!' Just like he always did.

I laughed, but it was a sad laugh. I knew that from that moment on, every time I walked past a slight figure slumped up against the wall of an underpass, sitting on a daggy piece of cardboard, I would have to check if it was Hamza.

Back in the office, Chris handed me a note with a wry smile. It was from Dimitra, who wasn't on shift today.

Gen, it has been nice knowing you. All the best. Dimitra.

Chris chuckled and then wrapped his arms around me in a bear hug.

'We have had a laugh, haven't we?' he said when he let go.

'It's not what I thought I'd be saying when I left prison, but yep, we sure have!' I replied.

I didn't exactly know how I was going to feel on my final walk through the prison. It's not as though I was anticipating a poignant and meaningful march through the gate with dramatic Hans Zimmer music playing as I went, but still – I hadn't expected it to feel this *final*.

I felt a shiver run down my spine as I locked the G-Wing door behind me for the last time. Then, as I strode away around the core, I heard someone singing.

'Ten green bottles, hangin' on the wall! Ten green bottles, hangin' on the wall! And if one green bottle should accidentally faaaall . . .'

I peered through the glass window on to the induction wing. I could see five officers staring up at a pair of skinny legs on the landing above them. Someone had hopped over the railings. I could see the toes of some prison-issue trainers wedged through the bars of the railings, the heels hanging over the eight-foot drop to the landing below.

I opened the wing door quietly and crept through to get a better look. There were officers checking their watches and busily trying to lock up other prisoners who wandered about looking amused. Other officers were talking into their radios and pacing around looking sweaty and cross. Then I heard the voice sing again in a playful lilt, 'And if I can't go to the pub tonight, then I'll tell you something, neither can all of you!'

I had a feeling I recognized that voice.

I took another few steps forward and sure enough, there was Bert. Grinning down at the mayhem he was causing, singing with all his heart.

Bert Harley, straight back into prison, the only home he, and too many others, had ever known.

Acknowledgements

First and foremost, I want to thank the very real people behind the characters in this book. To the prisoners, for all the lessons you taught me, both good and bad, for your openness and, more often than people would believe, for your kindness. To my most outstanding colleagues – it's the highest form of trust to have felt safe beside you on even some of the most testing days. Thank you for giving me reason to trust you, thank you for trusting me in return and thank you ever so much for all the laughs. And, of course, to prison staff serving all over the country for your endurance and for your sacrifices in the face of an underappreciated role – you have a lot to be proud of and things are going to change.

To my family, my boundless web of love and support. To the three women who raised me and the strongest women I know: my mum, Katie Glaister, and my sisters, Cosima Glaister and Dini McGrath, for their infectious ambition, sense of adventure and fierce love.

To my dad, Ricky Glaister, who, through his slightly unorthodox ways, has taught me resourcefulness, creativity and how to always find the good in people. To my partner, Fred Light, who wangled a work relocation which meant I got to write my book from a sunny rooftop in Mexico City and who bore the brunt of my writer's block with open arms and endless patience. To my friends, both those who are decades old and years old, for your interest. To Rosie, I hope you remain the only person I ever have to write a card to which reads 'I'm sorry a prisoner spat in your mouth,' but I can safely say that as two young prison officers living five minutes apart during a pandemic we gave 'support bubble' a whole new meaning. To Lucy Hall, for always being at the end of a phone with an explanation. To Lucinda Fraser, who has been the catalyst at so many stages in my career. To Vernel Dolor, who I worked with after leaving the prison service, who has consistently defied the odds of the hand he was dealt and who's friendship and stories have enriched this book to no end. To one teacher from school in particular, Nathan Shrubb, who taught me the power of having someone fight your corner when no one else would.

The most enormous thanks to the team around my book. My agent, Katie Fulford at Bell Lomax Moreton, for navigating me through this unknown world with so much wisdom right from the start. My whole team at Transworld, both old and new. Kate Fox and Liz Sheppard for guiding my writing and bringing all of these stories to life. Stephanie Duncan, Melissa Kelly and Emma Fairey for bringing so much energy and creativity to the later stages of the process. To Dan Balado, my copy-editor, Vivien Thompson for her guidance on these acknowledgements and to Lottie Chesterman for her hard work in finding me a narrator who would fit my many demands. To Katie Hickman and Josh Roberts, two brilliant authors who so kindly helped and advised in the early days.

To a number of people in and around the prison service who have given me opportunities, advice and inspiration: Dom Ceglowski, Bruce Houlder, Mary Gibson, Rupert and so many more. To some devoted and exceptionally impressive people who I have both worked alongside and adored: Lily Birkett, Samira Kelay, Steph Ilsley, DeeDee Illsley, Rosie Mackintosh, Nicky Slevin, Connie Sale and once more for good luck, Vernel Dolor.

Thank you to you all, your support has been a privilege.

© Charlie Hopkinson

Gen Glaister had her heart set on being a prison officer since she was fifteen. Just three months after leaving university she finally got the keys to one of London's largest male prisons, where she learned more about humans than she could ever have imagined.

Since leaving the prison service, Gen has remained determined to change the public's approach to people in prison and to get the UK excited about justice reform.